Discipline and Punishment
in Global Politics

Discipline and Punishment in Global Politics

Illusions of Control

Edited by Janie Leatherman

palgrave
macmillan

First published in 2008 by
PALGRAVE MACMILLAN™
175 Fifth Avenue, New York, N.Y. 10010 and
Houndmills, Basingstoke, Hampshire, England RG21 6XS.
Companies and representatives throughout the world.

PALGRAVE MACMILLAN is the global academic imprint of the Palgrave
Macmillan division of St. Martin's Press, LLC and of Palgrave Macmillan Ltd.
Macmillan® is a registered trademark in the United States, United Kingdom
and other countries. Palgrave is a registered trademark in the European Union
and other countries.

ISBN-13: 978-0-230-60584-8
ISBN-10: 0-230-60584-2

Library of Congress Cataloging-in-Publication Data

Discipline and punishment in global politics: illusions of control / edited by
Janie Leatherman.
    p. cm.
    Includes bibliographical references and index.
    ISBN 0-230-60584-2
    1. International relations—Political aspects. 2. International relations—
Sociological aspects. 3. Criminal justice, Administration of—International
cooperation. I. Leatherman, Janie, 1959–

    JZ1251.D57 2008
    327.1'17—dc22   2007047314

A catalogue record for this book is available from the British Library.

Design by Macmillan India Ltd.

First edition: June 2008

10 9 8 7 6 5 4 3 2 1

Printed in the United States of America.

With special appreciation to Ken Brown, Robert and Ruthann Johansen, Raimo Väyrynen, and Marc Ross for the years of support and mentoring

Table of Contents

Preface

With a sabbatical stretching out before me in the spring of 2003, I decided I would spend some of my time reading again the works of Michel Foucault. I was then a professor in the Department of Politics and Government at Illinois State University—formerly known as a "normal university"—which follows very much in the tradition of the French *école normale*. The university was located in the town of Normal. Although the university had since dropped the designation Normal University (teaching college), the town was stuck with the name. Living in Normal would probably have amused Foucault. But I often joked that I did not live in Normal, but on the edge of Normal, the outer limits of Normal, and so on. Vacations always presented the opportunity to go back to Normal. The name gives rise to endless possibilities, so I leave it to the reader to invent them. Thus, one of Foucault's central premises in *Discipline and Punish*—that nonconforming is punishable—was hardly an abstract proposition.

During that spring, I took *Discipline and Punish* in hand and was reading the first pages of it when the U.S. invasion of Iraq began. I was suddenly struck that the public spectacle of "shock and awe" raining down upon Baghdad with such fury, televised live around the globe, was hardly different in many respects from the gruesome account of the spectacle of the quartering of the criminal with which Foucault begins his own account of *Discipline and Punish*. Hence, in many respects, the origins of the present volume.

I was, however, also engaged at the time in the preparation of another volume that Palgrave Macmillan published in 2005, *Charting Transnational Democracy: Beyond Global Arrogance* (which I co-edited with Julie Webber). That study set out to examine the first of a set of two Gramscian propositions I was considering at the time about the loss of hegemony: as the consent to govern erodes, the hegemon resorts to force. *Charting Transnational Democracy* took up the first part of this formula—examining the ways that a consensual regime of global hegemony was eroding as transnational movements around the globe challenged its central tenets (myths). That study led to some hopeful conclusions about the possibility of transnational movements opening up democratic space. Yet the impact of September 11 and the failure of the global community, despite massive demonstrations around the world and concerted diplomatic efforts in the United Nations to halt the U.S. attack on Iraq, suggested that those openings were closing down. This present volume on *Discipline and Punishment in Global Politics* consequently addresses the second aspect of Gramsci's argument.

This research project has benefited from many enriching opportunities I have had to meet with the contributors over the past four years. This includes panel sessions at the International Studies Association's annual convention in Honolulu, Hawaii, in 2005, and at the International Studies Association Midwest meeting in St. Louis in October 2005, and other meetings. Many of the audience members and panel discussants also helped to shape our work for this volume. I also enjoyed several opportunities to teach graduate seminars around the topic of discipline and punishment in global politics at Illinois State University from 2005 to 2006. These seminars generated stimulating conversations and insightful student papers on a range of related case studies. One of those students, Anthony DiMaggio, now pursuing a Ph.D. at the University of Illinois at Chicago, was later asked by Dr. Ali Riaz to work under him on chapter 6 of this volume. From 2003 to the present, I also benefited from lively discussions at several forums where I had opportunities to lecture on topics relating to the framework of this book. This included lectures to the Institute for Retired Professionals at Fairfield University on October 12, 2006; a lecture on "UN-Making the World: The US, UN and Iraq War" for the Mornings with Professors series sponsored by Illinois State University and hosted by the St. John's Lutheran Church in Bloomington, Illinois, on October 17, 2003; and my participation at "The United Nations and Global Security" town hall meeting sponsored by Americans for Informed Democracy (AID) and the Stanley Foundation at the University of Illinois at Urbana-Champaign on April 5, 2005.

I owe special thanks to Professor Stacy D. VanDeveer for his close reading and helpful comments on an early draft of chapter 1. I want to thank Professor Jyl Josephson as well, for the many insights she has shared with me as I worked on this project. Anonymous feedback from the reviewers of the book was pointed and useful to enhancing the clarity and scope of the arguments in the book. I express my gratitude as well for those insightful comments. I also wish to thank Fairfield University for a summer research grant in 2007 for the final preparations of this manuscript.

As before, it is a delight to work with Anthony Wahl, senior editor at Palgrave Macmillan, in the preparation of this volume, and with his able and patient editorial assistant, Emily Hue. Lydia Mulyk, an undergraduate research assistant to the international studies program during the summer of 2007, also proved invaluable in helping to format the manuscript. Thanks also go to Anne Frank, graduate research assistant, who has so ably helped prepare the index. I also want to thank all of the contributors to the volume, because working closely with each of them has been rewarding and has also helped me to work through the exposition of the argument in the introduction and conclusion. I would also like to express my gratitude to Dr. Iris Bork-Goldfield, Associate Director of International Studies at Fairfield, who has graciously and with ever-good cheer kept the office going while I have had to discipline myself to complete this volume.

Finally, I would like to say a word about the faculty who have mentored me from the start of my academic training. In many ways, their voices, along with those of many other colleagues, have also helped shape my thinking on this project. I want to especially thank Professors Robert and Ruthann Johansen, Ken Brown, Raimo Väyrynen, and Marc Ross, who have given so generously of their time and support over the years. I dedicate this book to them. I am solely responsible for any of its shortcomings.

Janie Leatherman
Fairfield University
Fairfield Connecticut
October 17, 2007

Contributors

Evelyn L. Bush is an assistant professor of sociology at Fordham University. She received a Master of Arts in sociology from the College of William and Mary in 1996 and a Ph.D. in sociology from Cornell University in 2005. She has an article in *Social Forces* journal (June 2007) on secularization and the measurement of religion in global civil society and a book chapter on how European unification shapes farmers' protest in *Contentious Europeans: Protest and Politics in an Integrating Europe* (Doug Imig and Sidney Tarrow, eds.; Rowman and Littlefield, 2001). Her current research focuses on religion and HIV/AIDS.

Michael Dartnell is professor of political theory at Georgian College in Barrie, Ontario, Canada. His work is situated at the intersections of cultural studies, security studies, and ethnography. He is the author of *Insurgency Online: Web Activism and Global Conflict* (University of Toronto Press, 2006); *Action directe: Ultra-left terrorism in France, 1979–1987* (London: Frank Cass, 1995); and articles on information technologies and conflict/security, terrorism, political violence, and conflict in such journals as *Millenium, Terrorism and Political Violence, and Small Wars and Insurgencies.*

Anthony DiMaggio is the author of *Mass Media, Mass Propaganda: Understanding American News in the "War on Terror."* He has taught Middle East politics and American government at Illinois State University, and is currently finishing his Ph.D. at the University of Illinois at Chicago. He is a regular contributor to popular political publications such as *Counter Punch* and *Z Magazine.*

David S. Gutterman is assistant professor of politics at Willamette University. He has published work on the conversion narrative of George W. Bush, narrative theory, religious social movements in the United States, and gender and politics. His first book is *Prophetic Politics: Christian Social Movements and American Democracy* (Cornell University Press, 2005), and he is currently working on a book entitled *Narrating America: Political Discourse in the Bush Years.*

Krista Hunt is adjunct professor of women and gender studies and formerly a SSHRC postdoctoral fellow at the Munk Centre for International Studies, University of Toronto. Her recent articles include "The Strategic Co-optation of Women's Rights Discourse in the War on Terrorism" in the *International Feminist Journal of Politics,* and "Challenging and Reinforcing Dominant Myths: Transnational Feminists Use the Internet to Contest the War on Terrorism" in *Beyond Global Arrogance: Charting Transnational Democracy* (Janie Leatherman and Julie Webber, eds.; Palgrave Macmillan, 2005). She is co-editor with Kim Rygiel of *(En)Gendering the War on Terror: War Stories and Camouflaged Politics* (Ashgate, 2006).

Graham Knight is chair of the Department of Communication Studies and Multimedia at McMaster University, Hamilton, Ontario, Canada. His current research interests lie in the areas of corporate public relations and social responsibility, social activism, and media politics. His recent publications have appeared in *Communication and Critical/Cultural Studies;* the *International Review for the Sociology of Sport;* the *Australian Journal of Communication; Italian Canadiana;* and *Social Movement Studies.*

Janie Leatherman is director of international studies and professor of politics at Fairfield University in Fairfield, Connecticut. Her most recent publications include *Charting Transnational Democracy: Beyond Global Arrogance,* edited with Julie Webber (Palgrave Macmillan, 2005); *From Cold War to Democratic Peace: Third Parties, Peaceful Change and the OSCE* (Syracuse University Press, 2003); and *Breaking Cycles of Violence: Conflict Prevention in Intrastate Crises* (Kumarian, 1999). She is published in several languages and has authored numerous articles and book chapters on the OSCE, conflict early warning and prevention, gender and violence, sex-trafficking, gender and foreign policy, and transnational politics. She is currently preparing a book on *Sexual Violence and Armed Conflict,* under contract with Polity Press.

Julie Mertus is associate professor and co-director of the MA program in ethics, peace and global affairs at American University. Her prior appointments include Senior Fellow, U.S. Institute of Peace; Human Rights Fellow, Harvard Law School; Writing Fellow, MacArthur Foundation; Fulbright Fellow (Denmark 2006 and Romania 1995); and Counsel, Human Rights Watch. Her book *Bait and Switch: Human Rights and U.S. Foreign Policy* (Routledge, 2004) was named "human rights book of the year" by the American Political Science Association Human Rights Section. Her other books include: *Human Rights and Conflict* (edited with Jeffrey Helsing; United States Institute of Peace, 2006); *The United Nations and Human Rights*

(Routledge, 2005); *Kosovo: How Myths and Truths Started a War* (University of California Press, 1999); and *The Suitcase: Refugees' Voices from Bosnia and Croatia* (University of California Press, 1999).

Dawn Nowacki is professor of political science at Linfield College, Oregon. During the 1980s she worked as a staff analyst for Radio Liberty's Soviet Area Audience and Opinion Research department in Paris, France, and as an assistant editor for Central Asian Survey. Her research has focused on the election of women to Russian federal and regional parliaments, and more recently on women and war. Her publications include contributions to *Women's Access to Political Power in Post-Communist Europe* (Richard E. Matland and Kathleen Montgomery, eds.; Oxford University Press, 2003) and to the *Journal of Communication*.

Kristin Rawls is a graduate student in philosophy at Pennsylvania State University. She completed a Master of Arts in ethics, peace, and global affairs at American University and a Bachelor of Arts in political science and English at the University of North Carolina at Chapel Hill.

Ali Riaz is associate professor and chair of the Department of Politics and Government at Illinois State University. He has previously taught at Claflin University in South Carolina, Lincoln University in the United Kingdom, and Dhaka University in Bangladesh. His publications include *Islamist Militancy in Bangladesh: A Complex Web* (Routledge, 2008); *Paradise Lost? State Failure in Nepal* (with Subho Basu; Lexington Books, 2007); *Unfolding State: The Transformation of Bangladesh* (de Sitter Publications, 2005); and *God Willing: The Politics of Islamism in Bangladesh* (Rowman & Littlefield, 2004). His forthcoming book is *Faithful Education: Madrassahs in South Asia* (Rutgers University Press, 2008).

Kim Rygiel is a SSHRC postdoctoral fellow at the Institute on Globalization and the Human Condition at McMaster University. She taught in the politics department at Trent University prior to her fellowship. Her research focuses on investigating the technologies and practices of governing through citizenship in the "post-9/11" and "war on terror" environments. Her most recent work has investigated the gendered impacts of the "war on terror" and the study of detention arrangements in the post-9/11 period. She is co-editor with Krista Hunt of *(En)Gendering the War on Terror: War Stories and Camouflaged Politics* (Ashgate, 2006) and has published in edited collections, including *The Logics of Biopower and the War on Terror: Living, Dying and Surviving* (Elizabeth Dauphinee and Cristina Masters, eds.; Palgrave Macmillan, 2007); *Cities of the South: Citizenship and Exclusion in the 21st Century* (B. Drieskens, F. Mermier, and H. Wimmen, eds.; Saqi

Books, 2007); and *Recasting the Social in Citizenship* (Engin F. Isin, ed.; University of Toronto Press, 2008).

Jackie Smith is associate professor of sociology and peace studies at the University of Notre Dame. Her most recent book on globalization and popular movements is *Social Movements for Global Democracy* (Johns Hopkins University Press, 2007). She is also a co-author of *Global Democracy and the World Social Forums* (Paradigm Publishers, 2008). Smith has co-edited three books and more than thirty articles on transnational activism, including *Coalitions Across Borders: Transnational Protest in a Neoliberal Era* (with Joe Bandy), which explores transnational alliances among people of widely varying cultural, political, and economic backgrounds.

Abbreviations

ABM	Anti-Ballistic Missile
ACFUN	Alliance for a Corporate-Free United Nations
ACLU	American Civil Liberties Union
AI	Amnesty International
AIDS	Acquired Immune Deficiency Syndrome
ANEM	Association of Independent Electronic Media
API	Advanced Passenger Information
BBC	British Broadcasting Corporation
BMD	Ballistic Missile Defense
CANPASS	[Facilitates efficient and secure entry into Canada for pre-approved, low-risk travelers]
CAPPS II	Computer Assisted Passenger Pre-Screening System
C.A.T. Eyes	Community Anti-Terrorism Training Institute (United States)
CBSA	Canadian Border Services Agency
CCRA	Canadian Customs Revenue Agency
CEDAW	Convention on the Elimination of All Forms of Discrimination against Women
CIC	Citizenship and Immigration Canada
CNN	Cable News Network
CSR	Corporate Social Responsibility
EFF	Electronic Frontier Foundation
EBSVERA	Enhanced Border Security and Visa Entry Reform Act (United States)
EU	European Union
FAIR	Fairness and Accuracy in Reporting
FAST	Free and Secure Trade
FBI	Federal Bureau of Investigation
FBO	Faith-Based Organization
FISA	Foreign Intelligence Surveillance Act (United States)

FISC	Foreign Intelligence Surveillance Court
FY	Fiscal Year
GAO	Government Accounting Office
GC	Global Compact
HIV	Human Immunodeficiency Virus
ICAO	International Civil Aviation Organization
ICHRDD	International Centre for Human Rights and Democratic Development
IGLHRC	International Gay and Lesbian Human Rights Commission
IMAU	Islamic Medical Association of Uganda
IMF	International Monetary Fund
INGO	International Nongovernmental Organization
IRPA	Immigration and Refugee Protection Act (Canada)
ISP	Internet Service Provider
IR	International Relations
IT	Information Technology
IWF	Independent Women's Forum
MDA	Missile Defense Agency
MDAA	Missile Defense Advocacy Alliance
MDS	Missile Defense System
MP	Member of Parliament
MSNBC	Microsoft/National Broadcasting Company
MRTD	Machine Readable Travel Documents
NASA	National Aeronautics and Space Administration (United States)
NFL	National Football League
NATO	North Atlantic Treaty Organization
NEXUS	[United States and Canadian Program for Frequent Business/Leisure Travelers]
NGO	Nongovernmental Organization
NRO	National Reconnaissance Office
NSA	National Security Agency
NSS	National Security Strategy
OIC	Organization of the Islamic Conference
OIWI	Office of International Women's Issues (United States Department of State)
PA	Palestinian Authority
PATRIOT Act	Uniting and Strengthening America by Providing Appropriate Tools Required to Intercept and Obstruct Terrorism Act of 2001 (Public Law 107–56); also known as the USA PATRIOT Act

PEPFAR	President's Emergency Plan for AIDS Relief
PNR	Passenger Name Record
RAWA	Revolutionary Association of Women of Afghanistan
RFE	Radio Free Europe
RTS	Radio Television Serbia
STAR	Satellite Television Asian Region
TIPS	Terrorism Information and Prevention System (United States)
TNC	Transnational Corporation
TSA	Transportation Security Administration (United States Department of Homeland Security)
UK	United Kingdom
UKPS	United Kingdom Passport Service
UN	United Nations
U.S.	United States of America
US-VISIT	United States Visitor and Immigrant Status Indicator Technology
VOA	Voice of America
WMD	Weapons of Mass Destruction
WTO	World Trade Organization

CHAPTER 1

Challenges to Authority in Global Politics

Janie Leatherman

The al-Qaeda attack on the United States on September 11, 2001, was a crime against humanity and a challenge to U.S. hegemonic leadership and the entire post–World War II political order. Although the "war on terror" has replaced the once-familiar Cold War confrontation between communism and capitalism, the discourse and the power behind the war on terror mask a larger political process underfoot in global politics. Thus, this volume seeks to unsettle the predominance of the war on terror lens through which much of the post–Cold War international relations have been cast since September 11. There are many actors on the global stage competing for power and authority—some of them using punitive means, others consensual. Global capitalism, global civil society, global governance institutions and organizations, and a wide range of "illicit" networks—ranging from al-Qaeda to drug smugglers and human traffickers—present a bewildering array of stakeholders that variously confront and collaborate with one another using different strategies of power. Among the questions that must be asked are, on this crowded global stage, who is in charge of what, how do they stay in charge, and what are the effects of their strategic maneuvers?

To answer these questions, this volume draws on Michel Foucault and his extensive body of work on power and its effects (e.g., Ransom 1997; Rabinow 1984; Dreyfus and Rabinow 1982). Special focus is placed, however, on his work *Discipline and Punish* (1991) because of the disciplinary and punitive technologies of power that have emerged out of the Cold War and that have been increasingly deployed by the United States through various institutions—national and global—under the rhetoric and technologies

of the war on terror. Such maneuvering reflects nostalgia for a simpler era
when it was feasible to try to impose imperial solutions on global "disorder."
This is fundamentally a Gramscian argument. The main contention of this
study thus centers on the loss of hegemonic control by the United States
and, with it, the demise of soft power or the consent to govern. Hence, the
resort to threats and the use of force (see Cox 1996, 127; Leatherman and
Webber 2005). For these reasons, drawing on Foucault's concept of disciplinary power provides an important analytics underpinning the analyses of
hegemonic decline that are presented in the chapters that follow. It is, nonetheless, important to unsettle the predominance of the war on terror as the
principle driving force of global politics in the twenty-first century. The
contestations are complex and multifaceted, and the power dynamics are
multiple, fluid, and diffuse. Thus, the case studies that follow draw broadly
upon Foucault's work on power, ranging from sovereign power in premodern
periods to modern techniques of discipline, regulation, and pastoral power,
and how these are used in different combinations, with different effects (see
for example, Foucault 1994a). The present volume encompasses a heteroge-
neity of power and governance as conceived by Foucault.

Foucault's work has been applied to a variety of contexts that relate to international relations and globalization from various disciplinary perspectives,
including ethnography, aesthetics, political theory, ethics, the politics of insecurity and fear, and political economy and governance (some examples include
Ong and Collier, eds. 2004; Agamben 2005; Bauman 2004; Butler 2004;
Dauphinee and Masters 2006; Larner and Walters, eds. 2004; Perry and Maurer,
eds. 2003; Hardt and Negri 2000). Jabri (2007) has also written of Foucault's
analytics of war in the context of the social and the international, and from the
perspective of postcolonial studies. She notes in particular that his

> analytics are centered on the effects of Western modernity, in practices that
> he associates with the trajectory of modernization in modern European soci-
> eties. While we in the contemporary era might extrapolate from Foucault's
> writings in our analyses of the international domain and its transformations,
> seeing the logic of imperialism as the spatial connotation of his concept of
> biopower, Foucault himself only makes minor reference to the political
> economy of this form of power.
>
> (2007, 79)

Thus, bringing Foucault to bear on the changes under way in an era of
hostile unilateralism and hegemonic decline poses some problems. As Jabri
notes,

> Foucault's engagement with the international comes in minor writings, and
> specifically in his interpretation of the Iranian Revolution, the analysis of

which relocates Foucault in the international sphere, a relocation that both underpins the postcolonial critique while raising significant points of departure relating to Foucault's distinctly culturalist understanding of the international, an understanding that pits the modernizing imperatives of Western rationality against what he saw as the resistance(s) of the other.

(2007, 79)

For Jabri, one important challenge is to bring a "differentiated understanding of both power and resistance" (2007, 79).[1]

This volume takes up this challenge by problematizing the use of power through technologies, discourse, and institutions. Following Foucault, the objective is to "ascertain[ing] the possibility of a new politics of truth ... It's not a matter of emancipating truth from every system of power (which would be a chimera, for truth is already power), but of detaching the power of truth from the forms of hegemony, social, economic, and cultural, within which it operates at the present time" (1984a, 75). To this end, this volume provides a methods-testing approach for applying Foucault to the study of global politics in terms he would accept as an "ethics of the interaction between theory and practice"—of linking the two, of holding political leaders to account by showing how we can unblock history and invent a future for ourselves (1984b, 376). In this sense, the case studies in this volume—on the use of torture in U.S. foreign policy; on surveillance and regimes of supervision (e.g., the missile defense shield); on the role of the global media in the war on terror; on the disciplining of religious discourse at the United Nations (UN); and on the role of women in the neoliberal economy—seek to challenge the political, economic, and institutional production of "truth."

The conceptual approach is framed by looking at the role of norms and discourse, at rituals and ceremonies of power, and at the techniques or technologies of discipline and punishment and other forms of power, including sovereign, biopower, governmentality and regulation, and pastoral (or an ethic of caring); at how these powers can be overlapping, insidious, or leaky; and at how power can be used against power as a means of resistance. One theme that runs through many chapters is the loss of democratic accountability through pervasive and encroaching regimes of supervision and surveillance through, for example, the coincidence of interests and the colonizing of state power by corporate power, and vice versa. Many of the case studies document a variety of dilemmas that other actors, including activists from global civil society, face in reining in global capital to make it more socially and democratically responsible.

Complex patterns of discipline and punishment between different sets of actors in global politics (the global media vs. the state; the global media vs. the citizenry; civil society activists and global governance authorities vs. corporate power; the state with and working against corporate power, etc.) also give way to novel ways of redrawing boundaries between them, and to new challenges to identities. One of the ubiquitous effects of much of the disciplining in global politics is the rendering of docile bodies and the internalization of regimes of supervision so that at the individual level they become self-regulating. This also thwarts civic participation and demands for the democratic accountability of public authorities and governing institutions.

Applying Foucault's analytics of power to global politics—and using his work *Discipline and Punish* as a key point of departure—is, therefore, timely for several reasons. First, the end of the Cold War fundamentally changed the strategic environment and the role of the United States in global politics. The Cold War brought everything under its frame of reference with a host of "successful" disciplining devices that colonized politics, culture, economics, and military strategy, as well as academics, research agendas, and education. Reisman reminds us, however, that the Cold War "created a system of neither war nor peace, but constant preparation for war, a high expectation of violence on the part of all actors, a tolerance for institutionalized violations of international law, called euphemistically 'rules of the game,' and the conduct of proxy wars" (1991, 27–28).

This system of discipline and punishment ended with the fall of the Berlin Wall and the collapse of the Soviet Union. Since then, the United States has sought to reassert its authority by defining as the new archetypal enemy aggressive third world states that are acquiring weapons of mass destruction (WMD). General Carl E. Vuono, the Army chief of staff, had articulated the scenario in 1990 that "the proliferation of military power in what is often called the 'Third World' presents a troubling picture. Many Third World nations now possess mounting arsenals of tanks, heavy artillery, ballistic missiles, and chemical weapons ... . The United States cannot ignore the expanding military power of these countries" (as quoted in Klare 1995, 23–24). The George W. Bush administration justifies such policies in the war on terror by pointing to the "convergence of common interests" among extremists groups and their worldwide network whose aim is to hurt the United States and its allies. The U.S. response is two-pronged: coercive and preemptive action against its foes, if necessary (Tenet 2002, 3); and a protective policy for its friends through military aid, stationing of troops, development of new bases and military agreements, a missile defense shield, and so forth.

Framing the key challenge to authority in global politics as primarily a threat from global terror is, however, flawed on several grounds. The security frame precludes a deeper analysis of the causes of global disorder and malcontentment, while justifying repressive measures that undermine democracy and co-opt and violate human rights—as many chapters in this volume show. Moreover, the emphasis on the use of force belies a worldwide loss of consent to U.S. hegemonic rule (Leatherman and Webber 2005). It also ignores the widespread challenges to political authority that arise not only from networks of illicit actors, but also from other interconnected and competing global systems of power and authority, including global corporate power.

Second, along with the changing political landscape of the post–Cold War period, globalization presents new challenges to political authority (Archibuigi, Held, and Köhler, eds. 1998). Politics is no longer based just on the inter-state system—if it ever truly was (Sassen 1996; Appadurai 1996, 2001; Hoffman 1998). The inter-state system has been weakened by the erosion of nation-state sovereignty and the rise of other systems, such as global civil society and global networks of "illicit" actors (Camilleri and Falk 1992; Hall and Biersteker 2002; Price 2003). These developments have put into question the state's authority and monopoly of violence (Tilly 2002). It is now displaced through various mechanisms that operate below, above, and through the state; these mechanisms include the transnationalization of public-order enforcement and policing, the privatization of war, and the rise of global terrorist networks (Kaldor 1999; Barkawi 2006; Gunaratna 2003; Kaldor 2003; see also Friman and Andreas 1999, 8; O'Neill 2004). In so-called failed states like the Congo, Sierra Leone, Afghanistan, and Colombia, global profit-seeking networks link up with local political economies of violence, challenging not only definitions about where the licit and illicit markets begin and end, but also in whose hands the monopoly of violence lies (Friman and Andreas 1999; Pugh and Cooper 2004; Nordstrom 1999). Global networks of discipline and punishment are like figure eights—or perhaps more like a mobius band[2]—where opposing identities collude, overlap, or meld, obscuring the distinction between the world of the licit and the illicit and between friend and foe. Even nongovernmental organizations (NGOs), which have gained moral authority since the end of the Cold War (and the end of the welfare state) by picking up from the failures of the state system in complex humanitarian emergencies (Rose 1996; Lipschutz and Fogel 2002; Price 2003), face numerous ethical and operational dilemmas in their efforts to provide relief and promote postconflict development in countries where the shadow economy is the only system in place (Prendergast 1996; Duffield 2001; Leatherman and Negrustueva, forthcoming 2008).

Third, in addition to the outsourcing of the functions of "failed" states, many of the routine functions of "healthy" states are also being extended or redirected through global networks involving transnational corporations, global governance institutions, and NGOs. This is prevalent in such areas as law enforcement, the judiciary, and regulators in various fields, including commerce, health, finance, immigration, and the environment (Slaughter 2004; see Rygiel, chap. 5 in this volume). In sum, states are increasingly sharing the stage with "sovereignty free actors" (William 2002, 161), and they are also developing complex relationships with them that are often outside democratic controls. Even though fighting global terrorism provides a new raison d'être for states to retain their place of privilege, there are many other reasons to call for state protection (e.g., to respond to local or global environmental or health threats). Key questions are not whether or how the state provides or fails to deliver, but with and against whom it disciplines and punishes, how it does this, and with what effect.

Disciplinary Power and Its Effects

Foucault addresses the idea of discipline and punishment in a seminal work, *Discipline and Punish: the Birth of the Prison*. The French title, *Surveiller et punir* is, however, difficult to render precisely in English. As a 1977 translator of this work notes, the verb *surveiller* has no direct equivalent in English—although it evokes the idea of surveillance, to inspect or observe. It was Foucault himself who settled on the English-language title *Discipline and Punish* (Sheridan 1991, p. ix).

Discipline and punishment serve complementary functions, though punishment is often associated with a direct, legal response, while discipline need not be a specific or a judicial response to a violation, as Mertus and Rawls point out in chapter 2. However, the study of discipline and punishment is not only about specific responses or regimes, but, more importantly, about the effects of power in particular contexts and historical settings. It is not enough to study disciplinary measures in themselves. Foucault argues that one has to "situate them in a whole series of their possible effects, even if these seem marginal at first" (1991, 23). He tells us to "regard punishment as a complex social function" (1991, 23). The most obvious forms of punishment are *overtly* punitive: censorship, repression, violations of rights and freedoms, sanctions, threats, surveillance and control, and acts of destruction. However, Foucault is especially interested in the less visible, more hidden, or "productive" effects of disciplinary power, which may be more significant, if only because we tend not to be aware of them. Here, discipline is the power to identify, order, manage, administer, examine, diagnose, prescribe, and so forth.

Foucault begins his volume on discipline and punishment with a dramatic narrative of an execution by quartering of an accused in 1757. This comes in part 1 of the book, which Foucault devotes to torture and the historical development of an alternative—the penal system. As he explains:

> In monarchical law, punishment is a ceremonial of sovereignty; it uses the ritual marks of the vengeance that it applies to the body of the condemned man; and it deploys before the eyes of the spectators an effect of terror as intense as it is discontinuous, irregular and always above its own laws, the physical presence of the sovereign and of his power ... [However,] in the project for a prison institution that was then developing, punishment was seen as a technique for the coercion of individuals; it operated methods of training the body—not signs—by the traces it leaves, in the form of habits, in behaviour; and it presupposed the setting up of a specific power for the administration of the penalty.
>
> (1991, 131)

Throughout the remaining parts of *Discipline and Punish*, Foucault analyzes both the emergence of the prison and the way in which its disciplinary technique pervades modern society in institutions as diverse as those of education, the hospital, and capitalism. Discipline becomes routine and internalized by the subjects. Hidden forms of discipline function continuously in society through such mechanisms as standardization (e.g., rampant violence in videos and cultural entertainment); efficiency achieved through spatial organization (e.g., the factory production line in the early twentieth century or information technology in the twenty-first); and other means, such as the reduction of signification through repetition (e.g., the flow of travelers through airport detectors), and so on.

Foucault's methodology is to study disciplinary mechanisms within a grid of analysis to see how relations of power and authority are working themselves out in historical movements and events. Part of the task of analyzing a grid of power relations—including those in global politics—is to see how cultural practices are shaping them at present, while looking back to see how and why they have arisen and what the effects have been. Foucault used the French term *dispositif* to describe this grid of analysis, a network of relationships constantly in tension (Dreyfus and Rabinow 1982, 109). The objective is to uncover how knowledge is linked to power and is inseparable from it, how authority is invested in such knowledge and power, and who is resisting it. Foucault argues that "power and knowledge directly imply one another" (1991, 27). There is no knowledge separate from power.

As Dreyfus and Rabinow explain Foucault, "Power and knowledge are not external to one another. They operate in history in a mutually generative fashion." So, "knowledge does not offer a way out; rather it increases the dangers that we face" (1982, 114). Knowledge claims equal power. Or as Foucault puts it, "there is no power relation without the correlative constitution of a field of knowledge, nor any knowledge that does not presuppose and constitute at the same time power relations" (1991, 27). This is the essence of expertise and the setting and controlling of agendas. Knowledge is a central component of historical transformation of various regimes of power and truth (Edelman 1992). Political ideologies, religions, and nationalism, for example, all provide narratives with truth claims. The nation-state has used these discursive strategies for discipline and punishment (Sassen 2006; Conversi 2004).

Indeed, normality is shaped around such discourses. Norms are thus at the center of the acceptability of discipline and punishment in society. They are used to express what is acceptable and what is not. The boundaries that establish the standards of normality are drawn and maintained by the disciplining and punishing of those labeled deviants, rogues, evil, barbarous, and so forth. As Foucault tells us, "the art of punishing in the regime of discipline" serves not to expiate or repress as such, but "compares, differentiates, hierarchizes, homogenizes, excludes. In short, it *normalizes*" (1991, 183, italics original). Hence, the policing function of authority revolves around notions of "normality."

But norms and discourse are constantly being challenged in society, too.[3] New understandings and awareness push the envelope of what is acceptable and lead to the abolishment of, or prohibitions on, some practices (e.g., slavery or apartheid), and/or the expansion of the realm of acceptance of other practices (e.g., women's suffrage or gay rights). The end to which normative claims are deployed is, however, a question of the effects of power. For example, in chapter 3 of this volume, Krista Hunt explores the Bush administration's co-optation of women's rights to justify the war on terrorism.

To understand discipline and punishment, one must closely examine the cultural practices and discourse that make us who we are today. But, in an effort to develop a more complex analysis of power, Foucault was also interested in the long-term continuities of cultural practices. As Dreyfus and Rabinow (1982) explain, the objective of genealogy is to concentrate on relations of power, knowledge, and the body in modern society. In his discussion of televisual narratives of the Iraq conflict in chapter 7, Michael Dartnell captures these relationships. He selects images of captive Westerners in the Iraq conflict from 2003 to 2004 and brings in the cultural context by relating them to "literary narratives of captivity that appeared in colonial North America." Dartnell argues that "like earlier preelectronic storylines, televised captivity narratives discipline and punish those who veer from particular gender, racial, and sexual roles."

To understand the effects of power, Foucault looks at maneuvers, techniques, and the functioning of power as it is exercised through a network of relationships in the social, cultural, political, and economic fields. One technique that Foucault pays particular attention to is the "meticulous rituals of power" (Dreyfus and Rabinow 1982, 188). He develops this line of analysis in *Discipline and Punish* by looking at specific sites where rituals of power take place—such as in schools, monasteries, the military, or prisons; in the exercise of military power or the punishment of the accused; and through the "Panopticon," a prison building designed by Jeremy Bentham for maximum surveillance and control. In the Panopticon, prisoners can always be observed in their cells without ever seeing that they are being observed. As Foucault puts it, for the prisoner, "visibility is a trap" (1991, 200). Rituals and ceremonies are important vehicles for discipline and punishment, and they are often deployed in the service of discourses like nationalism or the war on terror. The ritualistic abuse of prisoners at Abu Ghraib, for example, serves such functions for the war on terror. In chapter 2, Mertus and Rawls discuss the humiliation of Muslim prisoners as a public spectacle.

Discipline itself is not an institution, but rather a *technique* (Dreyfus and Rabinow 1982, 153). Thus, discipline does not replace other forms of power; rather, it invests or colonizes institutions that already exist in society (Foucault 1991, 216)—such as globalization, the war on terror, homeland security, missile defense, and other forms of militarization; or the media, gendered relations, and so on. The effects may be widespread in society—for example, a Campbell's soup that substituted traditional alphabet noodles for the sexier Star Wars satellites (Enloe 2000, 1). Discipline works through many mechanisms and maneuvers, including the most mundane or improbable, and leads to the militarization of a child's lunch. Or, as Foucault puts it, this makes it possible "to bring the effects of power to the most minute and distant elements" (1991, 216).

One of the tasks of genealogy is to show that "the body is also directly involved in a political field: power relations have an immediate hold on it; they invest it, mark it, train it, torture it, force it to carry out certain tasks or perform ceremonies, to emit signs" (Foucault 1991, 25). The body is "the place where the most minute and local social practices are linked up with the large scale organization of power" (Dreyfus and Rabinow 1982, 111). The combination of knowledge and power localized on the body is a general mechanism of power. The practices of globalization spread this mechanism through networks of technology that are articulated on the body. For example, sweatshop factories (enclosed by wired fences and watchtowers; places where abuse includes not allowing workers to take bathroom breaks) produce human beings who are "docile bodies" that are productive for the global market (Bender 2004). Indeed, Dreyfus and Rabinow (1982, 135) argue that Foucault considered that "the development of political technology ... preceded the economic" (see also Foucault 1991, esp. 218–22). As Dreyfus and Rabinow explain, "It was the disciplinary technologies which underlay the growth, spread, and triumph of capitalism as an economic venture. Without the insertion of disciplined, orderly individuals into the machinery of production, the new demands of capitalism would have been stymied. In a parallel manner, capitalism would have been impossible without the fixation, control, and rational distribution of populations on a large scale" (1982, 135). Indeed, in chapter 9 of this volume, Knight and Smith argue that poverty was not a concern to capitalists—but rather the solution. The real problem was pauperism—"the tendency for many of the poor to be undisciplined, licentious, dissolute, unreliable, prone to criminality, and so on." Addressing this kind of social problem was an educational enterprise to reform their conduct.

The regulatory and disciplining strategies of global capitalism are generally geared to keeping the poor where they are and taking the manufacture of the goods to them; there, the poor can be pitted against the poor to ensure the lowest labor costs and the greatest profit margins for global capitalists (Bonacich and Appelbaum 2000). In chapter 5, Kim Rygiel explores how new techniques that rely on biometric technologies contribute to this by the "strengthening of citizenship as a governing regime." Some travelers have fast passes—these are the elite managers whom the heads of global capital need to move quickly and comfortably around the world—while others are relegated to a second-, third-, and even fourth-class status that progressively limits and denies their movements. Alternatively, slave labor can be moved through shadow networks of human trafficking that are designed to subvert or co-opt these controls (Farr 2005).

Discipline and punishment render bodies docile through other techniques, too, as Nowacki and Gutterman show in chapter 4 in their discussion of the missile defense shield and its gendered and patriarchal effects, or as Krista Hunt, in chapter 3, illustrates with the war on terror and the disciplining of third world women to work for the global market. In chapter 9, Knight and Smith assess the possibilities and limitations of the UN's Global Compact (GC) as a mechanism with which to discipline global corporate power to adhere to certain standards of social responsibility in such areas as human rights, labor rights, and environmental protections and sustainability.

In sum, disciplinary power has many forms and effects that actors use to exert and challenge authority in global politics. A key assumption of this volume is that none of the five principal systems of global politics (the nation-state system, global governance, civil society, illicit or shadow systems, and global capitalism) functions autonomously. In one way or another, they work with, or react to, one another while attempting to protect, defend, and expand their power and authority. These challenges involve policing or renegotiating boundaries, including those of nationality, gender, class, race, sexuality, or religion. The discussion below explores the role of three kinds of disciplinary mechanisms in these contestations: (1) norms and discourse, (2) disciplinary techniques and technologies, and (3) rituals and ceremonies.

Mechanisms of Discipline and Punishment

Norms and Discourse

Discipline and punishment are a means by which to reinforce normality, to determine what fits and what does not, what measures up to the rule, and what departs from it. As Foucault puts it, "the whole indefinite domain of the non-conforming is punishable" (1991, 178–79). Thus, discipline functions as a corrective—as a means by which to bring people back into the range of normality. Norms have various communicative functions. Norms allow people to relate to one another along a range of actions and purposes. They "allow people to pursue goals, share meanings, communicate with each other, criticize assertions, and justify actions" (Kratochwil 1989, 11). Norms also provide a range of solutions to social problems. For example, some classes of norms put limits on unacceptable behaviors and ban egregious practices. Other types of norms provide common standards to help parties avoid situations that could cause the escalation of conflict (e.g., cease-fires or arms-control agreements), or standardize rules of competition, as the World Trade Organization (WTO) does with free trade. Norm entrepreneurs (e.g., states, leaders, NGOs) that push for the adoption of new norms (e.g., the norm to ban slavery, genocide and torture, or landmines) or the norm to expand rights (e.g., women's right to vote) push the envelope of "normal" in society (Finnemore and Sikkink 1998). "Runaway norms" are a special class of norms in that they push "normal" in society in insidious ways—for example, by loosening prohibitions on, and normalizing, the acceptability of egregious behaviors, such as genocide, ethnic cleansing, systematic rape, and torture (Leatherman 2007).

Discourse encompasses rhetorical functions in discipline and punishment that are normalizing. In chapter 4, Nowacki and Gutterman point to the disciplining functions of the term *shielding* that surrounds Star Wars technology. They note that this rhetoric "produces (and defines) both those inside and outside of the conceptual space evoked in the public mind" as the family, not the country as a whole, or cities, or military installations. The critics who refuse to buy into the language of shielding are deemed "'unpatriotic' and willing to leave the United States vulnerable to attack, implying at best shortsightedness and at worst sympathy with enemies and terrorists," and unmanliness.

Discourse involves numerous disciplining mechanisms that reinforce accepted social norms. Repetition, as Foucault points out, is a mechanism for enforcing norm compliance that is used in schools and other institutions for correcting defects in behavior. Conservative media such as Fox News *repeatedly* call on "outlyers" like Jordan Eason, a former CNN news executive, and others (e.g., Dan Rather) to "correct themselves." Eason, for example, was disciplined for reportedly saying at the 2005 Davos World Economic Forum that the U.S. military was targeting both American and foreign journalists. Such was the fury launched by bloggers that Eason was forced to resign from CNN. On the February 14, 2005, *O'Reilly Factor* television show, Bill O'Reilly *repeatedly* asked his guest Rony Abovitz (who had attended the Davos panel session in question and had initiated the blogging deluge) whether Eason had apologized and admitted that he had misspoken and whether he had corrected himself on the record, and, if so, whether he had done so right way. Later in the interview, O'Reilly thanked Abovitz for putting the story out: "You can't be saying, running around, if you're the person from CNN or any other news organization, that American troops are killing journalists. Because you know that's going to be used for propaganda against us. We already have enough problems from throughout the rest of the world. So nice job. We appreciate it" (O'Reilly 2005, 3).

One of the most important functions of discourse is controlling the definition of the "problem," whether it be poverty, hunger, crime, illiteracy, youth vandalism, and so forth. Constructing and using social problems for such normative ends involves several hegemonic maneuvers. First, the process of constructing problems reduces the issue at hand to a certain origin. This excludes other perspectives and interpretations and thereby reinforces the dominant ideology and its justifications for certain courses of action or solutions (Edelman 1992, 265). In a democracy, the stability of authority is maintained by carefully controlling what the definition of the problem is, what the legitimate, competing solutions to solving it are, whether and why it can be elevated to a crisis, and who the appropriate authorities are for debating the problem and providing solutions. There are numerous means by which to confer status on the work of experts—for example, providing funding for them, organizing conferences for them to attend, and asking them to write reports, serve as expert witnesses, or be interviewed by the media. Such maneuvers also discipline (marginalize, ostracize) those who identify different problems as needing the urgent attention of society, or those who advocate paying attention to root causes and deep structural changes that threaten entrenched power and authority (Edelman 1992).

Discipline is also affected by manipulating such terms as *problem* and *crisis*. For Edelman, they are "inducements to acquiesce in deprivations. For most people they awaken expectations that *others* will tolerate deprivations" (1992, 273). A poignant illustration of such failures is found in the collapse of the WTO talks in Cancún on September 14, 2003, over agricultural subsidies. A delegate from Uganda "singled out the dispute over cotton subsidies as a major disappointment. Four of Africa's poorest nations had asked that the subsidies given American and European farmers be reduced, and the African farmers be paid $300 million in compensation for the losses they suffered because of unfair competition from wealthy farmers. Instead, a draft proposal suggested the question be studied and the African farmers plant other crops." The Ugandan delegate concluded, "When it came down to negotiations, our daily problems were ignored" (Becker 2003, A4).

The war on terror is an example of a discourse that relies fundamentally on the invocation of crisis. The permanency of the crisis allows political elites to achieve certain goals, to protect themselves from criticism, and to deter, marginalize, and punish dissent. In their chapter (2) on the U.S. regime of torture, Mertus and Rawls show that the permanent state of crisis also justifies that others will suffer deprivations—even extreme forms of deprivation that amount to torture—and it produces docile bodies within the American public who acquiesce in policing themselves and the "other."

Disciplinary Techniques and Technologies

Discipline is achieved through many different kinds of techniques and technologies. At the outset of *Discipline and Punish*, Foucault provides the example of the torture by quartering of the accused as a tool of the sovereign. As Dreyfus and Rabinow explain (1982, 145):

> Public torture was a political ritual. The law, it was held, represented the will of the sovereign: he who violated it must answer to the wrath of the king. A breach of the law was seen as an act of war, as a violent attack on the body

of the king; the sovereign must respond in kind. More precisely, he must respond with excessive force; the sheer strength and magnitude of power underlying the law must be publicly displayed as awesome. In the ritual of violence, the criminal was physically attacked, beaten down, dismembered, in a symbolic display of the sovereign's power. Thus, the power and integrity of the law were reasserted; the affront was righted.

Torture is not without its own limitations as a form of power and discipline. There were various ways in the eighteenth century, for example, that the authority could find itself mocked, and the criminals turned into heroes. The confession was one such opportunity. If the criminal confessed with great emotion and appealed for mercy, he or she could bring the crowd to the outlaw's side. Alternatively, the crowd could come to the criminal's rescue if he or she showed great defiance in the face of an unjust accusation, or even a just one, or if the machinery of death failed—then the mob might free the criminal and pursue the executioners (Dreyfus and Rabinow 1982, 146). Foucault writes that at these spectacles of atrocity, "there was a whole aspect of the carnival, in which rules were inverted, authority mocked and criminals transformed into heroes" (1991, 61). Even in death, the executed could still hold sway over society through the publication of the ritual confession, or death speech, so that either "the repentance of the criminal or the majesty of the crime took on epic proportions" (Dreyfus and Rabinow 1982, 146).

Foucault's *Discipline and Punish*, though subtitled *The Birth of the Prison*, is not simply a story about the history of detention. However, he uses the account of how disciplinary strategies move from torture to detention as a means to a larger analysis of the functions of knowledge, power, truth, and regulation and control in society as they have evolved in the modern era. Thus, prisons are only one example of the development of disciplinary technology. However, there are many others that draw upon the same logic of discipline, surveillance, and punishment. Foucault's analysis of the Panopticon—Jeremy Bentham's plan for a pentagonal prison with a watchtower in the center and cells all around it, with windows in front and back to ensure that the prisoner would be visible from the tower at all times—is a powerful analogy of the disciplinary function of technology.

The ubiquitous cameras in public forums—such as schools, school buses, shopping malls, grocery stores, parking lots—are a constant reminder of the mechanisms of discipline that pervade daily lives. Such surveillance depends partly on the internalization of norms of transparency. People accept these intrusions because the norm of transparency underpins the concepts of an open society, democracy, and free-market enterprise. Florini argues expectantly, however, that the end of the secrecy of states represents a profound change in the distribution of power (2000, 13). Transparency is a preferred means of enforcement under a global capitalist system—not by coercion or surveillance alone, but by revelation. "Transparency provides the basis for a highly democratic, albeit nonelectoral, system of transnational governance based on the growing strength of global civil society. It made sense to cling to secrecy in a world truly divided into discrete nation-states. But in this era of global integration, transparency is the only appropriate standard" (Florini 2000, 27). However, as the Panopticon suggests, transparency is its own double-edged sword. The control of international travelers through passenger-records systems, biometrics, and risk profiling leads citizens not only to become self-governing, but also to "profile" their fellow passengers, as Rygiel notes in chapter 5. The Panopticon thus performs a key reversal: it puts the citizen in the spotlight and government in the shadows, as Nowacki and Gutterman point out in chapter 4. Transparency for *whom?* then is the real question in the context of globalization—and with what *effects?*

Rituals and Ceremonies

Discipline and punishment are also imposed through ritual performances. In the eighteenth century, torture was a public spectacle that drew on ritualistic and ceremonial functions to reinscribe the authority of the sovereign. Since the end of the Cold War, the United States has repeatedly used shock-and-awe campaigns as a ritual answering to the wrath of the global hegemon ("king") and as a maneuver to reinscribe its authority (a short list of examples includes Panama, 1989; the Gulf War, 1990; Kosovo, 1999; Afghanistan, 2001; Iraq, 2003). The U.S. strategy of shock and awe deployed against Saddam Hussein, his regime, and, inevitably, the people of Iraq, is a twenty-first century spectacle of condemnation and torture. It is not so far removed as it might seem from the medieval practices of torturing and quartering the condemned that Foucault graphically details in the opening of *Discipline and Punish.*

How is this possible? Foucault argues that the modern state has moved away from spectacle as a form of discipline, which was part of the culture of antiquity, and in favor of surveillance. Indeed, Foucault associates this historical transition with the imperial figure of Napoleon, whose regime bridges both the spectacle and the move to surveillance. As he notes, "the importance, in historical mythology, of the Napoleonic character probably derives from the fact that it is at the point of junction of the monarchical, ritual exercise of sovereignty and the hierarchical, permanent exercise of indefinite discipline" (1991). This characterization of the Napoleonic moment is relevant precisely for understanding the function of ritual and ceremony in the Bush administration's own nostalgic imperial gestures. Foucault comments on Napoleon:

> At the moment of its full blossoming, the disciplinary society still assumes with the Emperor the old aspect of the power of spectacle. As a monarch who is at one and the same time a usurper of the ancient throne and the organizer of the new state, he combined into a single symbolic, ultimate figure the whole of the long process by which the pomp of sovereignty, the necessarily spectacular manifestations of power, were extinguished one by one in the daily exercise of surveillance.
>
> (1991, 217)

The ceremonial role of bowing to the imperial power of the Bush administration fell first to the U.S. Congress in the preparations for the war against Iraq and then later to the UN Security Council—which nonetheless resisted. The congressional debate on the joint resolution authorizing the war was a ritual performance for the imperial power of the presidency marking the total abdication of congressional authority. Bush went to Congress in early September 2002 to seek authorization. On Sunday morning talk shows on September 8, administration figures, including Vice President Cheney, abandoned a unilateralist approach and began making arguments for the development of a broad coalition against Iraq. The next move was to pressure Congress for a speedy resolution before the November adjournment for elections. The House Committee on Foreign Affairs, which reported the resolution, developed only five pages of text for its analysis. In it, the committee expressed the hope that the resolution authorizing the president to use force would be a signal to Iraq of the United States' resolve in the matter and that in the end it would be the best way to avoid having to use force. Thus, as Fisher notes, "the legislation would decide neither for nor against war. That judgment, which the Constitution places in Congress, would now be left in the hands of the President" (2003, 404). On October 8, 2002, the actual resolution passed in the House with 296 votes in favor and 133 against, and in the Senate, 77 to 23.

Robert Byrd, Democratic senator from West Virginia, was one of the few legislators to take strong exception to this public spectacle. "To Byrd, the fundamental question of why the United States should go to war was replaced by 'the mechanics of how best to wordsmith the President's use-of-force resolution in order to give him virtually unchecked authority to commit the nation's military to an unprovoked attack on a sovereign nation'" (as quoted in Fisher 2003, 406). He did not see the threat from Iraq justifying the "stampede" to authorize the president to use force. On the eve of the U.S. invasion of Iraq, Senator Byrd wrote, "The Chamber [the Senate] is, for the most part, silent—ominously, dreadfully silent. There is no debate, no discussion, no attempt to lay out for the nation the pros and cons of this particular war. There is nothing" (2003a, 1).

Shortly after the U.S. invasion of Iraq in March 2003, President Bush staged a dramatic event to announce a premature U.S. victory. On May 1, he donned a flight jacket and landed on the aircraft carrier USS Abraham Lincoln (when the ship was only a few miles off the coast of San Diego and easily accessible by helicopter). The entire drama was staged as a meticulous ritual of power by the White House; it included a presidential speech celebrating the battle of Iraq "as one victory in the war on terror." The speech was broadcast live at sunset against the backdrop of a large banner hung by a White House official on the carrier, boldly announcing, "Mission Accomplished."

Senator Byrd was again one of the sharpest critics of this grand spectacle. "We expect, nay demand, that our leaders be scrupulous in the truth and faithful to the facts. We do not seek theatrics or hyperbole. We do not require the stage management of our victories ... War is not theater and victory is not a campaign slogan" (2003b, 2).

Rituals and ceremonies can be used to invoke power and to resist it. The annual meetings of the WTO, the World Bank, the Group of 7/8, and regional development banks, as well as the World Economic Forum in Davos, Switzerland, serve ceremonial functions of reasserting the power and authority of global elites and the prevailing political and economic arrangements of neoliberal capitalism. That these rituals are forums for the powerful and provide opportunities for resistance has been made quite clear by the emergence over the last couple of decades of protest movements that have converged on the host cities and locales during these elite gatherings.

The protesters themselves have their own ceremonial functions, too. In an essay on "Transnational Protests: States, Circuses, and Conflict at the Frontline of Global Politics," O'Neill (2004) focuses on the performance and theater of the protesters as a means of promoting cooperation across diverse constituencies of the transnational protest movement, as well as a means of resisting the authority of the state and elite players. Part of their resistance stems from the fear that "states are ceding important powers to institutions and corporations that lack accountability and transparency and that the underlying dynamics of free market capitalism will undermine social and environmental policies and practices at the local, national and international levels" (238). The theatrical performances of the protesters also help them broadcast this message by using the colorful and playful nature of the protests to reach the media and a global audience.

The ritual nature of global elite meetings and protests has also spawned its own growth industry of discipline and punishment. One strategy of the elite is to constantly move the locales of the meetings to different points of the globe, sites that have become increasingly more remote. There has also been a transnationalizing of public-order enforcement through the policing techniques of surveillance, spatial organization, and control of protestors, so protests are out of view of the elite attendees of the global meeting in question, and thus unable to interfere with the event. National models of policing protests are also converging, through crowd-control techniques (paramilitarization of police tactics), prevention of protests, controlling (forbidding) activist travel, and infiltration and surveillance of protest activities (O'Neill 2004, 245). These policing strategies point in new ways to the strengthening of states and state agencies—rather than to their decline as predicted in much of the state literature.

Overview of the Volume

The chapters in this volume take up these themes of discipline and punishment in the broader context of Foucault's analytics of power. Several chapters focus on the discourse of the war on terror, the violations of rights, gender, and the rendering of docile bodies. In chapter 2, Mertus and Rawls develop an analysis of the disciplinary functions of torture and of the regimes of surveillance that support it. They argue that "current trends in U.S. torture policy are happening *in the context of modernity* and signify far more than a return to a feudal, monarchical past into which torturers acted to avenge a sovereign power." In chapter 3, Krista Hunt details how the war on terror co-opts women's rights to advance the Christian fundamentalist agenda of the Bush administration, leading to severe restrictions, controls, and punishments in the area of women's reproductive rights, including the denial of access to information about birth control and abortion, while promoting their integration into the global market economy in menial wage sectors. Nowacki and Gutterman also investigate the gendered aspects of power relations and discipline in the context of the rhetoric on the missile defense shield and its reification of domesticity. Rhetorical justifications of a missile defense shield for the United States present it seductively as the first line of defense in the war on terror and situate the failure to pursue this "antiterror," "antimissile" mission as irresponsible. In the rhetorical war to define and defend the "homeland," the missile defense shield serves as a magical vehicle that does not simply promise future safety, but reifies the mythical past of gender stability and domestic order.

A second set of chapters centers the analysis of disciplinary power around regimes of supervision and surveillance and illustrates the tension between the authority of the state and corporate power. In chapter 5, Kim Rygiel examines this in the context of new citizenship policies that have the intended effect of strengthening citizenship as a disciplining regime of governing populations. Drawing from Foucault's concept of governmentality, Rygiel focuses on citizenship policies and practices having to do with border controls and travel regulations using biometric technologies. She examines how the state's capacity to discipline populations is displaced on three levels to forces "above" and "below" the state. First, she shows that citizenship is internationalized, as state power is displaced to international organizations and as border controls and travel regulations are internationalized and standardized. She illustrates this argument through a discussion of biometric travel documents and Advanced Passenger Information (API) and Passenger Name Records (PNR) systems. Second, she shows how this internationalization is connected to other levels of governing, such as the privatization of citizenship. Third, she argues that citizenship is strengthened through disciplinary forms of power enacted directly on the body through biometric technology.

In chapter 6, Riaz and DiMaggio contend that the dramatic shift that characterizes the present century is the demise of the "state" as the central actor in global politics. The rise of electronic media is one of the most important developments in the reconfiguring of power. The international television networks, such as CNN, the BBC, and Al-Jazeera, have challenged the state's capacity to follow independent policies within domestic and international contexts, and they have undermined the authority and legitimacy of the state. National boundaries and, to a great extent, sovereignty are being violated. However, the erosion of the state's ability to control has not created a void wherein the media are acting without "supervision." The logic of international capitalism has been one such means of "disciplining" the media, but since the 1990s we have also seen the emergence of a "regime of supervision." Several national responses (e.g., by the United States, Israel, the Palestinian Authority, and Qatar) to these challenges and to the media's subversive techniques are illustrated.

In chapter 7, Michael Dartnell brings the analysis of the power of the media full circle back to the media's effects on the individual by discussing the role that images of captivity—including those of torture—play in the war on terror. Images and representations project and sustain the power to discipline and punish. He notes that "the power to 'evoke emotional responses, demand attention, threaten us, influence memories, and change ideas of what is natural' (Reeves and Nass 1998, 251) underlies the influence of images." To discuss how television blurs distinctions between representation and lived experience, Dartnell examines select images from the Iraq conflict from 2003 to 2004 and relates them to literary narratives of captivity that appeared in colonial North America. Dartnell argues that, like earlier preelectronic storylines, televised captivity narratives discipline and punish those who veer from particular gender, racial, and sexual roles.

Despite the typical binaries that the war on terror sets up between the West and Islam, white and brown, and racialized others, Evelyn Bush demonstrates in chapter 8 that the disciplinary function of diplomatic discourse does not break down along these same lines. In recent years, religious groups have been increasingly assertive in their efforts to exert influence within international institutions. Bush examines the discursive tactics that both religious and secular actors use to assert competing claims at the UN. First, she argues that "diplomatic speech privileges a discourse of 'rationalizing progress'" that expresses a purposive orientation, with attention to measurable goals, procedures, and effectiveness, and a commitment toward progress similar to that which is embedded in the concept of "development." The privileged status of this discourse constrains actors to state claims in ways that, at least on the surface, tacitly reinforce secular viewpoints. Second, however, she also shows that religious groups are as equally adept as their secular counterparts at using secular discourse to achieve their objectives, and that they have done so in ways that actually create space for religious resistance. Bush introduces the contours of this discursive terrain by exploring UN conflicts over Human Immunodeficiency Virus/Acquired Immune Deficiency Syndrome (HIV/AIDS) prevention and treatment programs. What this discourse obscures, however, is the fact that the debates over the UN Declaration of Commitment on HIV/AIDS involved conflicts that cut across multiple, intersecting dimensions of identity and authority: religious vs. secular, conservative vs. liberal, global North vs. global South, state vs. civil society, individualist vs. collectivist, women vs. patriarchy. Thus, in the global politics of discipline and punishment, the identities of friend and foe are not stable and predictable across the spectrum. Foes in one context become allies in the employment of disciplinary strategies in other contexts.

A common theme that pervades all the chapters is the challenge that neoliberal globalization presents to the territorially organized state system and, with it, to democratic accountability. In chapter 6, Riaz and DiMaggio reach this conclusion in their analysis of the relationships between the media, the state, and the globalization of neoliberalism. As they note, "now that the society is no longer attached to a specific location, thanks to the globalization process, a new kind of Panopticon is needed ... to normalize 'judgment'" and "to tell what is important and what deserves to be known, and conversely what needs to be marginalized."

In chapter 9, Knight and Smith suggest that the core problem is "how the balance of cultural, political, and economic power has been shifting in a direction that undermines democratic governance." Their chapter analyzes activists' challenges to the growth of corporate power at the expense of the state using the UN's GC. According to its advocates, the GC represents an initiative to promote the movement for corporate social responsibility (CSR) as a way of "[e]mbedding the global market within shared values and institutional practices" (Ruggie 2004). The political-economic context for this initiative is the hegemony of neoliberal economism and the new forms of social inequality, division, exclusion, and resistance to neoliberalism that have grown apace since the end of the Cold War and China's embracement of unfettered capitalism. The GC and CSR generally represent a response to the way that neoliberal globalization has accelerated the autonomy of the economic system and reduced the capacity and ideological will of the nation-state to intervene in the market in order to satisfy social demands. The GC is an attempt to rationalize the terrain on which criticisms of, and challenges to, economic and political power centers take place, and incorporate civil society actors within an institutional apparatus that normalizes their activities in the name of consensus-building and social responsibility. The GC, however, cannot simply be dismissed as an instrument for the social control of social activism. Social movements and NGOs that criticize and challenge power centers like the state and transnational corporations over issues such as CSR do so not by opposing power per se but by attempting to exploit alternative modes of power and by mobilizing the discourses of legitimacy associated with them. Knight and Smith introduce those in terms of Foucault's work on other technologies of power, including pastoral forms, the leakiness of power, and modes of resistance.

The concluding chapter examines the possibility that discipline and punishment, as well as other forms of power that work in conjunction with it, are contestable or leaky. It summarizes the challenges facing those seeking to produce alternatives in order to unblock history and open new space. The discussion problematizes the kinds of global regimes of supervision and surveillance covered in the preceding chapters and looks at their productive effects in terms of their economies of power, their discourses, their undermining of democratic accountability, and the mechanisms behind the disciplining of identities, including racial and sexual. The analysis is sobering. These technologies, discourses, and institutions of power are overlapping, reinforcing, extensive, and insidious in many ways. In spite of such constraints, the final part of chapter 10 addresses the possibilities of resisting, especially in the context of capillary power—that is, the self-regulation or subjugation and policing of the Other on which the Panopticon ultimately depends for its productive effects. Here, power *can* be leaky. Contesting it depends, in the first instance, on individuals creating alternatives and open spaces in their own minds—to be true to themselves and then also to work collectively to achieve these ends.

Notes

1. Foucault's writing on martial law in Poland and the Solidarity movement, though also limited, is nonetheless helpful in this regard, too. See for example, Foucault (1994b).
2. A mobius strip or band is created by taking a strip of paper and giving it a half twist, and then merging the ends to create one continuous strip. One of its principle features is that it has only one boundary. The international symbol for recycling is inspired by the mobius strip.
3. Breully (1994), for example, argues that nationalism is a discourse that has been used to challenge nation-states.

Bibliography

Agamben, Giorgio. 2005. *State of Exception.* Translated by Kevin Attell. Chicago: University of Chicago Press.

Appadurai, Arjun. 1996. *Modernity at Large: Cultural Dimensions of Globalization.* Minneapolis: University of Minnesota Press.

———, ed. 2001. *Globalization.* Durham, NC: Duke University Press.

Archibuigi, Daniele, David Held, and Martin Köhler, eds. 1998. *Re-imagining Political Community.* Palo Alto: Stanford University Press.

Barkawi, Tarak, 2006. *Globalization and War.* Lanham, MD: Rowman and Littlefield.

Bauman, Zygmunt. 2004. *Wasted Lives: Modernity and Its Outcasts.* Cambridge, UK: Polity Press.

Becker, Elizabeth. 2003. "Delegates from Poorer Nations Walk out of World Trade Talks." *The New York Times,* September 15, A1, A4.

Bender, Daniel. 2004. *Sweated Work, Weak Bodies: Anti-Sweatshop Campaigns and Languages of Labor.* Piscataway, NJ: Rutgers University Press.

Bonacich, Edna, and Richard Appelbaum. 2000. *Behind the Label: Inequality in the Los Angeles Apparel Industry.* Los Angeles: University of California Press.

Breully, John. 1994. *Nationalism and the State.* Chicago: University of Chicago Press.

Butler, Judith P. 2004. *Precarious Life: The Powers of Mourning and Violence*. New York: Verso.

Byrd, Robert. 2003a. "We Stand Passively Mute." Senate remarks by Robert Byrd, February 12. http://byrd.senate.gov/speeches (accessed February 17, 2007).

———. 2003b. "Making the Military a Prop in Presidential Politics." http://byrd. senate.gov/speeches (accessed February 17, 2007).

Camilleri, Joseph, and Jim Falk. 1992. *The End of Sovereignty?* Cheltenham, UK: Edward Elgar.

Conversi, Daniele, ed. 2004. *Ethnonationalism in the Contemporary World: Walker Connor and the Study of Nationalism*. London and New York: Taylor and Francis.

Cox, Robert. 1996. *Approaches to World Order*. Cambridge, UK: Cambridge University Press.

Dauphinee, Elizabeth, and Cristina Master, eds. 2006. *The Logics of Biopower and the War on Terror: Living, Dying, Surviving*. New York: Palgrave Macmillan.

Dreyfus, Hubert L., and Paul Rabinow. 1982. *Michel Foucault: Beyond Structuralism and Hermeneutics*. Chicago: University of Chicago Press.

Duffield, Mark. 2001. *Global Governance and the New Wars*. New York: Zed.

Edelman, Murray. 1992. "The Construction and Uses of Social Problems." In *Jean Baudrillard: The Disappearance of Art and Politics*, edited by William Stearns and William Choloupka, 263–80. New York: St. Martin's Press.

Enloe, Cynthia. 2000. *Maneuvers: The International Politics of Militarizing Women's Lives*. Berkeley: University of California Press.

Farr, Kathryn. 2005. *Sex Trafficking: The Global Market in Women and Children*. New York: Worth Publishers.

Finnemore, Martha, and Kathryn Sikkink. 1998. "International Norm Dynamics and Political Change." *International Organization* 52, no. 4: 887–917.

Fisher, Louis. 2003. "Deciding on War against Iraq: Institutional Failures." *Political Science Quarterly* 118, no. 3: 389–410.

Florini, Ann. 2000. "The End of Secrecy." In *Power and Conflict in the Age of Transparency*, edited by Bernard I. Finel and Kristin M. Lord, 13–28. New York: Palgrave Macmillan.

Foucault, Michel. 1984a. "Truth and Power." In *The Foucault Reader*, edited by Paul Rabinow, 51–75. New York: Pantheon Books.

———. 1984b. "Politics and Ethics: An Interview." In *The Foucault Reader*, edited by Paul Rabinow, 373–80. New York: Pantheon Books.

———. 1991. *Discipline and Punish: The Birth of the Prison*. 2nd ed. Translated by Alan Sheridan. New York: Vintage Books.

———. 1994a. *Michel Foucault: Power*. Edited by James D. Faubion. Essential Works of Foucault 1954–1984 Series, vol. 3, edited by Paul Rabinow, translated by Robert Hurley et al. New York: New Press.

———. 1994b. "The Moral and Social Experience of the Poles Can No Longer Be Obliterated." In *Michel Foucault: Power*, edited by James D. Faubion, 465–75. New York: New Press.

Friman, H. Richard, and Peter Andreas. 1999. "Introduction: International Relations and the Illicit Global Economy." In *Illicit Global Economy and State*

Power, edited by H. Richard and Peter Andreas, 1–24. Lanham, MD: Rowman and Littlefield.

Gunaratna, Rohan. 2003. *Inside Al Qaeda: Global Network of Terror*. New York: Penguin.

Hall, Rodney Bruce, and Thomas J. Biersteker, eds. 2002. *The Emergence of Private Authority in Global Governance*. Cambridge, UK: Cambridge University Press.

Hardt, Michael, and Antonio Negri. 2000. *Empire*. Cambridge, MA: Harvard University Press.

Hoffman, Stanley. 1998. *World Disorders*. Lanham, MD: Rowman and Littlefield.

Jabri, Vivienne. 2007. "Michel Foucault's Analytics of War: The Social, the International, and the Racial." *International Political Sociology* 1, no. 1 (March): 67–82.

Kaldor, Mary. 1999. *New War and Old Wars: Organized Violence in a Global Era*. Palo Alto: Stanford University Press.

———. 2003. *Global Civil Society: An Answer to War*. Cambridge, UK: Polity Press.

Klare, Michael. 1995. *Rogue States and Nuclear Outlaws*. New York: Hill and Wang.

Kratochwil, Friedrich. 1989. *Rules, Norms and Decisions*. New York: Cambridge University Press.

Larner, Wendy, and William Walters, eds. 2004. *Global Governmentality*. New York: Routledge.

Leatherman, Janie. 2007. "Sexual Violence and Armed Conflict: Complex Dynamics of Re-Victimization." *International Journal of Peace Studies* 12, no. 1: 54–71.

Leatherman, Janie, and Julie Webber, eds. 2005. *Charting Transnational Democracy: Beyond Global Arrogance*. New York: Palgrave Macmillan.

Leatherman, Janie, and Nadia Negrustueva. Forthcoming. "Gendered and Ethical Dilemmas of Moving from Emergency Response to Development in Failed States." In *The Handbook of Conflict Analysis and Resolution*, edited by Sean Byrne, Dennis Sandole, Ingrid Sandole-Staroste and Jessica Senehi. Oxford, U.K.: Routledge.

Lipschutz, Ronnie D., and Cathleen Fogel. 2002. "Regulation for the Rest of Us? Global Civil Society and the Privatization of Transnational Regulation." In *The Emergence of Private Authority in Global Governance*, edited by Rodney Bruce Hall and Thomas J. Biersteker, 115–40. Cambridge, UK: Cambridge University Press.

Nordstrom, Carolyn. 1999. "Shadow Sovereigns." Occasional Paper no. 17: OP 2, Kroc Institute for International Peace Studies, University of Notre Dame, Indiana. http://www.nd.edu/~krocinst/ocpapers/index.shtml.

O'Neill, Kate. 2004. "Transnational Protest: States, Circuses, and Conflict at the Frontline of Global Politics." *International Studies Review* 6: 233–51.

Ong, Aihwa, and Stephen Collier, eds. 2004. *Global Assemblages: Technology, Politics and Ethics as Anthropological Problems*. Boston, MA: Blackwell.

O'Reilly, Bill. 2005. "CNN Executive Let Go after Controversial Comments on Troops. The O'Reilly Factor." Transcript. *Fox News Network,* February 14.

Perry, Richard Warren, and Bill Maurer, eds. 2003. *Globalization under Construction: Governmentality, Law, and Identity.* Minneapolis: University of Minnesota Press.

Prendergast, John. 1996. *Frontline Diplomacy.* Boulder, CO: Lynne Rienner.

Price, Richard. 2003. "Transnational Civil Society and Advocacy in World Politics." *World Politics* 55, no. 4: 579–606.

Pugh, Michael, and Neil Cooper, with Jonathon Goodman. 2004. *War Economies in a Regional Context: Challenges of Transformation.* Boulder, CO: Lynne Rienner.

Rabinow, Paul, ed. 1984. *The Foucault Reader.* New York: Pantheon Books.

Ransom, John S. 1997. *Foucault's Discipline: The Politics of Subjectivity.* Durham, NC: Duke University Press.

Reeves, Byron, and Clifford Nass. 1998. *The Media Equation: How People Treat Computers, Television, and New Media Like Real People and Places.* Stanford, CA: CSLI Publications.

Reisman, William Michael. 1991. "Allocating Competences to Use Coercion in the Post–Cold War World: Practices, Conditions, and Prospects." In *Law and Force in the New International Order,* edited by Lori F. Damrosch and David Sheffer, 26–48. Boulder, CO: Westview Press.

Rose, Nikolas. 1996. "The Death of the Social? Re-Figuring the Territory of Government." *Economy and Society* 25, no. 3: 327–56.

Ruggie, John G. 2004. "Reconstituting the Global Public Domain: Issues, Actors, and Practices." *European Journal of International Relations* 10, no. 4: 499–531.

Sassen, Saskia. 1996. *Losing Control? Sovereignty in an Age of Globalization.* New York: Columbia University Press.

———. 2006. *Territory, Authority, Rights: From Medieval to Global Assemblages.* Princeton, NJ: Princeton University Press.

Sheridan, Alan. 1991. "Translator's Note." In *Discipline and Punish,* translated by Alan Sheridan. 2nd ed. New York: Vintage Books.

Slaughter, Anne. 2004. *A New World Order.* Princeton, NJ: Princeton University Press.

Tenet, George. 2002. "Worldwide Threat: Converging Dangers in a Post 9/11 World." Testimony of Director of Central Intelligence George J. Tenet before the Senate Armed Services Committee, March 19. http://www.cia.gov/public?affairs/speeches/senate_hearing_03192002.html.

Tilly, Charles. 2002. "War Making and State Making as Organized Crime." In *Violence: A Reader,* edited by Catherine Besteman, 35–60. New York: New York University Press.

Williams, Phil. 2002. "Transnational Organized Crime and the State." In *The Emergence of Private Authority in Global Governance,* edited by Rodney Bruce Hall and Thomas J. Biersteker, 161–82. Cambridge, UK: Cambridge University Press.

CHAPTER 2

Crossing the Line: Insights from Foucault on the United States and Torture

Julie Mertus and Kristin Rawls

Introduction

Ever since the attacks of September 11, 2001, the U.S. government has argued that the extraordinary nature of terrorism[1] requires extraordinary responses that, in gentler days, would have been rejected as illegal and immoral. Under a crude utilitarian calculus, U.S. officials have contended that because Americans live in such dangerous and frightening times, the suspension of civil liberties—including the right to be free from torture— may be justified (Human Rights Watch 2006; also BBC News 2006).

The trajectory toward the mainstreaming of torture in U.S. policy has been swift and reactionary. Immediately after September 11, the George W. Bush administration secretly approved measures for interrogating suspected al-Qaeda operatives that were to stop just short of torture (Kelley 2004, 1A). Thus began the slippery slope toward the normalization of torture. By 2003, reports on the torture of U.S.-held war prisoners were surfacing,[2] and the "Bush administration lawyers [were contending] ... that the President wasn't bound by laws prohibiting torture and that government agents who might torture prisoners at his direction couldn't be prosecuted by the Justice Department" (Bravin 2004). The lawyers reasoned that the Geneva Conventions outlining the proper treatment of enemy prisoners did not pertain to inmates held at Guantanamo Bay, Cuba, who were designated as "enemy combatants," and thus the door was open for torture (Ross 2005).

Torture "American style" happens within the confines of prisons (originally conceived in lieu of torture) (Ross 2005, 119), under great secrecy, and without the public spectacle of earlier times where the actual body of the accused was grotesquely attacked, delimbed, and disemboweled before the masses. Torture today is an entirely different kind of spectacle. Its existence is widely known by political elites, but is ignored under utilitarian reasoning (as justified means to the ends of containing terrorism) and is leaked to the general public through a series of photographic images that are disseminated through the Internet and other world media outlets, where they are widely debated and discussed, although no action is ever taken and the torture and violence continue.

These new images of torture serve a clear political purpose, as they are closely connected to discourse on the "war on terrorism." As Richard Jackson observes, the language and images of the "war on terrorism [are] not simply a neutral reflection of reality." Rather, they are "a carefully constructed discourse that is designed to achieve a certain number of key political goals, to normalize and legitimize the current counter-terrorist approach [which employs torture], to empower authorities and protect them from criticism; to discipline domestic society by marginalizing dissent or protest; and to enforce national identity by reifying a narrow conception of national identity" (2005, 2). A torture image folded into this terrorist discourse becomes itself an exercise of power.

Today's torture chambers illustrate *an extreme perversion in the mechanism of power institutionalized in the prison system,* in the name of the American people and against a specific type of dehumanized "other." Described variously as animals, evildoers, parasites, and cancers and other diseases and scourges against humanity, the less-than-human accused terrorists can be subject to less-than-human torture. This chapter uses two frameworks developed by Michel Foucault—one related to the nature of prisons and one related to that of madness—in order to argue that this perversion is made possible precisely as a result of the politicization of discipline and punishment and the construction of the enemy other.

Discipline and Punishment in the Context of Terror

Current antiterrorist legal and penal developments closely illustrate the medieval and modern economies of power that Foucault (1995) describes in *Discipline and Punish.* In particular, parallels can be drawn between Bush administration policies and Foucault's analysis along three interlinked and overlapping themes: First, it is possible to draw connections between the administration's policies and the way that power is maintained and communicated through discipline and punishment. Second, these similarities may be expanded to consider the role of the body in public spectacle and the way that globalization and hegemony may figure into this discourse. Finally, the chapter explores the issue of secrecy as a dubious tool for use in the production of truth—and considers what this means in terms of whether or not sound intelligence is really the goal of torture.

Power through Punishment and Disciplinary Power

According to Foucault, the primary ways in which authority asserts its power are twofold: punishment and disciplinary power. Neither of these tactics is necessarily more important than the other, and they generally serve to complement each other. Both may be regarded "as ... complex social function[s] ... [and] as political tactic[s]" (1995, 23). While punishment is a legal response to a perceived crime committed by identified perpetrators against specific aggrieved victims, disciplinary power refers to systematic efforts to control "movement and operations of the body" and to exercise power over individuals in order to produce docility and submission (ibid.). Unlike punishment, disciplinary power is often preventive and is not necessarily responsive. Moreover, it does not apply only to criminals. That is, it is intended to deter the production of criminality; the threat of being branded as criminal and of being subjected to punishment may help discipline people to behave in specific ways deemed desirable by the authorities.

The target of disciplinary power is not just the accused individual whose body is on display, but *everyone and anyone*. The rituals and practices that entail disciplinary action remind everyone that the state maintains control over information and a monopoly over violence—and that at any time their bodies may be next on the block. "Discipline," Foucault writes, "has its own type of ceremony. It was not the triumph, but the review, the 'parade,' an ostentatious form of the examination. In it the 'subjects' were presented as 'objects' to the observation of a power that was manifested only by its gaze" (ibid., 130). As Andrew Neal (2005) has observed, "disciplinary power" then "amounted from the assemblage of multiple new technologies, knowledges, micro-mechanisms and tactics constructed around producing and regulating ever more utile, efficient and productive forms of life at the individual and in turn social level."

The beginnings of power are established through intensive mechanisms of surveillance that induce paranoia and create fear in the population. Foucault's quintessential example of a disciplinary institution is Jeremy Bentham's Panopticon, a famous design for a pentagonal prison that puts a premium on surveillance. Prisoners could be easily observed in their cells, as Foucault (1995, 200) explains:

> At the periphery, an annular building; at the centre, a tower ... pierced with wide windows that open onto the inner side of the ring; the peripheric building is divided into cells ... They have two windows, one on the inside, corresponding to the windows of the tower; the other, on the outside, allows the light to cross the cell ... All that is needed, then, is to place a supervisor in a central tower and to shut up in each cell a madman, a patient, a condemned man, a worker or a schoolboy. By the effect of backlighting, one can observe from the tower, standing out precisely against the light, the small captive shadows in the cells of the periphery ... Each actor is alone, perfectly individualized and constantly visible. The panoptic mechanism arranges spatial unities that make it possible to see constantly and to recognize immediately ... Full lighting and the eye of a supervisor capture better than darkness ... Visibility is a trap ... Surveillance is established in the prisons, yes, but also in the hospitals, the factories, and the schools ... and from there reaching even into the family.

The power of observation that Foucault describes is tremendous. After all, those who lack privacy cannot very well think their own thoughts, much less plan their own subversions. Even in the extreme disciplinary institution of the Panopticon, it is not just the warden or the guard who is a "bearer" of power with regard to power relations (ibid., 203). When prisoners are unable to distinguish when they are safe to behave as they desire, they are forced to behave as the guards wish them to. In the Panopticon, the inmate "becomes the principle of his own subjection" inasmuch as he exerts disciplinary power over himself—maintaining a docile, subjugated body even though he does not know whether or not he is under surveillance, precisely *because* he may be under surveillance at any moment (ibid.). Surveillance is a potent means of social control that renders individuals docile, obedient, and easily manipulated (themes that arise elsewhere in this volume, such as in chapter 5 on border control and in chapters 6 and 7 on the effects of the global media). Even in this extreme disciplinary situation, then, the inmate, like the prison guard, is also a "bearer" of power, a "vehicle" through which power circulates.

Since September 11, such coercive surveillance measures as the USA PATRIOT Act, as well as the activities undertaken by the much-maligned Department of Homeland Security, have created a veritable Panopticon within the United States. Indeed, in the aftermath of September 11, the executive branch of the government fought to arm the U.S. government with abilities to "secretly spy on individuals and organizations, ... search and seize records or personal belongings without a warrant, and ... legally detain without trial and/or deport thousands of Arabs, Muslims and South Asians" (Lipman 2004). These measures went against traditions of civil liberty and the right to privacy in the United States. "The law governing clandestine surveillance in the United States, the [1978] Foreign Intelligence Surveillance Act, prohibits conducting electronic surveillance not authorized by statute" (Eggen 2005, A1). To aggressively increase its surveillance tactics, the Bush administration had to either create new laws or break existing ones.

The government consistently claims that such new surveillance powers are aimed exclusively at suspected terrorists who threaten national security and that such powers are thus in America's collective national interest. Yet, the Patriot Act allows the Federal Bureau of Investigation (FBI) to collect information on anyone without a warrant or any probable cause. Beyond the now legal activities, the Bush administration has been criticized for running a secret domestic surveillance program that operates out of the National Security Agency (NSA). The NSA program goes further in permitting government officials to eavesdrop on the e-mail, telephone, and other forms of communication of anyone without a warrant. The program, authorized by a secret executive order in 2002, is supposedly aimed at al-Qaeda operatives in the United States. However, "the NSA's vast data-mining activities began shortly after Bush was sworn in as president, [which] contradicts his assertion that the 9/11 attacks prompted him to take the unprecedented step of signing a secret executive order authorizing the NSA to monitor a select number of American citizens thought to have ties to terrorist groups" (Leopold 2006).

The "NSA Activities to Safeguard Americans," as administration officials call them, are another example of political opportunism and disciplinary control, as they use the terrorist threat as a justification for exercising greater surveillance power. Fortunately, the new surveillance has not been without opposition. Indeed, "suits filed by the American Civil Liberties Union [ACLU] and resolutions passed against the Patriot Act by three states and over 215 communities ..., reflect significant opposition. At issue is the build-up of a state apparatus with the authority to intrude into every aspect of [Americans'] lives and to punish without legal recourse those singled out by the government" (Lipman 2004).

In spite of some opposition, however, this new American Panopticon has created a polity that is afraid to question its authority. Many of the citizens who comprise this polity remain content in their assumptions that the government is targeting only true wrongdoers. They believe that the punitive structures are not focused on them and assume that they must be necessary in order to inspire such radical, time-consuming, and expensive measures.

They participate with the state in overseeing their own discipline and ignore the undemocratic consequences of what is taking place. Ultimately, the citizens permit what Wendy Brown has called "the hollowing out of a democratic political culture and the production of the undemocratic citizen" (Brown 2006, 692).

These developments are easy for many to ignore, since it is just one population—Muslims—that is being scrutinized by the new and improved American Panopticon. Though Muslims represent a vast range of countries, religious ideologies, and political beliefs, they represent one singular population under the Panopticon—the population of people whom the government believes to be dangerous and lacking in the requisite docility and subservience—people, Americans are led to believe, who may perpetrate terrorist attacks against American citizens at any given time.

The American Panopticon is endowed with the ability to perpetrate racial and religious profiling to a tee. Indeed, the U.S. government condemns racial profiling, except for purposes of national security. An ACLU report makes note of guidelines "Regarding the Use of Race by Federal Law Enforcement Agencies," issued by the U.S. Department of Justice in June 2003 (ACLU Report 2004). The guidelines include a grave loophole in stating, "The above standards do not affect current Federal policy with respect to law enforcement activities and other efforts to defend and safeguard against threats to national security or the integrity of the Nation's borders ... " (ibid.). Through its own war on terror, the United States keeps a close eye on the Muslims and nonwhites within its own borders and around the world.

The Panopticon is what enables the government to target and find those people who will eventually become the victims of torture—even those who live outside the borders of the United States. That most of the world's Muslims live outside the legal mechanism contained within the United States means that it is that much easier to circumvent the laws in their treatment. *Because they are often excluded from the democratic legal system, they are easily exempt from the rights that it entails.* Therein lies a perversion of the legal system—in the sanitized, cut-and-dry nature of the international system, it is not at all difficult to bypass the system in order to perpetrate horrific, barbaric acts of extreme violence in indignation against the socially constructed monstrosity of a criminal. Foucault would not be surprised by the masterful manner in which the United States manipulates the legal system. It is under the cloak of legal authority that the U.S. government has assumed the vast role of punishing some people—some guiltier than others—in order to avenge the American people.

In the end, the Panopticon ensures that no act of violence can be perpetrated against the observers within the Panopticon. Moreover, it is light enough that it precludes observers from committing acts of violence within its walls. While the Panopticon may prevent barbarous acts from occurring in daylight, it also exists within a power structure that gives its observers ultimate control over those in prison. Thus, the prisoners live at the whims of the observers and may therefore be removed from within the Panopticon's walls—something that Foucault did not foresee. Indeed, the Panopticon gives observers total domination over the condemned. Given that all people possess agency, it is no surprise that the structure may give way to horrific excesses; even in the most advanced of disciplinary structures, sovereign power, as Foucault warned, continues to circulate and subsist alongside of disciplinary power.

No longer the enemy just of a sovereign, the criminal was now conceived as "the enemy of all, whom it is in the interest of all to contain. He falls outside the pact, disqualifies himself as a citizen, and emerges, bearing within him, as it were, a wild fragment of nature; he appears as a villain, a monster, a madman, perhaps a sick and, before long, 'abnormal' individual" (Foucault 1995, 101). Now, the criminal was something less than human. A rigid mechanism of power could sufficiently keep these prisoners at bay by isolating them from other individuals. Though they were constructed as monsters and as abnormal, a rigid mechanism could theoretically succeed in limiting the pain that officers of the law could legally inflict upon criminals. In order to mitigate the hatred that it would undoubtedly inflame against the criminal, the regime would have to be exceptionally rigid and exceptionally strong, making sure to ingrain each of its officers and its citizens with the required legal limitations. The larger the economy of power became—and the more criminals it encompassed—the more difficult it would be to limit the degree of pain inflicted upon the criminal. This is precisely what has happened in the United States.

At any time, the observer may remove the condemned from the Panopticon structure and proceed to torture him. In this context, the criminal has been condemned for a crime *against all*; surely, no punishment could be too great for him. Vast surveillance has perpetuated the view that the condemned is less than human; thus, he does not deserve the due process to which humans are entitled. The observers internalize the notion that the condemned is an animal. It is not surprising—given that the observers hold the keys to the Panopticon—that they may sometimes choose to remove the condemned, resituate him in a dark place, and do unspeakable and abusive things to him—things that they might do to an animal as punishment. If anything, the American people should be surprised—given the stark construction of the Muslim, brown-skinned person as evil and subversive—that more torture has not been alleged.

The Role of the Body in Public Spectacle

In the end, the human body neatly incarcerated in the Panopticon—and wrested out for the purposes and at the whims of the observers—is a crucial factor in this analysis. Foucault's work explains how the prison represented a new era in controlling the human body, of utilizing it more efficiently for the purposes of power through knowledge (1995, 193). He explains: "As [society] switched [its] focus from the infliction of pain to an analysis of the inner workings of the criminals mind, we began to peer at the basic mechanisms which allow him to operate at his very soul" (ibid.). This means that the focus shifted to the mind, but the preoccupation with the body's symbolic dimensions did not diminish.

Indeed, if today's penal system attempted to move away from torture, an element of coercion exists in the fact that human bodies are forced into containment from which they cannot escape. The body is not simply the object of punishment, but the site of the production of the government's case and the inscription of the symbolic and material reality of sovereign power. That is, the body is the location in which the work on the soul and the mind of the condemned begins. As Foucault suggests, "The body, several times tortured, provides the synthesis of the reality of the deeds and truth of the investigation, of the documents of the case and the statements of the criminal, of the crime and the punishment. It is an element, therefore, in a penal liturgy, in which it must serve as the partner of a procedure ordered around the formidable rights of the sovereign, the prosecution and secrecy" (1995, 47). While Foucault suggests that this type of torture has disappeared in modernity, he allows for the fact that it persists in today's penal system, and, moreover, it is clear that it exists even in America's modern Panopticon.

Successful discipline creates "docile bodies," as Hunt, Rygiel, Nowacki and Gutterman, Dartnell, and others document in their chapters in this volume. A body is docile, Foucault explains, when it is both obedient and teachable. In the Panopticon, the human body, watched constantly, begins to achieve the desired malleability, the subservient demeanor, and the repentant posture. The process of torture simply expedites this process such that "the body interrogated in torture [constitutes] the point of application of the punishment and the locus of extortion of truth. And just as presumption was inseparably an element in the investigation and a fragment of guilt, the regulated pain involved in judicial torture was a means of both punishment and of investigation" (1995, 42). The sovereign relies on public displays of bodies in pain as reminders of its own power—and of the powerlessness of its subjects. "Its aim is not so much to re-establish a balance as to bring into play, at its extreme point, the dissymmetry between the subject who has dared to violate the law and the all-powerful sovereign who displays his strength" (Foucault 1995, 48–49).

Foucault illustrates how torture was used in medieval times in order to demonstrate the criminal's offense and warn others against following in his footsteps. In some ways, Muslim prisoners whose abuse becomes public are branded before their own peers and compatriots—humiliated before their own communities, the communities to which they will ultimately return if they survive. This humiliation represents one form of feudal public spectacle that remains. In some ways, this trend represents a globalized form of Foucauldian public humiliation—the creation of images that will never be erased from the public consciousness. While the government may no longer brand the condemned through the use of irons, the pictures taken at Abu Ghraib prison and at Guantanamo Bay are evidence of a new trend—physical branding in the form of a digital photograph that may never be erased, branding, then, via digital camera.[3] The message is clear: Let anyone who dares to perpetrate any aggression against the American people be warned.

Secrecy and the Production of Truth

Ultimately, Foucauldian insights can help to shed light on the production of truth and of knowledge in society. First, Foucault enables us to theorize around ways that U.S. policy has been based upon the criminality and inhumanity of perpetrators—as animalistic criminals who have wronged all citizens of a sovereign state. Foucault's work sheds light on how state involvement in the production of truth forms part of a complex economy of power. Sovereigns seek to create a narrative that justifies their monopolization over the instruments of violence and their ability to use violent instruments in acts of retaliation. Acts of terrorism, then, are viewed as strikes not only against the individual victims, but also against the state and against all citizens of the state.

In medieval times, criminal acts were understood as acts against the sovereign head of state. Thus, punishment, "require[d] that the king take revenge for an affront to his very person. The right to punish, therefore, was an aspect of the sovereign's right to make war on his enemies" (Foucault 1995, 48–49). Now, criminal offenses are said to constitute acts against all citizens of a sovereign state. Thus, punishment is carried out on behalf of citizens and against the criminal who has wronged them. Because citizens, including those citizens who act as observers for the Panopticon, have internalized the wrongs that the condemned has done, it is arguable that this type of torture—that which occurs in modernity—has the potential to take on a particularly cruel and vengeful nature. In other words, those who carry out torture do it on behalf of the citizens of their state—whom they understand to be the victims of the criminal act. The pictures released from Abu Ghraib reflect examples of intense cruelty; after all, these acts of torture were carried out on behalf of all American victims of terrorism, indeed against all Americans who view themselves as the victims of this new age of terrorism.

This torture serves to influence the way that states produce truth (read: intelligence) and impairs the transparency of criminal procedures. Foucault illustrates how, in premodern times, "the secret ... form of the procedure reflects the principle that ... the establishment of truth was the absolute right and the exclusive power of the sovereign" (ibid., 35). Foucault observes further that "the entire criminal procedure, right up to the sentence, remained secret: that is to say, opaque, not only to the public but also to the accused himself. It took place without him, or at least without his having any knowledge of the charges or of the evidence. In the order of criminal justice, knowledge was the absolute privilege of the prosecution" (ibid., 35). The state's desire to control information and resources only intensified in the age of Enlightenment, in which barbarities of the past were tossed aside and there was invented "a legal limit" (ibid., 74) to the sovereign's power to punish. Sovereigns who cross the line and violate this legal limit try their best to limit public oversight of their misdeeds.

There is ample evidence that the United States is mistreating detainees held at Guantanamo Bay. The atrocities committed at Guantanamo have been leaked to the press, despite attempts to seal the area off from the public and shroud it in secrecy. There is only one exception to the ban on outside observation. The International Red Cross is the only group, other than the U.S. government, that is able to access the over 600 suspected al-Qaeda operatives held in captivity there. "In exchange for access, the [Red Cross] committee has agreed to take any initial complaints directly to Washington" (BBC News 2003). This arrangement exemplifies the power of secrecy and the threat of observation. The Red Cross was granted controlled access to appease suspicion of mistreatment, and only on condition that it would not publicize its observations, thus preserving U.S. power and secrecy. Yet, even these control mechanisms did not prevent Christophe Girod, the senior Red Cross official in Washington, from making a critical public statement in October 2003. He said that "it was unacceptable that the 600 detainees should be held indefinitely at Guantanamo Bay without legal safeguards" (ibid.).

Today's new allegations of torture suggest a strange development in the republican system, reflecting, as they do, a system that has gotten out of control, that has grown far beyond its ability to keep the rigidity of legal mechanisms in check. As a result of the September 11 attacks, Americans—indeed, anyone, according to Bush, who "loves freedom"—are now a nation of victims, and the perpetrator, an entire group of people—Muslims. Whether or not the specific people being tortured actually perpetrated terrorist or otherwise criminal acts becomes immaterial. Just as the actual, physical victims of terrorism were deemed immaterial, so now the actual perpetrators are immaterial. Arab and South Asian Muslims now represent the crime that was done to the American people. They must be punished. Moreover, "the punishment must take into account the profound nature of the criminal himself, the presumable degree of his wickedness, the intrinsic quality of his will" (Foucault 1995, 98). Above all, though, the punishment must sufficiently deter those who empathize with the criminal, the "potentially guilty" (ibid., 8–9).

Foucault's analysis is persuasive and compelling in its suggestion that the modern age is characterized by "the disappearance of the tortured dismembered, amputated body" and the appearance of a new form of punishment in which "punishment [tends] to become the most hidden part of the penal process" (ibid.). Nevertheless, Foucault points out that "there remains ... a trace of 'torture' in the modern mechanisms of criminal justice—a trace that has not been entirely overcome, but which is enveloped, increasingly, by the non-corporal nature of the penal system" (ibid., 16). Indeed, this noncorporal nature is characterized by the various aspects of modern prison life that cause an inmate to suffer, since it is considered "just that a condemned man should suffer physically more than other men" (ibid.). It is that trace of torture that has seeped through, which the system of power has been unable to contain as a result of its own monstrous size. Instead of small instances of torture, though, we are seeing torture wrought large—the uncontestable consequences of the social demonization of the enemy.

Foucault's Theory of Deviance

Premodern torture was usually perpetrated against the poor—often for petty morality crimes, as a result of the fact that society could not figure out what to do with poor people. This historical form of torture punished undesirables that authorities did not know how to account for in their own societies, but current prisoners accused of terrorist activity have very little in common with premodern peasants. Moreover, no instance of U.S. torture has anything to do with national undesirables or with class in and of itself. Now, torture victims are flown to Guantanamo Bay and to various prisons in the Muslim world from many parts of the world. The victims are not victims because they are poor, although they may *happen* to be poor, but just as many are functioning members of their respective societies—for example, successful engineers and scientists and those in other generally well-respected positions. Here, Foucault's theorization of the social deviant is useful.

Foucault theorizes heavily about deviance and its construction by systems of power. One could write quite a tome on this issue, since the radicals being fought now are often radicals constructed by the U.S. system of power in order to serve its own interests in projecting power abroad. If not Cold War–era freedom fighters, today's terrorists are, more often than not, people who have been influenced, trained, and funded by Cold War–era thugs in Pakistani and Afghan training camps. Fortunately, Americans have short attention spans. So, when these freedom fighters began to act against U.S. interests, it became possible to reconstruct their identity. No longer freedom fighters, they were now a destructive alien force that needed to be contained.

In his discussions of madness, Foucault focuses on constructions of madness by the psychological profession. He points out:

> The notions found again and again through this set of [psychological] texts are: "psychological immaturity," "a poorly structured personality," "a poor grasp of reality." These are all expressions ... in the reports of psychiatric experts: "a profound affective imbalance," "serious emotional disturbance." Or again: "compensation," "imaginary production," "display of perverted pride," "perverse pride" ... "Don Juanism," etc.
>
> (1999)

Foucault suggests that these characterizations "emerge against a background in which they are measured against an optimum level of development ('psychological immaturity,' 'poorly structured personality,' 'profound imbalance'), a criterion of reality ('poor grasp of reality'), moral qualities (modesty, fidelity), and ethical rules" (ibid., 16). Thus, a criminal is constructed who "is incapable of integrating himself into the world, who loves disorder, commits extravagant or extraordinary acts, hates morality, who denies its laws and is capable of resorting to crime" (ibid., 17).

American power structures were so successful in their construction of the Islamic radical deviant that they would convince the American public that they must be *fearful* of the radicals infiltrating their democratic society. In order to combat these enemies, extreme measures would need to be taken, since Americans were dealing with an unpredictable, undetectable, and evil group. This construction of all Arabs and all Muslims as potentially evil deviants would ultimately serve to justify the use of torture in the war on terror. Extreme forms of coercion would be needed in order to control this otherwise growing and uncontrollable group; hence the Bush administration's policies.

Conclusion

The United States is turning the clock back hundreds of years with respect to its disregard of human rights and its attempt to carve out a space for torturing the accused. In so doing, the United States is following a well-worn path of autocratic sovereigns seeking to use torture and other public forms of punishment to impose discipline and compel obedience. Some point out that the new trend hearkens back to the times of authoritarian kings and their torture chambers, but today's practice of torture and its techniques are decidedly postmedieval. This essay demonstrates that current trends in U.S. torture policy are happening *in the context of modernity* and signify far more than a return to a feudal, monarchical past into which torturers acted to avenge a sovereign power.

Notes

1. The use of the term "terrorism" in this essay refers to international terrorism, defined as "incidents in which terrorists go abroad to strike their targets, select domestic targets associated with a foreign state, or create an international incident by attacking airline passengers, personnel, or equipment." Domestic terrorism, on the other hand, involves "incidents perpetrated by local nationals against a purely domestic target." See www.tkb.org/RandSummary.jsp.
2. One of the most authoritative reports was by an international fact-finding team. See "United Nations, Economic and Social Council" (2006).
3. See generally Fulwider, Greenhill, and Weaver (2007) and also Dartnell, chap. 7, in this volume.

Bibliography

American Civil Liberties Union. 2004. "Sanctioned Bias: Racial Profiling since 9/11." Report. February. www.aclu.org/FilesPDFs/racial%20profiling%20report.pdf.
BBC News. 2003. "Red Cross blasts Guantanamo." October 10. http://news.bbc.co.uk/2/hi/americas/3179858.stm.
———. 2006. "Amnesty Accuses US on Rendition." April 5. http://news.bbc.co.uk/2/hi/europe/4878096.stm.

Bravin, Jess. 2004. "Pentagon Report Set Framework for Use of Torture: Security or Legal Factors Could Trump Restrictions, Memo to Rumsfeld Argued." *The Wall Street Journal,* June 7.

Brown, Wendy. 2006. "American Nightmare: Neoliberalism, Neoconservatism, and De-Democratization." *Political Theory* 34: 690–714.

Eggen, Dan. 2005. "Bush Authorized Domestic Spying: Post–9/11 Order Bypassed Special Court." *Washington Post,* December 16, A01.

Foucault, Michel. 1975. *Surveiller et punir: Naissance de la prison.* Paris: Editions Gallimard. Translated by Alan Sheridan as *Discipline and Punish: The Birth of the Prison.* 2nd ed. (New York: Vintage, 1995).

———. 1999. *Abnormal: Lectures at the College de France, 1974–1975.* New York: Picador.

Fulwider, John M., Kelly M. Greenhill, and David A. Weaver. 2007. "The Power of Pictures? A First Look at the Evidence from the Case of Abu Ghraib." Paper prepared for delivery at the annual meeting of the International Studies Association, Chicago, Illinois, February 28–March 3.

Human Rights Watch. 2006. "Human Rights Watch World Report 2006: US Policy of Abuse Undermines Rights Worldwide." January 18. http://www.hrw.org/english/docs/2006/01/13/global12428.htm.

Jackson, Richard. 2005. *Writing the War on Terrorism: Language, Politics and Counter-Terrorism.* Manchester: Manchester University Press.

Kelley, Mark. 2004. "Justice Department Repudiates Torture Memo Bush Reserved Specific Right to Ignore Geneva Conventions." *Charleston Gazette,* June 24, 1A.

Leopold, Jason. 2006. "Bush Authorized Domestic Spying Before 9/11." *Truthout Perspective,* January 13. http://www.truthout.org/cgi-bin/artman/exec/view.cgi/48/16920.

Lipman, Pauline. 2004. "Education Accountability and Repression of Democracy Post–9/11." *Journal for Critical Education Policy Studies* 2, no. 1. http://www.jceps.com/index.php?pageID=article&articleID=23.

Neal, Andrew W. 2005. "Foucault in Guantanamo: National Sovereignty, Disciplinary Exceptionalism." April 12. http://www.libertysecurity.org/article199.html.

Ross, James. 2005. "Bush, Torture and the Lincoln Legacy." Human Rights Watch, August 1. http://hrw.org/english/docs/2005/08/05/usdom11610.htm (accessed May 22, 2005).

United Nations, Economic and Social Council. 2006. "Situation of Detainees at Guantánamo Bay." Report of the Chairperson of the Working Group on Arbitrary Detention, Leila Zerrougui, the Special Rapporteur on the independence of judges and lawyers, E/CN.4/2006/120, February 15. http://news.bbc.co.uk/2/shared/bsp/hi/pdfs/16_02_06_un_guantanamo.pdf#search=%22Situation%20of%20detainees%20at%20Guant%C3%A1namo%20Bay%22 (accessed October 5, 2006).

CHAPTER 3

Disciplining Women, Disciplining Women's Rights

Krista Hunt

Building on their discourse of women's liberation that has figured prominently in the war on terror, the George W. Bush administration has developed and started to implement its "pro-women" foreign policy agenda. Through the U.S. State Department's Office of International Women's Issues (OIWI), the Bush administration has declared its commitment to "the worldwide advancement of women's issues" (Powell 2002). According to former secretary of state Colin Powell, promoting women's issues is "not only in keeping with the deeply held values of the American people; it is strongly in our national interest as well" (Powell 2002). Currently, the Bush administration claims that it has embarked on a mission to empower Afghan, Iraqi, and Middle Eastern women by granting them economic and political rights. It contends that as "Muslim-majority countries" become more respectful of women, the United States and the rest of the world will become more secure and more prosperous.

In contrast to this official war story (Hunt and Rygiel 2006), I argue that the Bush administration is using its pro-women foreign policy agenda as a disciplinary mechanism—an argument similar to that made by Mertus and Rawls in their analysis of U.S. torture policy in chapter 2—to reassert neoimperial power and control within the international system, especially within "Muslim majority" countries. With economic and political issues topping the agenda, Bush has defined the liberation of women in terms of the liberation of markets, the spread of democracy, and respect for (certain) human rights. For the Bush administration, promoting women's issues means installing democratic—or, more to the point,

U.S.-friendly—governments; empowering women to become workers in the global economy; and granting women political rights that do not seriously challenge patriarchal power. In reality, women's issues are not an end in and of themselves, but rather a means to securing access and control over targeted countries, resources, and labor. Therefore, I argue that the OIWI is disciplining women in Muslim-majority countries, as well as feminist conceptions of women's rights, according to the interests of Western imperialism, global capitalism, and patriarchal power. As such, this redeployment of women's issues by the Bush administration is a significant attempt to threaten women's rights.[1]

Disciplinary Power

Before discussing Bush's pro-women foreign policy, it is necessary to examine the theoretical framework for this analysis. In *Discipline and Punish,* Michel Foucault urges us not only to study the repressive effects of punitive measures (in this case war), but also to situate these measures "in a whole series of their possible positive effects, even if these seem marginal at first" (1995, 23). Although discipline and punishment are conventionally viewed as negative (e.g., the power to repress, censor, violate, or destroy), Foucault argues that this is only one aspect of disciplinary power. Foucault insists on examining disciplinary power as productive, and includes the power to identify, order, manage, and administer. As the war on terror illustrates, military campaigns against Afghanistan and Iraq should not be viewed simply as deadly punishment for "the terrorists and those that harbour them" (White House, 2006), but, more importantly, they should be examined for their positive effects. These might include constructing the United States as (women's) liberators; producing a pro-women foreign policy agenda; initiating a global campaign to civilize and democratize Muslim-majority nations starting with the rights of Muslim women; gaining access to new markets, resources, and labor; and, overall, constructing the war on terror as a practice of granting, rather than restricting, freedoms. The purpose of the war on terror is not to destroy targeted nations, but rather to discipline their governments and societies into becoming compliant members of the U.S.-led democratic, neoliberal global system.

In order to understand such disciplinary measures, Foucault undertakes an analysis of how discourses, institutions, and power relations intersect in what he calls the "discursive field." For Foucault, disciplinary power is "exercised within discourses" that constitute and govern individuals, societies, and institutions (Weedon 1987, 113). Of particular interest is how certain (dominant) discourses come to have greater legitimacy, power, and authority than others. As such, it is necessary to examine the discursive field in question "in order to uncover the particular regimes of power and knowledge at work in a society and their part in the overall production and maintenance of existing power relations" (ibid., 107–8). In this case, how have feminist definitions of women's rights been co-opted and redefined by the Bush administration to serve its own interests? The purpose of such an examination is not only to understand how dominant discourses produce and maintain power through various disciplinary measures, but also to challenge and destabilize the dominance of these discourses through the production of alternative discourses.

In terms of the Bush administration's pro-women foreign policy agenda, this chapter undertakes a discursive analysis of the field of women's issues focusing on OIWI policies, reports, "fact sheets," and press releases. Following David Campbell, I hold that these foreign policy texts do not "simply offer strategic analyses of the 'reality' they [confront,]" but actively script both "reality" and identity (1992, 33). This includes the identity of the United States, its enemies, its security threats, the disciplinary measures related to managing those threats, and the conception of women's issues that are under attack and thereby in need of defense. Of particular importance to this examination is an analysis of the disciplinary effects of OIWI women's issues discourse; the kinds of subjects, institutions, and power relations it produces; the interests it serves; and the potential strategies for resistance. In order to resist the Bush administration's regressive redeployment of women's issues, one must "understand the intricate network of discourses, the sites where they are articulated and the institutionally legitimized forms of knowledge to which they look for their justification" (Weedon 1987, 126). Using this methodology, I demonstrate how women's rights are being used by the Bush administration to discipline Muslim countries into conforming to a democratic, neoliberal agenda, and in the process, how these rights, redeployed as women's issues, are being disciplined and deradicalized.

Imperial Discipline

Through the war on terror, women's rights became tied to U.S. security and international relations. Capitalizing on the horrific treatment of Afghan women by the Taliban, the oppression of women became a central discourse casting the terrorists as misogynists and the coalition as women's liberators. In speeches justifying the war on terror, the Bush administration detailed the abuses that women faced under the Taliban regime and stated that one of its top priorities was the liberation of Afghan women. According to Bush, freedom and civilization hung in the balance as terrorists waged a "war against civilization" (G. W. Bush 2003b).

The Bush administration stressed that it was not only Afghan women's rights that were at stake. According to Bush,

> the central goal of the terrorists is the brutal oppression of women—and not only the women of Afghanistan. The terrorists who help rule Afghanistan are found in dozens and dozens of countries around the world. And that is the reason this great nation, with our friends and allies, will not rest until we bring them all to justice.
>
> (G. W. Bush 2001)

Speaking for an administration that saw itself as the champion of universal women's liberation and the protector of freedom, First Lady Laura Bush (2001) declared that the "fight against terrorism is also a fight for the rights and dignity of women" worldwide.

Their discourse about protecting women expanded after Bush proudly announced that coalition forces had "liberated" the women of Afghanistan— a claim that remains widely contested by Afghan women's rights activists and human rights organizations. In his first State of the Union address, President Bush sermonized that the September 11 attacks had transformed a self-centered nation into a self-sacrificing global leader. He told the American people that "we have a great opportunity during this time of war to lead the world toward the values that will bring lasting peace ... In every region, free markets and free trade and free societies are proving their power to lift lives" (G. W. Bush 2002a). As such, Bush defined the next chapter in the war on terror as one that would defend liberty and justice by spreading democracy and free markets throughout the "uncivilized" world. Occupying the moral high ground, the Bush administration argued that "we do not choose to use force as the way to promote either democracy or women's rights," but will do so if it is necessary to protect women, freedom, and civilization (Ponticelli 2003b).

In the months that followed, the Bush administration intensified its focus on women's issues. In remarks to the United Nations (UN) on International Women's Day, Laura Bush (2002) stated that September 11 "galvanized the international community" to "look closely at the roles women play in their societies." She urged them to remain dedicated "to respecting and protecting women's rights in all countries" in order to achieve "a peaceful, prosperous, and stable world." As leaders of this fight for women's rights, Secretary of State Colin Powell and President Bush declared their commitment to "fully integrating [women's issues] into American foreign policy" (Powell 2002). According to Powell,

> the worldwide advancement of women's issues is not only in keeping with the deeply held values of the American people; it is strongly in our national interest as well ... Women's issues affect not only women; they have profound implications for all humankind. Women's issues are human rights issues. They are health and education issues. They are development issues. They are ingredients of good government and sound economic practice. They go to the heart of what makes for successful, stable societies and global growth. Women's issues affect the future of families, societies and economies, of countries and of continents. We, as a world community, cannot even begin to tackle the array of problems and challenges confronting us without the full and equal participation of women in all aspects of life.

Through the development of its pro-women foreign policy, the United States vowed to create a world where free individuals "can live in free societies that no longer threaten each other" (Ponticelli 2003b).

In order to achieve this, the Bush administration charged the State Department's OIWI with developing and implementing its foreign policy agenda. Women's economic opportunities and political participation were placed at the top of the OIWI's agenda. Although violence against women, trafficking in women and girls, female genital mutilation, and Human Immunodeficiency Virus/Acquired Immune Deficiency Syndrome (HIV/ AIDS) are also mentioned, they are considered to be secondary (and unrelated) issues. While the OIWI claims that these issues "are important to American women and women throughout the world," its efforts are almost entirely directed toward women in Afghanistan, Iraq, and the "Middle East" (excluding Israel) (OIWI homepage). By virtue of this focus, Bush's pro-women foreign policy agenda remains fundamentally tied to the countries, region, and issues targeted by the war on terror.

According to the Bush administration, its foreign policy agenda regarding women in Muslim-majority countries is part of a greater mission to create a more secure and more prosperous world. However, critics of the war on terror continue to argue that the Bush administration is engaged in a neoimperial project to remake the world in its own image (Bacchetta et al. 2001; Ali 2002; Chomsky 2002; Talbot 2003). Characterizations by the Bush administration that this war is a crusade; a mission to protect civilization; a fight to save Other women from their barbaric, primitive, premodern societies; and an operation to spread (the good word about) democracy, human rights, and neoliberalism reinforce perceptions around the world that the United States has embarked on an imperial project. In response to these charges, Bush maintains that the United States is a force for freedom, rather than a force for occupation or imperial expansion, and that the United States has "no desire to dominate, no ambitions of empire. Our aim is a democratic peace—a peace founded upon the dignity and rights of every man and woman" (G. W. Bush 2004). Bush stresses that "America will always stand firm for the non-negotiable demands of human dignity; the rule of law; limits on the power of the state; respect for women; private property; free speech; equal justice; and religious tolerance" (G. W. Bush 2002a). For Bush, enforcing these "universal" freedoms differs fundamentally from imposing culturally specific values.

In its efforts to present itself as protecting universal rights and freedoms, the Bush administration has sought legitimacy through recourse to the UN's Universal Declaration of Human Rights. For instance, though the Security Council did not back the U.S. invasion of Iraq in 2003, the United States maintains that it acted in defense of the universal rights and freedoms that the UN proved unwilling to defend. In a speech that served to both chastise the UN for failing to help liberate the people of Iraq and construct the United States as *the* protector of universal rights and freedoms, Bush stated that "because there were consequences [for Iraq's noncompliance], because a coalition of nations acted to defend the peace, and the credibility of the United Nations, Iraq is free" (G. W. Bush 2003b). Despite serious disunity on the issue of Iraq, Bush realigned the United States with the UN, telling the General Assembly that "there remains unity among us on the fundamental principles and objectives of the United Nations. We are dedicated to the defense of our collective security, and to the advance of human rights." In closing, Bush argued that the United States would continue fighting to "fulfill the U.N.'s stated purpose, and give meaning to its ideals" even in the face of opposition from the institution itself. This construction of the United States as the unfailing protector of universal human rights highlights the moral and political power of human rights discourse. Even though Bush seriously challenged the relevance of the UN, he has appropriated the discourse, as well as the responsibility for interpreting, redefining, and enforcing these "universal" rights. In so doing, Bush claims to be defending the "moral law that stands above men and nations" (G. W. Bush 2003b).

However, these appeals to universal human rights do not counter charges of imperialism, since human rights discourse is often invoked to serve imperial interests (Grewal 1998; Nair 2002). According to Inderpal Grewal, violations of women's rights in third world countries are not simply used "to bring to light and to voice the oppression of women," but to support and "enable the deployment of imperial discourses by powerful states" (1998, 511). This is evident in that the Bush administration's solutions to both terrorism and the abuse of women "rely on a colonial, Manichean model whereby 'advanced capitalist freedom and liberty' is venerated over 'backward extremist Islamic barbarism'" (Bacchetta 2001). Grewal argues that women's rights have and continue to be used to construct the "third world" as violent and uncivilized and "third world women" as victims in need of protection and liberation from benevolent Westerners. In addition, women's rights discourse is invoked to construct the rescuers as "authoritative and objective" enforcers of these rights, with no other interests than to uphold the rights and freedoms of all human beings (1998, 502). Although the Bush administration maintains that it is committed to promoting women's issues (defined as economic and political rights), its goal is not to secure women's rights but rather to secure the civilized world by replacing "terrorist regimes" with democratic, U.S.-friendly governments committed to promoting neoliberal economic restructuring. Exemplifying "states' authoritative and creative reinvention of the human rights agenda" (Nair 2002, 257), the Bush administration is using women's issues to discipline "uncivilized nations" into conforming to a process of democratization and market liberalization. Women's rights, redeployed as "women's issues," are being used as a disciplinary mechanism, and in the process, women and their rights are being disciplined by the Bush administration's agenda to remake Muslim-majority countries.

Disciplining Women, Liberating Markets

In support of the Bush administration's imperial project, the OIWI cites traditional culture, authoritarian rule, and an undeveloped economy as the key impediments to Muslim women's empowerment and to the progress of their societies. This claim reflects the World Bank's contention that women's subordination is the result of a "lack of sufficient contact with modern ideas and markets" (Bergeron 2003, 403). Reinforcing neoliberal evangelicalism, Bush argues that "as trade expands and knowledge spreads in the Middle East, as women gain a place of equality and respect, as the rule of law takes hold, all peoples of that region will see a new day of justice and a new day of prosperity" (G. W. Bush 2003a). As such, the Bush administration forwards a neoliberal agenda for economic and political reconstruction characterized by freeing markets from government interference, building a self-financing public sector, and opening the economy to trade and private investment.

In order to reach this goal, the United States is focused on integrating Afghan, Iraqi, and Middle Eastern women into the global economy by providing economic and political opportunities for women through basic educational programs, job-skills training, support for women's nongovernmental organizations (NGOs), political training for women, and aid to female entrepreneurs. The assumption is that through economic and political liberalization, women will become full and equal participants in political and economic life. Once women are integrated into the market, they will be both "the major beneficiaries of economic globalization" and the "new 'enterprise zones' to fuel globalization further" (Runyan 1999, 214). This agenda exemplifies how women and "women's issues" are being disciplined by the dictates of global capitalism.

At the moment, the OIWI's only detailed plan for improving women's economic and political opportunities focuses on Afghanistan. However, the strategies adopted by the United States in Afghanistan reflect the economic and political priorities outlined for Iraq and the Middle East. The OIWI's 2003 report "U.S. Support for Afghan Women, Children, and Refugees" calls for establishing an environment that promotes growth in the private sector—growth that it contends will result in women's empowerment. It urges a democratic Afghan government to "establish institutions, law and policies that foster private sector economic growth, sustainable development, poverty reduction and social stability," all while maintaining a self-financing public sector (OIWI 2003, 2). Although the government should provide vocational training, education, income-generation programs, and opportunities for women to participate in politics, most women will depend on a "vibrant market economy" rather than on the public sector for employment, social security, and opportunities for advancement (ibid.). According to the report, "the degree of success achieved by a broad national reconstruction and economic revitalization program will be a crucial determinant for the future of the country's women" (OIWI 2003).

The OIWI's focus on the private, rather than the public, sector for women's opportunities for advancement raises serious concerns. In developed countries, the downsizing of government, the dismantling of the welfare system, and the privatization of social security have been and will continue to be imposed by states in concert with global financial institutions in the name of global competitiveness. Barbara Evers argues that "women are disproportionately disadvantaged by the effects of restructuring," since cuts in government spending "affect the production and reproduction of human beings" (Evers 1994, 118). Goods and services once provided by the state (e.g., health care, education, child-care subsidies, baby bonuses) are either privatized or downloaded onto women in the family and community.

By way of contrast, developing countries targeted for "national reconstruction and economic revitalization" are unable even to develop a public sector that includes a social safety net. The OIWI's plan for the Afghan government to support and facilitate economic liberalization by maintaining a "self-financing" public sector exemplifies this trend. In war-torn Afghanistan, decades of civil war have resulted in a large number of widows and female-headed households. The question now becomes: How will Afghan women be able to "revitalize the economy" while single-handedly caring for their families? While the small number of educated, middle-class women who secure government positions will have access to child-care facilities, there are no provisions for the majority of women who will be employed (and unemployed) by the private sector. As Gayatri Spivak warns, "the poorest in the South are at the bottom of a society where a welfare structure cannot emerge because of globalized exploitation" (Spivak 1996). U.S. plans for free markets and a self-financing public sector in Afghanistan reinforce the reality that political and economic reconstruction takes place without consideration for these "women's issues."

This privileging of economic restructuring represents the tenor of the entire report in which women's advancement is promised to be the result of economic liberalization. To this end, the United States plans to increase trade and private investment through several measures, including granting duty-free status to some Afghan exports; finalizing a textile trade agreement between Afghanistan and the United States; working with the World Bank to facilitate global trade; facilitating Afghanistan's membership in the World Trade Organization (WTO); encouraging foreign investment; and creating a transparent business climate (OIWI 2003, 5). The United States is also working with U.S. and transnational corporations, including Gateway, Daimler, Time Warner, Smith Richardson, and the Fortune 500 group, all of which have donated money, equipment, and services to women's projects in exchange, to be sure, for lucrative reconstruction contracts (OIWI 2003, 8). Women are expected to contribute to this plan by participating in programs that will train women to weave carpets and produce traditional embroidered cloth; to grow cash crops; to make garments; and to run bakeries—all highly feminized, low paying, and likely nonunionized work (OIWI 2003, 9–10). The report maintains that Afghan women will benefit from the increased quality of life that results from a strong economy. According to the OIWI, "women, children and refugees constitute the vast majority of this country's entire population, so they will be massively helped simply by being ensured their inclusion in general economic growth" (OIWI 2003, 16). Afghan women are promised the benefits of trickle-down economics as they take their places as low-paid workers producing "traditional" goods for the global market.

This incorporation of Afghan women into the global economy is exemplified by their employment as carpet weavers supplying Afghan "war rugs" to the Western market. Since September 11, Western demand for the rugs has increased dramatically, providing a market for Western dealers to capitalize on. Stories about war rugs have been featured in the major Canadian and American media and are characterized as traditional folk art made by Afghan women needing an outlet to express their feelings about the effects of war on their country (Ross 2004; Helman 2003). Although Afghan women began weaving images of war and messages of resistance into their rugs in opposition to the Soviet occupation, the post–9/11 war rugs for sale in the West are uncritically supportive of the war on terror, showing how readily radical activities and sentiments are subverted by incorporation into the marketplace. Highlighting the fact that these rugs are being manufactured for the U.S. market, the rugs depict appropriately pro-American images and messages (warrug. com). One rug shows planes hitting the World Trade Center, with a peace dove emblazoned below, and another features military planes over Afghanistan with the message "Root out terrorism with the help of America and Britain." According to the website, these rugs are purchased by an American dealer from U.S. Special Forces personnel who buy them from Afghans. Although Western dealers market the rugs as expressing "authentic political sentiment" within Afghanistan, the blatant pro-Americanism, the presence of spelling errors, the reality that the women weaving the rugs are not literate in English, and reports from Afghan women that the war has worsened their situation indicate that the messages are a reflection of Western demand rather than of Afghan women's political positions on the war. The rugs, which cost anywhere between U.S. $400 and $7,500, reflect the Western market for traditional/exotic/ "primitive"/Oriental goods, the exploitation of Afghan women's labor-made-cheap, and a disturbing commodification of the war on terror. Reinforcing Bush's claims about America's role in liberating Afghan women, the rugs are marketed not only as a way to commemorate the victims of 9/11, but also as a way to "help" Afghan women financially. Although the owner of warrugs.com will not disclose how much Afghan women earn for the six weeks of work that it takes to make an average rug, one can reasonably conclude that it is only a fraction of the amount that Afghan middlemen, U.S. soldiers, and then the American dealers earn off the labors of Afghan women weavers. Not only has the United States invaded Afghanistan under the guise of liberating women, it now claims to be empowering Afghan women by exploiting their labor and their experiences of the war on terror.

With reference to the gendered, racialized, and class-biased effects of the global market, feminist economists maintain that neoliberal restructuring has far from empowered (most) women (Bakker 1999; Bergeron 2003; Runyan 1999). Through its escalation of feminized labor; women's triple burden of paid, unpaid, and community work; cuts in the social safety net; downloading of social reproduction to the private sphere; environmental degradation; and the feminization of poverty, so-called free-market feminism serves to liberate the market rather than liberate women (Mohanty 2003, 6; Runyan 1999, 218). The motive of capitalist expansion is not the empowerment of women, but rather the "further commodification, or packaging for the world market, of nature, commonly-held resources, and human labour" (Turner, Brown, and Kaara 2001, 95), which is illustrated clearly in the case of Afghan war rugs. As Zillah Eisenstein argues, "global capital thrives because of a racial-patriarchal transnational sexual division of labour" that "disproportionately locates women and girls, especially those of color, in low-wage assembly and information jobs and in sexual ghettos elsewhere in the market" (2002, 134). In contrast to Bush's claims that Afghan women will be "liberated" by producing goods for the global market, Afghan women will remain at the bottom of the global economic system earning a nonliving wage for casual, part-time, nonunionized, unsafe, insecure work. Afghan women's empowerment is not the concern of Bush's pro-women foreign policy agenda; rather, the Bush administration is disciplining Afghan women (and their rights) according to the dictates of the global economy.

The mass-marketing of women's issues by the Bush administration has been used to frame the war on terror and the reconstruction of Muslim-majority countries. Women are guaranteed liberation and empowerment by becoming workers and, following that, consumers in the global market. Recently, major U.S. cosmetics companies, including Revlon, L'Oréal, and Clairol have targeted Afghan women as both workers and consumers of their products. These corporations are backing a new project to "liberate" Afghan women called Beauty Without Borders. According to the organization's website, the program seeks to "provide women in Afghanistan with access to a comprehensive educational program that teaches both the Art and Commerce of beauty" (Beauty Without Borders website). The organizers maintain that the program will provide their graduates with businesses that will help them support their families, and will supply the "thriving" demand for beauty products and treatments coming from women able to afford such luxuries (women likely married to politicians, military generals, warlords, and those involved in the lucrative drug trade) (Ghafour 2004, A1). If capitalist expansion thinly veiled behind the pretense of liberation (marked by the co-optation of the world-renowned humanitarian organization Doctors Without Borders) was not enough, the organization's spokeswoman, Debbie Rodriquez, seeks to liberate Afghan women from their primitive beauty rituals. According to Rodriquez,

> When I first came to Kabul, oh my God, I was shocked at what these women did to their hair and face ... They would use henna, which is horrible for your hair. The scissors looked like hedge trimmers. And they used buckets from nearby wells outside to rinse hair. I asked one of the girls to do my makeup once and I looked like a drag queen.
>
> (Ghafour 2004, A16)

Rodriquez, with backing from these cosmetic corporations, has received Bush's message that women's empowerment depends on integrating them into the global economy, and she has taken the extra step of targeting Afghan women as a new consumer market. Just as the liberation of Afghan women was used to sell the war on terror, beauty products are now being marketed as vehicles by which Afghan women can gain empowerment through entrepreneurship and consumerism.

This case exemplifies a Western-capitalist-patriarchal disciplining of women's liberation. Women's empowerment has become an excuse to integrate targeted countries, people, and resources into the global economy in the name of liberation rather than of imperial expansion or capitalist exploitation. Afghan women, once forbidden from wearing "fashionable" clothes or painting their nails, are considered to be liberated by Westerners who consider shedding the burqa, wearing makeup, and following fashion trends to be a sign of women's emancipation. Reinforcing the mass-marketed images of empowerment that continue to sell products to "liberated" American women (think of Nike or Special K ads), this Western conception of empowerment is now being marketed to Afghan women. It is used not only to sell makeup, but also to reinforce conservative ideas about women's empowerment. When women in the West and beyond see liberation as purchasing power, capitalist patriarchy reinforces its ability to contain and discipline women.

Disciplining Women's Rights, Reinforcing Patriarchy

Reinforcing both imperial and patriarchal practices, the Bush administration has assumed responsibility for defining and enforcing women's issues. It is not surprising that "women's issues" rather than "women's rights" have become the favored discourse of the Bush administration. While feminists, along with the UN, have for decades actively defined and promoted women's rights internationally, the Bush administration's focus on women's issues allows them the flexibility to diverge from established definitions deemed either too "radical" or not in their interests. Recently we have witnessed this in the Bush administration's sustained resistance to the UN Convention on the Elimination of All Forms of Discrimination against Women (CEDAW), a resistance based on patriarchal fears that CEDAW will threaten the family by enshrining reproductive rights. However, women's issues do not have the same feminist connotations as women's rights, something that is particularly important for a U.S. administration that stridently advocates patriarchal family values and actively challenges women's right to choose. While reproductive and sexual rights are widely seen by women's rights activists to be fundamental human rights protected by international law, women's issues are much more flexible and better able to be disciplined around the Bush administration's staunch antichoice agenda. The shift away from women's rights has resulted in the Bush administration dropping the fundamental second wave feminist demand for reproductive freedom, and instead promoting such programs as nonfamily-planning clinics that abstain from giving women information about contraceptives and abortion; from managing mother-to-child HIV transmission through education and "safer" nursing techniques; and from equating women's health with maternal health. By redefining women's rights, the Bush administration can promote women's participation in the democratization of their societies and in the liberalization of their economies without extending women's issues to include such things as reproductive and sexual rights.

This disciplining of women's rights attempts to scale back definitions of women's issues to early twentieth-century calls for women's liberation in Western nations. Although Bush's pro-women foreign policy envisions women's inclusion in education, politics, and the workforce, it holds the line on rights considered to threaten women's roles as wives and mothers. In contrast to the way contemporary feminists define women's rights, the Bush administration defines women's issues in ways that, it argues, will strengthen, rather than destroy, family values. According to the Bush administration, "When women participate in the economic and political life of their country, they can take charge of their lives and improve the situation not only for themselves, but also for their children, families and society at large" (Ponticelli 2003a). Women's issues are not considered to be an end in and of themselves, but rather a strategy for modernizing and liberalizing "uncivilized" nations. In other words, women are granted rights by the Bush administration only by default.

However, the Bush administration's plan to integrate Muslim women into political and economic activities does necessitate the eradication of certain patriarchal practices. The message to targeted nations who engage in practices the Bush administration deems oppressive is this: In order to establish a nonaggressive relationship with the United States, enjoy the prosperity of neoliberal globalization, and hold on to power, you will have to (at least on paper) change your position with respect to women's economic and political participation. Yet, it is important to note that this challenge is not "to the masculinist privilege of Islamic states and third world nations, but to the way the gendered borders of these traditional discourses hinder the global market and marketing of women" (Eisenstein 1996, 140). This point was made most clearly by L. Paul Bremer, administrator of the Coalition Provisional Authority in Iraq. According to Bremer (2003),

> To educate women, to permit them to take their place in society as teachers, as doctors, as lawyers, and, yes, as police officers and presidents, violates no religion, destroys no family ... To encourage women to go to school, to educate themselves to the best of their ability, takes nothing away from anyone. An educated woman can be an integral part of any family. An educated wife and mother is a better, stronger wife and mother.

Male privilege in Muslim-majority countries is not challenged by the Bush administration; rather, it is disciplined in ways that will facilitate economic growth and democracy. As the Bush administration maintains, the development of free societies and free markets need not threaten traditional families and cultures. The administration sells its campaign to fellow patriarchs in Muslim-majority countries by arguing that (a) families and societies will benefit from granting women nominal rights and (b) everyone will become more liberated and prosperous, so the increase in women's freedoms is really only relative.

This reality is playing out in Afghanistan with respect to women's political participation. When the interim Afghan government was established, two Afghan women were granted posts as evidence of the commitment of the governments of the United States and Afghanistan to women's political participation. For the Bush administration, these token Afghan women in the Karzai government were proof that Afghan "women [were] free and are part of Afghanistan's new government" (G. W. Bush 2002a). After the constitution was approved in early 2004, Afghanistan's ambassador to the United States stated that "accepting equality between men and women [in the constitution] marks a revolutionary change in the roles women are able to play in Afghan government and society" (Khalilzad 2004). Echoing this, the OIWI maintained that "women continue to play a significant role" in Afghan politics and that the Bush administration would actively support Afghan women's participation as voters and candidates in the 2004 elections (OIWI 2003). This rhetoric reinforces the Bush administration's contention that it is successfully transforming Afghanistan into a democracy that respects women's rights.

Despite official optimism, the future for women in Afghan politics remains highly uncertain. During her first few months as interim minister of women's affairs, Sima Samar reported that she had not received an office, funds, equipment, or staff to run the ministry, indicating the relative importance of the ministry within the government (ICHRDD 2002). By the spring of 2002, Minister Samar had been run out of office after receiving death threats for being "too radical" in her campaign for women's rights. Samar was accused of criticizing Islamic law, and as a result was labeled the Salman Rushdie of Afghanistan. In response to her opponents within the Afghan government, and in keeping with the Bush administration's own version of women's liberation, Samar stated, "I am not asking for abortion, just equality" (Edwards 2003). Nevertheless, the message to current and future female politicians was that challenging patriarchal power would result in their own loss of political power.

The remaining female politicians in the Karzai government quickly learned their lesson. In contrast to Samar, the other female interim minister, Sohaila Siddiqi, vocally distanced herself from Afghan women's rights activists, thereby aligning herself with a less threatening position on women's issues (Mahoney and Honey 2001). Similarly, Samar's replacement, Habiba Sorabi, took a moderate stand on women's rights, stating that "women have to learn about their rights and duties so that they can defend themselves in everyday life without crossing the borders of Islam" (Petersmann 2004). Her position that Afghan women should only be granted rights that do not threaten Islam echoes the new constitution, which enshrines equality between all Afghan citizens, yet includes a notwithstanding clause stating that no laws can be "contrary to the beliefs and provisions of the sacred religion of Islam" (Sunder 2004).

The disciplining of Afghan women in Parliament does not end there. In May 2007, Malalai Joya, the youngest member of Parliament (MP) and the most outspoken defender of women's rights, was expelled from Parliament for stating that "the legislative body was worse than a stable" (*Daily Telegraph* 2007). Joya reports that during her term fellow MPs had "[thrown] water at me, threatened me with death, and one of them shouted, 'Take her out and rape her' ... Then they turned off my microphone" (*Daily Telegraph* 2007). This, in response to her unwavering commitment to represent her people and expose the undemocratic actions of the U.S.-backed Karzai government. However, after five years and many war stories from the Bush administration and the Karzai government about the successful rebuilding of post-Taliban Afghanistan, unwavering and undisciplined voices like Joya's threaten to destabilize the official war story that democracy is flourishing in Afghanistan.

That female politicians within the Afghan government survive only when they do not appear to take radical positions on women's rights has led the Revolutionary Association of Women in Afghanistan (RAWA), the oldest women's rights organization in Afghanistan, to declare that the Ministry of Women's Affairs can do nothing for women (Rawi 2004). According to RAWA member Mariam Rawi, while the Karzai government has established a Ministry of Women's Affairs in order to convince the international community that it (like the Bush administration) is committed to promoting and protecting Afghan women's rights, there is no real power behind the ministry. While the Afghan government has taken symbolic steps towards including women in politics, such as ratifying CEDAW (something the United States still refuses to do), setting aside one-quarter of the seats in Parliament for women, and addressing equality rights in the constitution, even President Karzai admits that these are only theoretical rights (Sunder 2004). Like the attention paid by the Bush administration, this symbolic attention to women's issues masks an enduring reality about women in high politics: that female politicians remain in positions of power only after demonstrating that they have "learned the lessons of masculinized political behaviour well enough not to threaten male political privilege" (Enloe 1989, 6–7). As evidenced in the case of the Ministry of Women's Affairs, token attempts to include women in politics do not translate into a sustained commitment to women's political empowerment. Although the faces may change, the policies remain the same.

Both presidents Karzai and Bush are acutely aware of this, which is why they are willing to grant women token representation and to pay lip service to women's empowerment. By "allowing," and this is exactly what it is, a few compliant Afghan women to occupy political office, Bush and Karzai reinforce their message that the war on terror has liberated Afghan women and that Afghanistan is on the road to democracy, economic liberalization, and respect for women's rights. These successes are held up as evidence that Bush's plan to civilize Muslim-majority countries is working and that it should continue in Iraq and throughout the Middle East.

However, these supposedly "successful" attempts to discipline Muslim-majority nations into empowering women economically and politically continue to be challenged by conservative power brokers within targeted nations. Women's rights organizations in Afghanistan report that warlords, including the U.S.-backed Northern Alliance, continue to wage a war against women's rights in Afghanistan with widespread instances of sexual violence, forced marriages, and domestic violence (Rawi 2004). Whereas under the Taliban women were flogged for not following the rules, now they are raped (Rawi 2004). RAWA reports that women are confined to their homes out of fear for their safety. Amnesty International reports that the risk of rape and sexual violence by members of armed factions is extremely high (Amnesty International 2003). In the western province of Herat, Human Rights Watch reports Taliban-style restrictions on women's dress, freedom of movement, appearance in public, and relations with men (Zia-Zarifi 2004). In Kandahar and Logar, girls' schools have been set on fire. Throughout the country, women and girls have been forced out of school and work because of the insecurity that they face. Former UN secretary-general Kofi Annan, Human Rights Watch, and Amnesty International have agreed that a culture of violence against women persists in post-Taliban Afghanistan.

So why does the Bush administration continue to prioritize economic and political rights over Afghan women's security? After all, if women are to become the backbone of reconstruction efforts in Afghanistan, then they must be able to walk to school and to work without fear of being harassed, raped, or kidnapped. Similarly, they must have the freedom within their families to get an education and hold a job without fear of being beaten or accused of dishonoring their family. The reason the Bush administration continues to ignore these security concerns is simple: in order to root out the terrorists and those that harbored them, the Bush administration needed local forces on the ground to fight the Taliban and minimize the number of U.S. casualties. To this end, the United States backed, funded, and rearmed the Northern Alliance despite the fact that the Alliance was notorious for committing sexual crimes against women during its pre-Taliban reign. In exchange for its military support, the Northern Alliance now holds the vice presidency in the Karzai government and remains the most powerful military force in the country. Although RAWA warned the United States and the international community that reinstalling the Northern Alliance and other warlords would do nothing to improve the lives of Afghan women, the Bush administration chose military strategy over women's rights. In spite of OIWI's claims that they are "deeply committed to addressing issues that are important to American women and women throughout the world," (OIWI homepage) they continue to ignore Afghan women's rights activists who argue that security, rather than economic and political participation, is the most important issue facing Afghan women. Here again, we see how easily women's rights are disciplined and even bargained away in the interests of imperial, global capital, and patriarchal power.

Networks of Disciplinary Power

In this volume, Leatherman has called on contributors to address how states, state-based international organizations, global civil society, the underbelly of globalization (terrorists), and global capitalism "work with, or react to, one another while attempting to protect, defend, and expand their power and authority." In what follows, I map out the complex network of disciplinary power that is the basis of Bush's pro-women foreign policy agenda in order to highlight the interests and actors it serves. As I have argued, the Bush administration is using women's issues as a cover for imperial, global capital, and patriarchal interests and, in the process, is disciplining the definition of women's issues.

To begin, the Bush administration appropriated the discourse of women's rights from feminists (global civil society) and the UN (state-based international organization) in order to legitimize its imperial mission to oust terrorist regimes (the underbelly of globalization) and civilize Muslim-majority countries. When feminists and the UN spoke out against this appropriation of women's rights to justify the war on terror, the Bush administration accused them of failing to uphold universal rights and freedoms and presented itself as the only actor willing to protect these rights. In so doing, the Bush administration reinforced its role as arbiter and guarantor of women's rights and freedoms, deflected criticism that it is motivated by imperial interests, and set the stage for invading other countries that violate women's rights.

This redefinition of women's rights serves not only the imperial interests of the Bush administration, but also its close connection to global capitalism. We must not forget that the Bush administration is made up of high-ranking members who are financially connected to major oil companies. President Bush was the owner of Arbusto, a Texas oil company; Vice President Dick Cheney was the CEO of Haliburton; and Secretary of State Condoleezza Rice was a director at Chevron. It is no secret that the U.S. government continues to assert power and influence in the Middle East in the interest of controlling its vast oil reserves, which (literally) fuel the U.S. economy. However, their relationship with global capital extends beyond oil. As made clear in the OIWI report on Afghanistan, the United States, in partnership with the World Bank, the WTO, and a number of U.S./transnational corporations, has a keen interest in gaining access to new resources, labor, and markets in Afghanistan and other targeted countries. As demonstrated through their policies regarding Afghan women's economic empowerment, the United States has been disciplining women to become workers and consumers in the global economy. While the OIWI argues that women will be the beneficiaries of the free market, the OIWI's own policies make clear that Afghan women workers are simply a new pool of labor-made-cheap to feed globalization.

By appropriating women's rights from feminists and the UN, the Bush administration also has the power to redefine those rights. For all its rhetoric about protecting universal rights and freedoms, the Bush administration is militantly antichoice and reactionary against so-called radical feminist agendas. In keeping with its patriarchal position on women's issues, the Bush administration actively opposes women's reproductive rights both domestically and internationally. Although Bush's policies on women's economic and political empowerment in places like Afghanistan necessitate a loosening of patriarchal power within these countries, the Bush administration continues to bargain away women's rights in the name of both military and economic interests.

Having mapped how the Bush administration's imperial pro-women foreign policy agenda overlaps with both global capitalism and patriarchy at the expense of a women's rights agenda, it is important to address how this reassertion of imperial, capitalist, and patriarchal power can be resisted. Bush's disciplining of women's rights certainly reinforces Foucault's thesis that disciplinary power is produced through an intersection between discourse, institutions, and power relations. In this case, we see how a politically transformative discourse like women's rights is co-opted by the Bush administration, redefined as women's issues, institutionalized in the OIWI, and used to frame a Western imperial, global capitalist, patriarchal "pro-women" foreign policy agenda. As such, this appropriation and subsequent disciplining of women's rights by the Bush administration must be a major focus of feminist resistance. It is necessary to pay close attention to how, in its redefinition of "women's issues," the administration attempts to scale back or prevent women from gaining fundamental rights and freedoms. As Eisenstein warns, "Much political talk today, about women, acts to neutralize once-militant ideas" (Eisenstein 1996, 111). In resisting this disciplinary agenda, counterdiscourses are essential in order to illuminate how women's rights are being subverted rather than championed by the Bush administration. Such counterdiscourses should include how Bush's pro-women foreign policy agenda threatens Afghan and Iraqi women's rights, including reproductive rights, and civil liberties, and how it poses a similar threat to the rights of women in countries that will be targeted by the United States in the future. Most important, however, is that Bush's focus on women's oppression indicates that there is a critical mass of people within and beyond the United States that can be swayed by appeals to such issues. The key, then, is to expose how this co-optation of women's issues is not only disingenuous but also harmful to women, and on that basis rally support for an alternative conception of women's rights that puts women at the top of the agenda.

Conclusion

An analysis of OIWI policies finds that Powell was not mincing words when he stated that women's issues are the "ingredients of good government and sound economic practice" (2002). According to Bush's pro-women foreign policy agenda, this is about all they are. As previously discussed, the Bush administration has tailored its definition of "women's issues" to justify Western imperialism and global capitalism while being very clear about the fact that its promotion of women's issues is a means to an end: U.S. global dominance through the spread of free markets and democracy. In the process, the Bush administration is redefining women's issues in keeping with its patriarchal attitudes about women's role in society. As this examination details, the incorporation of "women's issues" by the Bush administration serves to create a global order in which markets are liberated; women become productive workers in the global economy; Muslim-majority countries become cooperative members of a neoliberal, democratic international system; and the United States, having cloaked its imperial agenda under the guise of protecting and enforcing universal human rights, further reinforces the power of Western imperialism, global capitalism, and patriarchy.

For the Bush administration, "women's issues" have been used to represent the United States as the global champion of freedom, civilization, women's rights, and democracy. Although the Bush administration would have us believe that its international activities are stemming terrorism, liberating oppressed people, and sowing the seeds of peace and prosperity, those targeted by these policies know differently. In sharp contrast to the Bush administration's image of itself, we see the Bush administration as the former backer of these (now) misogynistic terrorists; as the current supporter of regimes (such as the Northern Alliance) that stand accused of raping, beating, and abducting women; as the wager of wars that kill the very women the administration purports to protect; as the imperialist out to exploit the resources and labor of targeted countries; as the occupier awarding lucrative reconstruction contracts to itself and its friends; and as the patriarch intent on rescinding fundamental women's rights. Although it is hard to be optimistic when it appears so easy to co-opt progressive ideas as a cover for unjust and exploitative practices, I believe that it is in resisting the seduction of dominant understandings, in asking whose interests the official version serves, and in telling Other stories that those of us committed to a different conception of peace, justice, freedom, and liberation can begin to remake the world.

Note

1. See also chap. 4, where Nowacki and Gutterman argue that the Bush administration's disciplinary maneuvers related to missile defense are also deployed to fortify patriarchal power and to reify a mythical past of gender stability within domestic and international order.

Bibliography

Ali, Tariq. 2002. *The Clash of Fundamentalisms: Crusades, Jihads and Modernity.* London and New York: Verso Press.

Amnesty International. 2003. "Afghanistan: 'No one Listens to Us and No one Treats Us as Human Beings': Justice Denied to Women." Index no. ASA 11/023/2003. October 6. http://amnesty-news.c.tep1.com/maabwrGaa02Ggbb0iDWb/ (accessed October 6, 2003).

Bacchetta, Paola, Tina Campt, Inderpal Grewal, Caren Kaplan, Minoo Moallem, and Jennifer Terry. 2001. "Transnational Feminist Practices against War." http://chiaroscuro_aubade.tripod.com/911/Bacchetta.html (accessed September 15, 2003).

Bakker, Isabella. 1999. "Neoliberal Governance and the New Gender Order." Working Papers in Local Governance and Democracy, Vol. 1, no. 1: 49–59.

Beauty Without Borders. http://www.heavenspa.com/clientmanager/Live/Sites/index.asp?CID=194 (accessed February 24, 2004).

Bergeron, Suzanne. 2003. "The Post–Washington Consensus and Economic Representations of Women in Development at the World Bank." *International Feminist Journal of Politics* 5, no. 3: 397–419.

Bremer, L. Paul. 2003. "Equality for All." December 10. http://www.cpa-iraq.org/transcripts/20031210_Dec10_Human_Rights.html (accessed February 24, 2004).

Bush, George W. 2001. "President Signs Afghan Women and Children Relief Act." December 12. http://www.whitehouse.gov/news/releases/2001/12/20011212-9.html (accessed February 24, 2004).

———. 2002a. "State of the Union Address." January 29. http://www.cnn.com/2002/ALLPOLITICS/01/29/bush.speech.txt/ (accessed May 8, 2003).

———. 2002b. "President's Remarks at the UN General Assembly." September 12. http://www.whitehouse.gov/news/releases/2002/09/20020912-1.html (accessed January 20, 2004).

———. 2003a. "President Bush Presses for Peace in the Middle East." May 9. http://www.whitehouse.gov/news/releases/2003/05/print/20030509-11.html (accessed January 23, 2004).

———. 2003b. "President Addresses UN General Assembly." September 23. http://www.state.gov/p/io/rls/rm/2003/24321pf.htm (accessed October 16, 2003).

———. 2004. "State of the Union Address." January 20. http://www.whitehouse.gov/news/releases/2004/01/20040120-7.html (accessed January 21, 2004).

Bush, Laura. 2001. "Radio Address by Laura Bush to the Nation." November 17. http://www.whitehouse.gov/news/releases/2001/11/print/20011117.html (accessed January 31, 2003).

———. 2002. "Remarks by Mrs. Bush to the United Nations on International Women's Day." March 8. http://www.state.gov/g/wi/rls/8769pf.htm (accessed November 18, 2003).

Campbell, David. 1992. *Writing Security*. Minneapolis: University of Minnesota Press.

Chomsky, Noam. 2002. *9–11*. New York: Seven Stories Press.

Daily Telegraph. 2007. "Malalai Joya: US Makes Mockery of Afghani Democracy." June 19. http://www.rawa.org/temp/runews/2007/06/19/malalai-joya-us-makes-mockery-of-afghani-democracy.html (accessed July 9, 2007).

Edwards, Lucy Morgan. 2003 "Why Burqas Still Stifle Afghan Women." *Telegraph*, January 2. http://rawa.false.net/telegraph2.htm (accessed November 21, 2003).

Eisenstein, Zillah. 1996. *Hatreds*. New York and London: Routledge.

———. 2002. *Global Obscenities*. New York and London: New York University Press.

Enloe, Cynthia. 1989. *Bananas, Beaches and Bases*. Berkeley: University of California Press.

Evers, Barbara. 1994. "Gender Bias and Macro-economic Policy: Methodological Comments from the Indonesian Example." In *The Strategic Silence: Gender and Economic Policy*, ed. Isabella Bakker, 117–29. London: Zed.

Foucault, Michel. 1995. *Discipline and Punish: The Birth of the Prison*. New York: Vintage Books.

Ghafour, Hamida. 2004. "Beauticians without Borders Teach Basics to Afghan Women." *The Globe and Mail*, February 24, A1, A16.

Grewal, Inderpal. 1998. "On the New Global Feminism and the Family of Nations: Dilemmas of Transnational Feminist Practice." In *Talking Visions: Multicultural Feminism in a Transnational Age*, ed. Ella Shohat, 501–30. New York: MIT Press.

Helman, Christopher. 2003. "Carpet Bombing." *Forbes*, December 22. http://www.forbes.com/forbes/2003/1222/150_print.html (accessed February 24, 2004).

Hunt, Krista, and Kim Rygiel. 2006. "(En)Gendered War Stories and Camouflaged Politics." In *(En)Gendering the War on Terror: War Stories and Camouflaged Politics*, ed. Krista Hunt and Kim Rygiel, 1–24. London: Ashgate.

ICHRDD (International Centre for Human Rights and Democratic Development). 2002. "Take Action Now." http://www.ichrdd.ca/english/supportSamar.html (accessed February 22, 2002).

Khalilzad, Zalmay, "Afghanistan's Milestone," *Washington Post*, January 6, 2004. http://www.state.gov/p/sca/rls/rm/27702.htm.

Mahoney, Jill, and Kim Honey. 2001. "MD Aims to Better the Lives of Women." *The Globe and Mail*, December 6, A3.

Mohanty, Chandra Talpade. 2003. *Feminism without Borders*. Durham and London: Duke University Press.

Nair, Sheila. 2002. "Human Rights and Postcoloniality." In *Power, Postcolonialism and International Relations*, ed. Geeta Chowdhry and Sheila Nair, 254–84. London and New York: Routledge.

OIWI. http://www.state.gov/g/wi/ (accessed January 19, 2004).

OIWI. 2003. "Report Submitted to Congress by the Department of State under the Afghan Women and Children Relief Act 2001." June 16. http://www.state.gov/g/wi/rls/22436pf.htm (accessed November 25, 2003).

Petersmann, Sandra. 2004. "Hope for Women in Afghanistan." *Deutsche Welle*, January 3. http://www.dw-world.de/english/0,3367,1430_A_1075264,00.html (accessed January 25, 2004).

Ponticelli, Charlotte. 2003a. "Respect for Women: A U.S. Foreign Policy Imperative." March 17. http://www.state.gov/g/wi/rls/18767pf.htm (accessed November 24, 2003).

———. 2003b. "U.S. Outreach to Muslims on Women's Issues: From Theory to Practice." May 16. http://www.state.gov/g/wi/rls/21240.htm (accessed November 25, 2003).

Powell, Colin. 2002. "Remarks at Reception to Mark International Women's Day." March 7. http://www.state.gov/secretary/rm/2002/8691pf.htm (accessed May 8, 2003).

Rawi, Mariam. 2004. "Rule of the Rapists." *Guardian*, February 12. http://www.guardian.co.uk/comment/story/0,3604,1146134,00.html (accessed February 25, 2004).

Ross, Cecily. 2004. "Carpet Bombing." *The Globe and Mail*, January 24, L7.

Runyan, Anne Sisson. 1999. "Women in the Neoliberal Frame." In *Gender Politics in Global Governance*, ed. Mary K. Meyer and Elisabeth Prugl, 210–20. Lanham: Rowman & Littlefield.

Spivak, Gayatri. 1988. "Can the Subaltern Speak?" In *Marxism and the Interpretation of Culture*, ed. Cary Nelson and Lawrence Grossberg, 271–312. Urbana: University of Illinois Press.

———. 1996. "Woman as Theatre: United Nations Conference on Women, Beijing 1995." *Radical Philosophy* (January/February). http://www.radicalphilosophy.com/default.asp?channel_id=2187&editorial_id=10716 (accessed February 19, 2004).

Sunder, Madhavi. 2004. "The New Afghan Constitution: Will it Respect Women's Rights?" *CNN.com*, January 20. http://www.cnn.com/2004/LAW/01/20/findlaw.analysis.sunder.afghan (accessed February 25, 2004).

Talbot, Karen. 2003. "Afghanistan, Central Asia, Georgia: Key to Oil Profits." In *After Shock: September 11, 2001: Feminist Perspectives*, ed. Susan Hawthorne and Bronwyn Winter, 316–27. Vancouver: Raincoast.

Turner, Terisa E., Leigh S. Brown, and Wahu M. Kaara. 2001. "Gender, Food Security, and Foreign Policy Toward Africa: Women Farmers in Kenya and the Right to Sustenance." In *Ethics and Security in Canadian Foreign Policy*, ed. Rosalind Irwin, 95–110. Vancouver: University of British Columbia Press.

Warrug.com. http://www.warrug.com/ (accessed February 24, 2004).

Weedon, Chris. 1987. *Feminist Practice and Poststructuralist Theory*. Cambridge and Oxford: Blackwell.

White House. 2003. "Proposed Middle East Initiatives." May 9. http://www.state.gov/g/wi/rls/20491pf.htm (accessed January 13, 2004).

———. 2006. "Fact Sheet: The Fifth Anniversary of September 11, 2001." September 11. http://www.whitehouse.gov/news/releases/2006/09/20060911-2.html (accessed February 11, 2008).

Zia-Zarifi, Sam. 2004. "Losing the Peace in Afghanistan." Human Rights Watch World Report, January. http://www.hrw.org/wr2k4/5.htm (accessed February 26, 2004).

CHAPTER 4

Shielding America: Missile Defense and the Reification of Domesticity

Dawn Nowacki and David S. Gutterman

Imagine an impenetrable shield, impermeable to enemy missile attack, protecting the "homeland." A shield that guarantees national security and secures national prosperity. A shield that fulfills and enables America's destiny. This is the illusion that U.S. political leaders, defense contractors and their military clients, and conservative social advocates have presented to the American public under the guise of the "war on terror." Rhetorical justifications of a missile defense shield for the United States portray it seductively as being the first line of defense in the war on terror, and situate the failure to pursue this "antiterror," "antimissile" mission as irresponsible. The George W. Bush administration and its allied constituencies have presented the shield to the American populace as a package of policies—a presentation made through a gendered discourse that links defense of the country with defense of the family. We argue that, in the rhetorical war to define and defend the "homeland," the missile defense shield serves as a magical vehicle that does not simply promise future safety, but reifies the mythical past and a projected future of gender stability and domestic order.

In this chapter, we illuminate the arguments of the Bush administration, its defense contractor partners, conservative nongovernmental organizations (NGOs), and media outlets in their promotion of the erection of the missile defense shield. We do this in order to illustrate the language of traditional domesticity underpinning their rhetorical dynamic. We then discuss the desperate and impossible longing for hegemonic control that explains the irrationality of the missile defense shield in the face of strategic, scientific, and fiscal challenges. While the Bush administration relies on a conventional rhetoric of homeland defense to justify its plans for a costly and ill-conceived missile defense program, the current patriarchal discourse of watching and shielding the homeland adds disturbing new aspects to the debate on national security.

Disciplining the Homeland through (Gendered) Rhetorical War

Foucault's views on discipline as a modality of power offer insightful ways to think about the question of "shielding." As Sawicki observes, "Disciplinary practices ... aim to render the individual ... more powerful, productive, useful and docile. They secure their hold not through the threat of violence or force, but rather by creating desires, attaching individuals to specific identities, and establishing norms against which individuals and their behaviors and bodies are judged and against which they police themselves" (1991, 67–68). The rhetoric of shielding is a form of disciplining that produces (and defines) both those inside and those outside of the conceptual space evoked in the public mind. Rhetoric justifying the missile defense system places "the family"—with its corresponding desires, identities, and norms—in the center of what must be shielded and protected. It is the family that must be protected, rather than the general population, cities, economic entities, or military installations. In this formula, the normative family serves as a synecdoche standing in for the nation as a whole, and the desires of the nation, and its economic entities and military installations, are advanced under the protective cover of the "family." As a disciplinary mechanism, the rhetoric of missile defense functions to "create" and sustain the normative family and plays upon individuals' longing to be completely safe. Its appeal is more than attractive to those made uneasy and anxious in the aftermath of 9/11, particularly to women (see Huddy et al. 2005; Kliman 2006, chap. 5, on the support of Japanese housewives for missile defense).

Much conservative political and religious discourse argues that the American family has been under attack for a long time, not only from external enemies but from internal ones, and that this results in "unhealthy,"[1] and thus unacceptable, families. A vivid, but by no means atypical, illustration of the connection between the security of (a certain kind of) family and the security of the country was explicitly made by Senator Rick Santorum (R–Pennsylvania) on July 14, 2004, on the floor of the U.S. Senate. He argued that passing a constitutional amendment on the sanctity of heterosexual marriage would be the best step the Senate could take in the maintenance of homeland security: "I am for homeland security. But there isn't enough money in the world that you can spend to secure the home more than marriage. You want to invest in homeland security? You invest in marriage. You invest in the stability of the family" (Senate Republican Conference 2004).

The gendered nature of missile defense rhetoric consistent with the sentiment expressed by Santorum is further revealed by conservative NGOs that target women. Consider, for example, the "mission page" of the Eagle Forum website, which links familiar conservative antigay, anti-abortion, antitax, and antifeminist principles along with the seemingly unrelated objective of support for missile defense. Missile defense is the only specific military-technological program that is cited in the pantheon of the Eagle Forum's conservative principles (www.eagleforum.org). Or this illustration from the conservative think tank Independent Women's Forum (IWF), which proclaimed on September 1, 2001, that missile defense is a women's issue:

> It is in the nature of all human beings—and certainly the nature of women—to protect whom they love and what they value. On that premise our society has spawned whole industries to help us play it safe, and women take these precautions seriously. Because no man or woman would willingly leave a family vulnerable to danger, we assume that we are safe in our homes. Yet every home in America is lacking a crucial level of security. We have no protection against foreign and hostile missiles. Missiles, whether deliberately or accidentally launched, can enter our air space unimpeded, carrying weapons to destroy homes, families, and cities. Today, we can't stop them.
>
> (IWF 2001)

The IWF proclaims that it presents only the "facts": that the threat is real; that the technology to stop missiles in midflight is available; that there is entrenched opposition (which the writers of the piece find "baffling"); and that "we now have a President who recognizes the severity of the threat, the promise of the technology, and the government's obligation to shield the nation." Based on these "facts," the IWF concludes: "Now is the time for women to say that when it comes to the safety of our loved ones, we won't accept anything less than the best—a strong national missile defense" (ibid.).

The gendered dynamics that portray the United States as a traditional normative family that needs the protection of a missile defense shield like a father with a shotgun on the porch is not just evident among conservative women's organizations. An illustration of the overlap between hegemonic masculinist hierarchies—the National Football League (NFL) and the Pentagon—is demonstrated in the person of Riki Ellison, former NFL linebacker for the San Francisco 49ers, who is the founder and president of the Missile Defense Advocacy Alliance (MDAA). The MDAA conducts "opinion polls" and "focus groups," the purpose of which is to spread "awareness" about missile defense and to generate public support. Ellison himself makes speeches around the country at "Champions" meetings in support of missile defense in connection with protecting families. In a characteristic message, Ellison declared, "Missile defense provides the roof over our national home" (PR Newswire 2004).

In a bid to position itself as the best defender of America, the Republican Party explicitly connects the defense of the family against the internal threats to the nation with the defense of the homeland against the external threats to the nation. This defense of America, a thread that has run through Republican politics over the past hundred years, includes implicit definitions of America and the American family, and of their enemies.[2] Indeed, the language of shielding sets the terms of debate and punishes those who would challenge the terms of the shield. Those who question are "punished" as "unpatriotic" and willing to leave the United States vulnerable to attack, implying at best shortsightedness and at worst sympathy with enemies and terrorists. In a representative example, former Reagan administration official Frank Gaffney[3] approvingly cited then national security advisor Condoleezza Rice, who argued that "it makes no sense to 'put deadbolt locks on your doors and stock up on cans of mace and then decide to leave your windows open' to enemy attack. That, she correctly contended, would be essentially the effect if the Bush administration were to perpetuate its predecessors' practice of leaving the country undefended against missile-delivered [weapons of mass destruction] WMD" (Center for Security Policy 2004).[4] This failure is portrayed as unmanliness, as inviting weakness and disorder by failing in the duty to protect the home. As Senator Santorum proclaimed, homeland security in the United States has been eroded by the diminishment of the "definition of manhood [as] being 'provider' and 'protector'" (Senate Republican Conference 2004).

The rhetorical construction of males as protectors, of course, requires the construction of females and children as those in need of protection. Women who question protection by males are likewise seen as "unpatriotic" and "unnatural" and certainly not interested in protecting their families, unlike their more "naturally" maternal sisters, the "security moms." Just as shielding and defending the family legitimizes the missile defense system, the missile defense system legitimizes the shielding of a particular kind of family, one beholden to a particular set of gendered constraints.

In this era of the war on terror, rhetorics of defense serve to reify the redomestication of the American family. In *The Morning After*, a look at gendered international politics in the immediate post–Cold War period, Cynthia Enloe predicted that in the near future, "in each country someone will be making calculations about how masculinity and femininity can best serve national security ..." (1993, 261). Enloe has eloquently argued that traditional gender roles are required, and valorized, in the militarization of society (Enloe 2000). In short, as Bayard de Volo (1998) suggests, in conditions of perceived national insecurity, "in mobilizing a nation to war, differences are squelched as the individual voices of the citizens must appear to speak as one. Since a nation's way of life is to be protected, voices outside the mainstream appear as a threat. As with representations of ethnicity and race, the most traditional and extreme representations of masculinity and femininity are to be found during wartime" (241). The effort to craft national security around the protection of hegemonic visions of the normative family is particularly poignant in the United States where debates about sex, sexuality, and gender are especially contentious.[5]

Just as Foucault's notion of discipline and punishment gives us insights into the production of missile defense rhetoric, so too does his thinking about power. Power is seen by Foucault as "capillary." In conditions of Panopticism, Foucault argues "there is the penetration of regulation into even the smallest details of everyday life through the mediation of the complete hierarchy that assured the capillary functioning of power" (1979, 198). That is, it circulates through the social body as a whole, created not only by top-down relationships, but also from the bottom up through the interactions of ordinary people. From the top-down perspective, defending against effeminate (and feminine) weakness in America begins with the impulse for surveillance, for identifying and guarding against the "enemy threat." This emphasis on surveillance is, of course, central to Foucault's thinking about discipline and punishment. Today, new technologies of surveillance, including remote sensing satellites that have image resolution down to three inches, or with infrared capability, raise the specter of anyone at any time being watched from space. The rhetoric of missile defense is intended to create a populace that has internalized the terrorist threat; a citizenry anxious that "evil" can strike at any time, anywhere is all too willing to accept the "necessity" of surveillance from space, legitimating the "protective" watchfulness of a new order of Panopticon.[6]

At the same time, the effort to enlist all "good" citizens as agents in the war on terror complements this top-down call for surveillance with a demand for watchful citizens disciplining their neighbors. The most obvious illustration of this initiative was the development of the Terrorism Information and Prevention System (TIPS) as part of the National Homeland Security and Combating Terrorism Act of 2002. While this program, which emerged from John Ashcroft's Justice Department, was ultimately scuttled, the message delivered to citizens was clear: Watch what your neighbors say and do; sleeper cells and insurgents can be anywhere waiting for a vulnerable place and time to strike—and strike close to home. Even the more positive and less aggressive rhetoric of the administration reinforces this theme of citizen-soldiers protecting and comforting their families as the first line of national defense. Consider Bush's September 20, 2001, speech to the nation, in which he answers the rhetorical question: "Americans are asking, 'what can we do?'" with the instructions to pray, hug their children, and continue to shop in order to bolster the American economy and way of life.[7] In these everyday, normative ways, Americans are thus enlisted in the army of freedom in the battle of good and evil, the war over civilization. The political forces at work in justifying the missile defense shield are thus fighting a war on two fronts: simultaneously protecting and containing the nation from external force and internal dissension. In so doing, the politics of missile defense illustrates Foucault's argument that power is not simply a tool of suppression, but also a productive force:

> If power were never anything but repressive, if it never did anything but to say no, do you really think one would be brought to obey it? What makes power hold good, what makes it accepted, is simply the fact that it doesn't only weigh on us as a force that says no, but that it traverses and produces things, it induces pleasure, forms knowledge, produces discourse. It needs to be considered as a productive network which runs through the whole social body, much more than as a negative instance whose function is repression.
>
> (Foucault, in Gordon 1980, 119)

The missile defense shield exemplifies the ways in which power produces discourses that connect individuals' deepest fears with particular government activities that claim to alleviate those fears. But it is important to remember that missile defense, while being imposed from the top down, could not be used as a successful instrument of fantasy creation without some level of bottom-up buy-in by individuals. We return to these points later in the chapter. First we outline the more objective reasons that explain why the Bush administration has placed missile defense at the center of its national security policy.

Conventional Forms, New Stakes

The efforts of the Bush administration and its allies to link discourses of internal and external threats to the homeland have a storied history in conservative politics in the United States. Such themes resonate in America today in tones familiar and oddly comforting. The reasoning goes something like this: As an individual, my capacity to fight terrorism is limited, but if I strive to preserve the sanctity of my normative family, I too can contribute to homeland security. Yet, at the same time, the very conventionality of the rhetoric masks something fundamentally new: the stakes are much higher because of the nature of the technology involved and the intimate and complex relationship between private surveillance companies and the U.S. military. What can be seen as a greater threat to Americans than "terrorists" or external enemies is the fact that the "eyes in the sky" that purport to "protect" them are owned by private interests whose biggest client is the U.S. government. Extremely sophisticated technologies for snooping on private citizens have been under development for many years by corporations specializing in "security"—corporations that include some of the Defense Department's largest contractors (Brzezinski 2004). Meanwhile, the actions of government under the USA PATRIOT Act are more opaque, and the government is increasingly ceding surveillance authority and responsibility to private sources unbound by public accountability.[8]

In her critique of the USA PATRIOT Act,[9] and in her outline of the resistance of American communities to it, Elaine Scarry makes the broader argument that democracy requires the transparency of government and the opacity of its citizens' private lives. The PATRIOT Act reverses this formula by rendering the actions of government secret and by invading the privacy of the citizens (Scarry 2004). The technologies of missile defense perform the same sort of reversal. Surveillance from space by ultrasecret satellites makes private lives and homes open to inspection by the authorities. The remoteness of the instruments of surveillance, moreover, remain not just removed from the everyday lives of citizens, but more disconcertingly, in the hands of private corporations removed from the reach of a democratic populace. By legitimizing missile defense through a gendered rhetoric about who desires, needs, and deserves protection, domestic space is imagined in conventional ways that mask its surveillance in unconventional ones.

The Official Rationale and Ends of Missile Defense

So, what is missile defense officially supposed to accomplish? According to the Bush administration and the military, missile defense is necessary because "we can't say with any certainty where the threats of the future will come from. A variety of states and groups continue to seek to acquire [WMD] and the means to deliver them" (Garamone 2001). In a June 2001

meeting with North Atlantic Treaty Organization (NATO) defense minis-
ters, Secretary of Defense Donald Rumsfeld argued:

> We are leaving a world where our principal aim was to deter the Soviet
> Union, and we are entering a world where we will need to deter a variety of
> different actors, with a variety of different motivations, armed with a variety
> of different weapons. We need to take advantage of this period to ensure that
> NATO is prepared for the newer security challenges we will certainly face in
> the 21st century.
>
> (Gilmore 2001, p. 101)

Examples of such challenges enumerated by Rumsfeld were terrorism, cyber
attack, high-tech weapons, and ballistic and cruise missiles armed with
WMD. Administration officials were already conflating terrorist and missile
attack threats even before the events of September 11, 2001. After 9/11,
missile defense was named by President Bush as the nation's top national
security priority, cast in terms of the "war on terror." As Bush declared on
December 17, 2002, "Defending the American people against these new
threats [posed by ballistic missiles] is my highest priority as Commander-
in-Chief, and the highest priority of my administration" (quoted in Missile
Defense Agency 2004). The Bush administration has been undeterred in its
promotion of "high-tech" missile defense by the 9/11 terrorists' "low-tech"
methods. Yet a missile defense shield provides no protection against individual humans armed with box cutters and bent on suicide.

The Bush administration's National Security Strategy (NSS) document
of September 17, 2002, solidifies this proclamation into a policy agenda
(NSS 2002). The NSS document contains eight specific goals designed to
"make the world not just safer but better." Interwoven through the entire
document is the case for missile defense. A key theme, stated in several
places in the document, is that the United States will "prevent our enemies from threatening us, our allies, and our friends, with weapons of
mass destruction." Section 5 reiterates this theme and calls for missile
defense:

> We must be prepared to stop rogue states and their terrorist clients before
> they are able to threaten or use [WMD] against the United States and our
> allies and friends. Our response must take full advantage of strengthened
> alliances, the establishment of new partnerships with former adversaries,
> innovation in the use of military forces, modern technologies, including *the
> development of an effective missile defense system* [emphasis added], and
> increased emphasis on intelligence collection and analysis.
>
> (NSS 2002)

The NSS document offers an explicit justification for the use and maintenance of a broad range of military capabilities, especially in section 9, which
"reaffirm[s] the essential role of American military strength" and calls for a
transformation of the American military:

> We must ... develop[ing] assets such as advanced remote sensing, long-range
> precision strike capabilities, and transformed maneuver and expeditionary
> forces. This broad portfolio of military capabilities must also include the
> ability to defend the homeland, conduct information operations, ensure U.S.
> access to distant theaters, and protect critical U.S. infrastructure and assets
> in outer space.
>
> (NSS 2002)

Conventional deterrence will no longer work under the new conditions
of the war against terrorism, according to the NSS document. Instead,
overwhelming American military dominance is seen as a new kind of
deterrence.

The NSS document frames the argument for missile defense in a way
that overlooks concerns about its effectiveness against terrorists, its enormous cost, and the move from strategic deterrence to the possession of
overwhelming military capability. This latter move defies the logic of realist
theory, which posits that a balance of power between states promotes stability and peace. The superiority of U.S. military forces is unlikely to stop
other international actors from acquiring nuclear arms and ballistic missiles,
since the American strategy neglects the role that these kinds of high-status
armaments play in other actors' calculations of their national security,
national identity, and international prestige (e.g., Iraq pre-9/11, North
Korea, Iran).[10]

Embedded in overwhelming military dominance as a deterrent strategy is the missile defense system, as stated in the "National Policy on
Ballistic Missile Defense Fact Sheet" (The White House), dated May 20,
2003:

> Some states are aggressively pursuing the development of [WMD] and long-
> range missiles as a means of coercing the United States and our allies. To deter
> such threats, we must devalue missiles as tools of extortion and aggression,
> undermining the confidence of our adversaries that threatening a missile
> attack would succeed in blackmailing us. In this way, although missile defenses
> are not a replacement for an offensive response capability, they are an added
> and critical dimension of contemporary deterrence. Missile defenses will also
> help to assure allies and friends, and to dissuade countries from pursuing bal-
> listic missiles in the first instance by undermining their military utility.

However, the questions relating to whether missile defense technology will work, its costs, and its inability to deal with low-tech threats are still begged by its promoters.

Difficulties with Missile Defense

Despite the ballyhooing of missile defense by the administration and the military, evidence suggests that ballistic missile defense (BMD) won't work as intended—and it is exceedingly expensive. It is true that the current iteration of missile defense is a much scaled-down version of the "impenetrable" shield of the Reagan era, with its space-based lasers and network of satellites. (However, those of the public who remember Reagan's Star Wars program still imagine it that way, which works to the benefit of those trying to promote it.) While the BMD system, deployed in late 2004, ground-based, and consisting of only ten interceptors, is much simpler technologically than Reagan's grand design, the policy architects envision it as a complex, multilayered[11] set of defenses that, according to the Missile Defense Agency (MDA), will be space-based.

Foucault's insight into the productive nature of power is helpful in understanding the Bush administration's strategy of linking missile defense to Bush's reelection. Throughout his first term, Bush insisted that the first phase of missile defense become operational in 2004—coinciding with the presidential election—to demonstrate that there was something to show for the $31.9 billion he had requested, and received, from Congress for missile defense for fiscal years (FY) 2002 through 2005.[12] Despite evidence of severe technical difficulties with missile defense, the deployment of ten interceptors produces rhetoric vindicating Bush's strategy of using missile defense to justify his claim to be protector of the homeland.

The reality of missile defense belies its rhetorical success, however. In testimony before the Senate Armed Services Committee, the Senate Appropriations Committee, and the Strategic Forces Subcommittee of the House Armed Services Committee in March and April 2004, officials responsible for the program admitted that it was riddled with cost overruns, delays, and inadequate testing. The most sophisticated parts of the system, the space-based lasers, would not be available for ten or twenty years.[13] Moreover, parts of each layer are under the aegis of different branches of the military and are being built by different defense contractors. While spreading responsibility for the deployment across each of the branches of the military and a large number of defense contractors will undoubtedly make the resulting system extraordinarily complex, this generation of divergent partners does create a productive alliance for proponents of BMD. With the investment of revenue into each military branch and defense contractor, the Department of Defense is able to establish support for its plans in a context of military restructuring and economic competition that would otherwise be expected to lead to criticism and complaint from within the military-industrial complex—and this broad support has proven vital in the wake of test failures and political fallout.

Technical difficulties with BMD are demonstrated in Government Accounting Office (GAO) reports, testimony from experts (both proponents and critics of missile defense) to the House and Senate Armed Services and Appropriations committees, and analysis from outside groups, such as the Union of Concerned Scientists. Military experts have further testified to Congress that coordinating the layers of missile defense has proven to be a difficult problem. The failure of any part of the system means failure of the whole. "[Testing layered missile defense] is like deploying a military aircraft missing the wings, the tail and the landing gear. And without testing to see if that aircraft can do its mission without wings, a tail or landing gear," noted Philip E. Coyle, a former chief of operational test and evaluation at the Pentagon (Glanz 2004). Operational tests of the missile defense system have not been at all promising.[14]

Even the small steps taken toward a functional missile defense system have been very costly. While $9 billion in an overall military budget of $420 billion for FY 2005 does not seem very unreasonable, the cost becomes quite substantial if the billions already spent in the 1980s, 1990s, and into this century for BMD are included. (Total appropriations between FY 1985 and FY 2007 equal $106.9 billion, according to the MDA's figures). An assessment by Caldicott (2004), relying on information publicly available from defense contractors, outlined the major systems, the defense contractors responsible for each part of the systems, and the costs of missile defense. She demonstrated that the whole program would be worth hundreds of billions of dollars to defense contractors over the next fifteen years.

Even if we were to set aside the technical challenges and costs, deploying the missile defense system raises thorny strategic concerns. It makes irrelevant the Cold War strategy of banning the acquisition of ballistic missiles by other countries, since the "shield" can destroy such missiles. The technology used in missile "defense" could actually be used offensively. Consequently, other countries' efforts to acquire nuclear and missile capabilities become more legitimate, since they are wary of the "defensive" purposes of the American missile defense.

To take one illustration, in response to Bush's unilateral withdrawal from the 1972 Anti-Ballistic Missile (ABM) Treaty on June 17, 2002, President

Vladimir Putin changed Russia's strategic doctrine in 2003 to include the use of nuclear weapons in the event of an attack. In late 2004, Putin announced that Russia was developing "new missile complexes." He noted, "Not only are we conducting tests of modern nuclear missile systems, but I am sure that they will be added to the arsenals in the near future. Other nuclear powers do not have and will not have such weapons for a long time" (Melikova and Babakin 2004, 1).[15]

Finally, the pursuit of missile defense has meant the de facto weaponization of space, a dramatic departure from past policy. The firewall against placing offensive weapons in space is breached by missile defense. As a result, rather than being enhanced by missile defense, national and global security will be seriously compromised as other powers scramble to put their own weapons into space.

Disciplining Freedom

Considering the immense difficulties of fielding an operational missile defense system, its great costs, and its international political consequences, the advertised advantages of BMD do not fully explain the Bush administration's determined pursuit of unrealistic goals. We argue that there are important fantasy ends being served by the rhetorical project of missile defense. A standard definition of national security is a psychological perception of freedom from fear (Kegley and Wittkopf 2004, 450). In post-9/11 conditions, freedom from fear is a fantasy, yet the Bush administration must give the impression that it is doing everything possible to protect national security, to create a sphere that is fearless. As self-styled heirs to the Reagan era, the Bush team has promoted a similar kind of grandeur and optimism, made possible in part by the image of an invulnerable homeland. Much political capital can be amassed if people feel secure, or more accurately, if people believe that their government is working conscientiously to make them secure. And if people feel that the government is competent in securing the homeland, other administration goals can be accomplished more readily.

In line with this discursive strategy, pursuing missile defense is presented as "freedom" by the Bush administration and its Republican allies in Congress. For example, the freedom theme is prominent in the U.S. Senate's Republican Policy Committee document entitled "Reviewing the Progress of Missile Defense: Exploring the Freedom Afforded the United States by the Absence of the ABM [Anti-Ballistic Missile] Treaty." The document quotes Bush:

> We know that the terrorists, and some of those who support them, seek the ability to deliver death and destruction to our doorstep via missile. And we

must have the freedom and the flexibility to develop effective defenses against those attacks. Defending the American people is the highest priority as Commander in Chief, and I cannot and will not allow the United States to remain in a treaty that prevents us from developing effective defenses.

(quoted in U.S. Senate Republican Policy Committee 2003, 1)

Abrogating the 1972 ABM Treaty was defined as "freedom" by Bush three months following the 9/11 terrorist attacks. As a rhetorical move, it was masterful in creating a regime of discipline that punishes those who would oppose missile defense by lumping them together with terrorists.

Granted, in the new geopolitical realities post–Cold War and post-9/11, old treaties may no longer be relevant. The Soviet Union no longer exists; newer members of the nuclear club were not signatories to the ABM Treaty, in which the Soviet Union and the United States banned layered missile defense, prohibited tampering with each other's spy satellites, and prohibited working with allies to develop ABM systems.[16] Ironically, missile defense is an answer to the conditions that existed during the Cold War, when a single enemy power was armed with thousands of nuclear-tipped missiles. Promoting missile defense today serves to veil other options that might be more applicable to the new international security situation, and establishes a false dichotomy between missile defense or unilateral vulnerability.

The "Capillary" Effects of Power

We argued earlier that the fantasy ends of missile defense are achieved in part because power is productive. It produces an attractive myth of absolute protection for "perfect" American families, and thus fulfills many individuals' longing for complete security and control in the context of a perceived threatening environment. While some people's support for missile defense may be explained by their greater support in general for the military and the use of military force, there is a gender gap in this regard. Political psychological studies of women find them to be relatively more anxious than men in the face of an external threat (Huddy et al. 2005), but less willing to use military force (Eichenberg 2003; Conover and Sapiro 1993), which might explain some part of their support for missile defense: precisely because it is *defensive*. Fear creates docile bodies, and particularly gendered bodies. We can all be soldiers in the war on terror, not because we actually take up arms, but because we are properly docile. We can fight in the war on terror by having a proper, healthy family, and by watching other people to make sure they are doing the same.

Conclusion

Gibbs (2004) demonstrates that, at several post–World War II historical junctures, government and foreign policy elites of the day employed threatening external events as pretexts to undertake enormous buildups of military forces and to justify foreign interventions to skeptical publics. September 11 was just such a pretext, serving as justification for continuing the missile defense program. An impermeable "shield" produced by the rhetoric of missile defense is similar to the Bush administration's other sleights of hand that elide Osama bin Laden into Saddam Hussein and transfer the central front in the war on terror from Afghanistan to Iraq. Missile defense can do nothing to stop individual terrorists, but it is presented as a bulwark against "rogue states" that may launch a missile armed with WMD. Similarly, as we have argued, *who* is to be protected is elided from the general population to a certain subset of the population: the family, constructed as traditional, heterosexual, with multiple children, patriotic, nonimmigrant, and religious, which "deserves" this kind of absolute protection.

Missile defense is the pretext for other equally problematic elisions. First, it serves as a Trojan horse designed to get the public to accept something even more dangerous: the weaponization of space.[17] An obvious connection exists between the militarization and weaponization of space and the protection of U.S. commercial interests in space. The MDA overtly promotes the interdependence of private business and the military, encouraging private companies to invest in the development of technology and products for use in space. Conveniently, private companies' "assets" in space then provide the pretext for military protection, and the U.S. sphere of interest is projected into space.

Second, the rhetoric of missile defense is an important contributor to the ethos of insecurity and anxiety that generates public support for political candidates and policies that are "strong on defense," and it requires everyone to engage in the debate on these terms—or else be "disciplined."

Finally, to the extent that the public accepts the rhetoric and supports the policies, the influence of the military-industrial complex in the halls of government is strengthened, and the economic reach of those corporations behind the construction of the missile defense shield is expanded. Defense contractors are large contributors to political campaigns, especially those of Republicans, who are seen as stronger than Democrats on defense.[18] Key members of the Bush administration, including Vice President Cheney, have ties to key suppliers of missile defense technology. Several have served on the boards of, or have been top executives at, Northrop Grumman, Boeing, Raytheon, Lockheed Martin, and TRW.[19] Bluntly put, missile defense contracts reward friends of the administration and, at least indirectly, members of the administration itself.

These exercises of power at the top could not succeed without the capillary effects of power from the bottom up. Foucault reminds us that as subjects of the Panopticon, ordinary individuals seek, and even long for, discipline. They have internalized the rules and know that they are being watched as a way both to protect individuals from each other and to protect the larger society (Epstein 2007). People seek discipline because they cannot stand disorder, and in wartime they cannot stand weakness and submission to an "enemy." Not only are Americans being continually fed the messages that they are at war and should be fearful of terrorists from the top down, they also seek discipline and order from the bottom up. They expect, and indeed demand, that their leaders keep them safe.

In his analysis of why Bush really won the 2004 election, Mark Danner argues that the facts did not matter in the campaign. Voters were offered a choice: "either discard the facts, or give up the clear and comforting worldview that they contradicted. They chose to disregard the facts" (Danner 2005). Many Americans are willing to set aside their skepticism to support leadership that provides the *illusion* of safety, security, and stability. Bush, his administration, and his advisors and strategists are masters of illusion. They bludgeon people with the idea of "freedom" as a way to get them not only to support an imperialistic and reckless foreign policy, but also to ensure order and discipline at home. "Freedom" in Bush-speak actually means highly disciplined behavior. Similarly, a missile defense shield provides the illusion of safety from enemy missiles. The facts about costs, technological problems, and political consequences are not important. What is important is that people feel reassured and protected. Missile defense rhetoric constructs the traditional family as being most deserving of reassurance and protection, and produces the necessary identity for those who seek to live in the American homeland, shielded from external and internal dangers.

Notes

1. For example, according to recent legislation providing "welfare" incentives for families to remain "intact," which was introduced in the U.S. House of Representatives and the U.S. Senate, "healthy" families are those with fathers. Implicitly, "unhealthy" families are those without fathers. See HR240, "Personal Responsibility, Work, and Family Promotion Act of 2005" (S105 with the same text and title).
2. As a prominent example, consider Ronald Reagan's famous "evil empire" speech, delivered before the National Association of Evangelicals in Orlando,

Florida, on March 8, 1983. In this speech, Reagan linked the threat posed to the United States by the "atheistic" Soviet Union to unholy forces of "modern-day secularism" that are corrupting America from within, leading to an "increase in illegitimate births and abortions involving girls well below the age of consent." Together, Reagan argued, these threats endanger the United States in the "struggle between right and wrong and good and evil" (Reagan 1983).

3. Gaffney, a relentless promoter of missile defense through his Center for Security Policy and its "Decision Briefs," is a key figure linking the work of military experts, policy analysts, and organizations whose mission is to influence women to support the Bush administration's war on terror as a "family issue." In addition to writing his own influential opinion pieces, Gaffney, who got his start in the 1970s working in Washington, D.C., on defense matters under Richard Perle, is a founding member of the hardline neoconservative Project for a New American Century. He was instrumental in the creation of Family Security Matters, an organization whose mission, according to one of the editors of the organization's newsletter, is to "'… address women's fears about national security and family security and link those fears to the urgent need for a strong national defense,' Carol Taber, said. 'We'll inspire our audience to engage politically and support the laws and practices that ensure our nation's security'" (Stoll 2003).

4. For other illustrations of this line of argument among conservative commentators, see articles by John J. Miller in the *National Review* (e.g., Miller 2003); Frank Gaffney in the *Washington Times* (e.g., Gaffney 2004); Karl Zinsmeister, editor in chief of the *American Enterprise;* and news "analysis" by Baker Spring, of the Heritage Foundation, for Fox Television News.

5. For an exploration of the politics of gender during the George W. Bush presidency, see Ferguson and Marso (2007).

6. As Riaz and DiMaggio note in chapter 6, such pervasive regimes of supervision have the effect not only of creating docile bodies, but also of multiplying the 'asymmetries of power'.

7. See Bush (2001).

8. On the problem of public accountability, see also Rygiel (chap. 5 in this volume) and Knight and Smith (chap. 9 in this volume).

9. The official title is the Uniting and Strengthening America by Providing Appropriate Tools Required to Intercept and Obstruct Terrorism Act of 2001 (Public Law 107–56), also known as the USA PATRIOT Act—or just the Patriot Act.

10. As Knight and Smith—following Foucault—argue in chapter 9, it is for such reasons that "power is leaky; the problems it addresses and seeks to subsume can escape its embrace to some extent."

11. "Multilayered" means that several different missile defense systems are being developed as backups in the event of failure to shoot down a missile in the early "boost" phase of its launch. Different systems are designed for the initial boost phase, the midcourse phase, and the terminal phase of a missile's trajectory.

12. President Bush requested a total of $31.9 billion for FY 2002–2005. He requested another $17.1 billion for FY 2006 and FY 2007. The actual appropriations passed

by Congress totaled a slightly larger amount. See the official MDA website, http://www.mda.mil/mdalink/pdf/histfunds.pdf.

13. The officials testifying were Michael W. Wynne, acting undersecretary of defense (for acquisition, technology, and logistics); Lt. Gen. Ronald T. Kadish, U.S. Air Force, director of the MDA; Adm. James O. L. Ellis Jr., U. S. Navy, commander, U.S. Strategic Command; Lt. Gen. Larry Dogden, commander, Space and Missile Defense Command; and Thomas Christie, director of operational test and evaluation, Department of Defense.

14. Two examples of many failed tests occurred in December 2004 and February 2005 when the rocket carrying the interceptor missile, meant to smash into and destroy a mock warhead launched from Kodiak, Alaska, shut down (see Kaplan 2004; AP 2005).

15. Commentators and journalists speculated for a month about what Putin meant, and according to an interview with Col. Gen. Nikolai Solovtsov, commander, Strategic Missile Forces, in *The Russian Courier*, which reports on defense and security issues in Russia, "Tactical and technical characteristics of the new complexes will be different from the existing ones. It will truly be a new nuclear weapon, which other nuclear powers lack." The article continues:
"Does it mean that the matter concerns delivery means, and not the nuclear device as such? Yes, it does. It was officially confirmed by Deputy Foreign Minister Vladimir Chizhov, who said that Russia was not increasing its nuclear potential. 'It's just that we will upgrade it to increase precision and improve defense from enemy attacks,' the diplomat explained. It goes without saying that 'defense from attacks' does not mean terrorists. It means the ability to pierce ballistic missile defense systems" (*Russky Kurier* Dec. 15, 2004, 5).

16. "... including the development, testing, and deployment of sea-based, air-based, space-based, and mobile land-based ABM systems, and ABM system components" (United States Senate Republican Policy Committee. 2003, 2).

17. See Mowthorpe (2004) and Hays (2002) for the details on how the militarization of space is proceeding. It is, for the military, not a question of "if" but of "when."

18. Caldicott (2004) estimates that approximately two-thirds of contributions from defense contractors benefit Republican candidates for political office. (See also http://opensecrets.org for a breakdown of contributions by defense contractors to Democratic and Republican candidates. The top contributors are also the top recipients of missile defense contracts.)

19. In 2001 Bush appointed Peter Teets, former chief operating officer of Lockheed Martin, as undersecretary of the Air Force and director of the National Reconnaissance Office (NRO). In budgetary terms, the NRO is the United States' largest intelligence agency. Teets has been in the forefront of promoting missile defense and the weaponization of space, while his former corporation, Lockheed Martin, is receiving billions of dollars' worth of contracts to develop the necessary technologies (Johnson 2004, 79).

Bibliography

Associated Press, 2005. "Missile Defense Test Fails Again. Second Test Failure in Recent Months for Experimental Program." February 14.

Bayard de Volo, Lorraine. 1998. "Drafting Motherhood: Maternal Imagery and Organizations in the United States and Nicaragua." In *The Women and War Reader*, ed. Lois Ann Lorentzen and Jennifer Turpin, xx. New York: New York University Press.

Brzezinski, Matthew. 2004. *Fortress America: On the Front Lines of Homeland Security – An Inside Look at the Surveillance State*. New York: Bantam Books.

Bush, George W. 2001. "Address to a Joint Session of Congress and the American People." September 20, 2001. http://www.whitehouse.gov/news/releases/2001/09/20010920-8.html.

Caldicott, Helen. 2004. *The New Nuclear Danger: George W. Bush's Military-Industrial Complex*. New York: New Press.

Center for Security Policy. 2004. "Restructure, Don't Cut, the Missile Defense Program: Focus Should Be on Deployment of Near Term Anti-Missile Systems." Decision Brief No. 04-D 19, 2004-04-05. http://centerforsecuritypolicy.org/.

———. 2005. "Anti-anti-missile defense." Decision Brief No. 04-D 15, 2004-04-05. http://centerforsecuritypolicy.org/.

Conover, Pamela Johnston, and Virginia Sapiro. 1993. "Gender, Feminist Consciousness, and War." *American Journal of Political Science* 37, no. 4: 1079–99.

Danner, Mark. 2005. "How Bush Really Won." *New York Review of Books* 52, no. 1, January 13. Accessed at http://www.nybooks.com/articles/17690.

Eichenberg, Richard C. 2003. "Gender Differences in Public Attitudes toward the Use of Force by the United States, 1990–2003." *International Security* 28, no. 1: 110–41.

Enloe, Cynthia. 1993. *The Morning After: Sexual Politics at the End of the Cold War*. Berkeley: University of California Press.

———. 2000. *Maneuvers: The International Politics of Militarizing Women's Lives*. Berkeley: University of California Press.

Epstein, Charlotte. 2007. "Guilty Bodies, Productive Bodies, Destructive Bodies: Crossing the Biometric Borders." *International Political Sociology* 1, no. 2: 149–64.

Ferguson, Michaele L., and Lori Jo Marso, eds. 2007. *W Stands for Women: How the George W. Bush Presidency Shaped a New Politics of Gender*. Durham, NC: Duke University Press.

Foucault, Michel. 1979. *Discipline and Punish: The Birth of the Prison*. Translated by Alan Sheridan. New York: Vintage Books.

Gaffney, Frank, Jr. 2004. "Anti-Anti-Missile Defense." *Washington Times*, April 6, A15.

Garamone, Jim. 2001. "Why America Needs Missile Defense: Is There Really a Ballistic Missile Threat?" *Armed Forces Press Service*, August 17.

Gibbs, David N. 2004. "Pretexts and U.S. Foreign Policy: The War on Terrorism in Historical Perspective." *New Political Science* 26, no. 3: 293–321.

Gilmore, Gerry J. 2001. "Rumsfeld to NATO: Prepare Now for Emerging Threats." *American Forces Press Service*, June 7.

Glanz, James. 2004. "Star Wars: The Next Version." *New York Times*, May 4, F1.

Gordon, Colin, ed. 1980. *Power/Knowledge: Selected Interviews and Other Writings 1972–1977 by Michel Foucault.* New York: Pantheon Books.

Hays, Peter L. 2002. *United States Military Space: Into the Twenty-First Century.* INSS Occasional Paper 42, USAF Institute for Security Studies, USAF Academy, Colorado, and Air University Press, Maxwell AFB, Alabama.

Huddy, Leonie, Stanley Feldman, Charles Taber, and Gallya Lahav. 2005. "Threat, Anxiety, and Support for Antiterrorism Policies." *American Journal of Political Science* 49, no. 3: 593–608.

Independent Women's Forum. 2001. "Missile Defense: It's a Women's Issue." http://www.iwf.org/issues/issues_detail.asp?ArticleID=545.

Johnson, Chalmers. 2004. *The Sorrows of Empire: Militarism, Secrecy, and the End of the Republic.* New York: Metropolitan Books, Henry Holt and Company.

Kaplan, Fred. 2003. "Shooting Down Missile Defense: Even the Pentagon Admits the Program is in Trouble." *Slate*, August 7. http://www.slate.com/id/2086724/.

Kegley, Charles W., Jr., and Eugene R. Wittkopf. 2004. *World Politics: Trend and Transformation.* 9th ed. Belmont, CA: Thomson/Wadsworth.

Kliman, Daniel M. 2006. *Japan's Security Strategy in the Post–9/11 World.* Westport, London, and Washington, D.C.: Praeger and Center for Strategic and International Studies.

Melikova, Natalya, and Alexander Babakin. 2004. "The Diplomacy of 'Nuclear Non-Deterrence.'" *Nezavisimaya Gazeta,* November 18, 1–2.

Miller, John J. 2003. "Defensible: How Missile Defense Can Learn from Failure." *National Review.com,* June 23.

Missile Defense Agency. 2004. Ballistic Missile Defense System Overview. Pamphlet. http://www.acq.osd.mil/mda/mdalink/html/mdalink.html.

Mowthorpe, Matthew. 2004. *The Militarization and Weaponization of Space.* New York: Lexington Books.

PR Newswire. 2004. "Survey: Likely Democratic Voters Support a Missile Defense System." January 29. http://www.lexisnexis.com.ezproxy.linfield.edu:2048/us/lnacademic/results/docview/docview.do?risb=21_T2200497219&format=GNBFI&sort=RELEVANCE&startDocNo=1&resultsUrlKey=29_T2200495763&cisb=22_T2200497221&treeMax=true&treeWidth=0&csi=8054&docNo=2.

Reagan, Ronald. 1983. Speech to the National Association of Evangelicals. Orlando, Florida, March 8. http://www.luminet.net/~tgort/empire.htm.

Sawicki, Jana. 1991. *Disciplining Foucault: Feminism, Power and the Body.* New York and London: Routledge.

Scarry, Elaine. 2004. "Resolving to Resist." *Boston Review* (February/March). http://bostonreview.net/BR29.1/scarry.html.

Senate Republican Conference. 2004. "Chairman Santorum Marriage Remarks on Senate Floor." July 14. http://www.senate.gov/src/agenda/index.cfm?fuseaction=ViewArticle&article_id=318.

Stoll, Ira. 2003. "From Protest to Glitz to Pro-War Soccer Moms." *New York Sun,* December 4. Available at http://www.fatnetwork.net/~familyse/modules.php?name=Content&pa=showpage&pid=9.

United States Senate Republican Policy Committee. 2003. "Reviewing the Progress of Missile Defense: Exploring the Freedom Afforded the United States by the Absence of the ABM Treaty." December 10.

White House, The. 2002. "National Security Strategy of the United States." September 17. http://www.whitehouse.gov/nsc/nssall.html.

———. 2003. National Policy on Ballistic Missile Defense Fact Sheet. Release from the Office of the Press Secretary, May 20. http://www.whitehouse.gov/news/releases/2003/05/print/220030520-15.html.

CHAPTER 5

Citizenship as Government: Disciplining Populations Post-9/11

Kim Rygiel

Introduction

Much has been written on the growing tension that has emerged between the conflicting modes of political organization of a deterritorialized global capitalist system and an international political system based on the territorial nation-state system (e.g., Held and McGrew 1999, 2002; Scholte 2000). This tension is based on the fact that global economic processes often demand borders that are relatively open, enabling a less restrictive movement of goods and services (and some people) across them. In contrast, the nation-state and traditional modern notions of state security have been founded upon relatively fixed territorial borders and populations. These two principles seem to be at odds. Although this tension has existed for some time (Hollifield 2004 refers to this as the "liberal paradox"), it has become particularly visible since the events of September 11, 2001, with governments seeking to thwart terrorist attacks by exercising greater control over their borders, but in ways that do not jeopardize the global capitalist economy. New ways of disciplining populations through citizenship policies, such as border controls and travel regulations, have become increasingly important as a way of responding to these competing systems of governance. It seems that the moment of 9/11 has provided the opportunity for many countries to introduce disciplinary forms of governing populations, many of which had already been conceptualized prior to 2001. This chapter argues that countries have thus used the events of September 11, 2001, and the subsequent "war on terrorism" as an opportunity to implement new citizenship policies in response to this economic/security paradox. As a result, citizenship is becoming a more global disciplinary regime of governing populations. This chapter argues that this is occurring in part through a decentering of state control. Moreover, this decentering does not necessarily correlate with a weakening or a "crisis" of citizenship, as many have argued, but rather with the strengthening of citizenship as a governing regime.[1]

This argument is informed by an alternative Foucauldian-inspired reading of citizenship *as government*. Rather than the more common way of viewing citizenship as an institution, located within a defined political community (most often that of the nation-state), by citizenship as government, I mean to suggest the way citizenship involves policies, practices, discourses, and technologies of power, the purpose of which is primarily the governing over individuals and populations.[2] From this perspective, citizenship is associated with neither the state *per se* nor with a particular form of juridical power (legal rights and status), but rather it involves much broader power relationships that extend well beyond the state and juridical or sovereign forms of power. In particular, citizenship depends on disciplinary power, which, according to Foucault (1979), is particularly effective—first, because "discipline fixes; it arrests or regulates movement" (ibid., 219); and second, because it is "exercised through its invisibility, at the same time it imposes on those whom it subjects a principle of compulsory visibility" (ibid., 187). From the perspective of citizenship as government, then, it can be argued that globalization and the deterritorialization of the state do not necessarily mean a weakening of citizenship, but rather the strengthening of it as a governing regime in that it can provide for a more disciplinary regime of governing populations.

Integral to my argument is the idea that the modern notion of territorial state control over disciplining populations is displaced and shared among other state and nonstate governing authorities to create a *globalizing*—and the focus of this chapter—more *disciplinary* regime of governing. As I have argued elsewhere, by *globalizing* I am referring to the idea that as a regime of government, citizenship has as much to do with governing populations *between* and *across* states as it does governing *within* the state (see Rygiel, forthcoming). Citizenship functions through a cooperation between state authorities and a harmonization and standardization between states around policies governing mobility. This can be thought of as an *internationalization* of citizenship. Yet, more than this, citizenship also depends on the displacement of power traditionally located in agents of the state to other actors such as international organizations, but also to private companies and even to individuals themselves. In other words, citizenship has become a *globalizing* regime by depending not just on its *internationalization* but also on both its *privatization* and *individualization* (Rygiel, forthcoming).

In this chapter, I wish to focus on how such shifts in governing through citizenship (internationalization, privatization, and individualization) allow for a more *disciplinary* regime of governing. To do so I will look at examples of border controls and travel regulations implemented across industrialized countries in the North, such as the United States, Canada, the European Union (EU), and the United Kingdom (UK). On the one hand, citizenship is internationalized through an increased harmonization of border and travel controls between states, overseen by international organizations like the International Civil Aviation Organization (ICAO), so the regime becomes more disciplinary through an increased standardization in the area of travel regulation between and across North America and Europe. On the other hand, disciplinary power is also operationalized through a privatization of citizenship as governments increasingly employ private companies to oversee certain governing functions, especially in the areas of surveillance and the regulation of mobility. Finally, a more disciplinary regime is emerging as individuals increasingly internalize travel regulations and border controls and come to participate in their own self-governing as well as the governing of other citizens. This chapter examines each of these aspects of disciplinary power in turn. What such an examination reveals is that a more complex reading of world politics is required today. This is a reading that, as Janie Leatherman points out in this volume's introduction, views world politics as a series of competing, yet interconnected, global networks of governing that feed into one another much "like figure eights—or perhaps more like a mobius band—where opposing identities collude, overlap, or meld, obscuring the distinction between the world of the licit and the illicit and between friend and foe" (see chap. 1). Not only does this vision challenge the notion of distinct licit and illicit governing structures, but it also provides a more complex reading of the state, where the boundary between state and nonstate actors is blurred. It might be more useful to think of the state as assemblages and flows of spaces (Massey 1994; Deleuze and Guattari 1987; Hardt and Negri 2000) rather than as contiguously bounded territorial spaces.

Citizenship as the Discipline of Population

In *Discipline and Punish: The Birth of the Prison*, Foucault notes that disciplinary power is an efficient means of governing over mass numbers of people and of achieving the maximum amount of control with the minimum amount of resources (1979, 220). Disciplinary power, Foucault notes, works by fixing movement. He writes, "That is why discipline fixes; it arrests or regulates movements; it clears up confusion; it dissipates compact groupings or individuals wandering about the country in unpredictable

ways; it establishes calculated distributions" (ibid., 219). Globalization processes and the events of 9/11 have led to a greater desire on the part of
governments to regulate the mobility of populations in the face of accelerated border crossings and the mixing of peoples and, more recently, the
perceived need to "root out" undetected "terrorists." It is here where citizenship as government has become an important means of disciplining individuals and populations by fixing or controlling movement in space at
precisely a time when people are becoming ever more mobile and their
identities ever more fluid.[3]

This is partly about disciplining populations within the state. Citizenship
has always been about disciplining domestic populations, and particularly
about disciplining certain types of bodies within the body politic. Feminist
scholars and critical international relations and security scholars have long
noted the relationship between securing the inside of the state through
border controls and the way this is intrinsically connected to processes of
regulating the movement and rights of particular gendered, racialized,
classed, and sexualized bodies within and from the body politic (see for
example, Campbell 1998; Pettman 2005; Biemann 2000; Anthias and
Yuval-Davis 1992; Arat-Koc 2005).

In the case of the post-9/11 period, government officials have mobilized
particularly effectively around a discourse of fear of "terrorists" living undetected within "civilized nations," or as Canadian officials put it, "perpetrators
(who) have demonstrated their ability to move with ease from country to
country, from place to place" (Chrétien 2001) and who "have been able to
melt away into our cities and into our way of life" (Manley 2001). Within
this context, border control strategies are directed not just at international
borders, but also inward toward domestic security and the symbolic borders
of belonging to the body politic. Border controls revolve around notions of
expanding the border: it is no longer just the international border that is
of concern, but also the internal borders of domestic political communities
of neighborhoods, towns, and cities. Perhaps one of the most notable
expressions of this is in the United States with the actual formalization and
institutionalization of the new cabinet-level department, the Department of
Homeland Security. As Sunera Thobani explains, this securitization of the
state, and of the body politic within, has had a particularly disciplining
effect on particular bodies, especially peoples of color. As Thobani argues,
"What was initially presented as a threat at the nation's territorial borders
has now become a threat within the nation's body, and surveillance has
shifted to the localized sites where people of color live out their lives, that
is the malls where they shop and the apartments in which they live" (2004,
597). As government authorities stress the need to "root out" invisible

enemies, they do so by suggesting that the most effective way is to identify who does and does not belong to the community. It is here where a host of border controls and travel regulations, such as those using data-mining, biometrics, and risk-profiling technologies, become important for identifying individuals. They not only give government authorities the right to identify members of the population—they also force individuals to self-disclose their identities "voluntarily" by electing to participate in registered and trusted travel programs.

But citizenship is not just about disciplining particular bodies within the state, but also about constructing populations over which states can be said to legitimately govern. States divide the world into distinct political spaces and communities through an "inside/outside" binary (Walker 1993). As David Campbell (1998) has explained, "the constitution of identity is achieved through the inscription of boundaries which serve to demarcate an 'inside' from an 'outside,' a 'self' from an 'other,' a 'domestic' from a 'foreign'" (ibid., 8). Thus citizenship policies not only discipline populations within the state but also demarcate domestic populations from those outside the state's borders. Citizenship thus establishes and reaffirms the boundaries of the state—both its territorial and conceptual boundaries of identity. Through such policies, the demarcation of a particular population is constituted, over which the state can be said to legitimately govern. This is why, as John Torpey (1998) has so accurately noted, scholarship on the state needs to understand the way national identities are not just "imagined" (Anderson 1983), but also created through routine and bureaucratic means of governing populations. This includes border controls and travel regulations using identification systems (e.g., national identity cards, passports, registered travel passes, and other travel documentation). As Torpey argues, "identities must become codified and institutionalized in order to become socially significant" (1998, 246). He also maintains that, historically, states and the international state system have come to "monopolize the legitimate means of movement" and that an important part of this process has been the role that identification systems have played (see Torpey 1998, 2000; and Salter 2003 for more on this with respect to the historic role of the passport). Given this, it is not surprising that after September 11, 2001, industrialized countries in the North (particularly the UK, the United States, Canada, and countries in the EU) have turned towards implementing border controls based on the identification and registration of populations as a way of exercising greater discipline over their domestic populations.

But if citizenship has always been about disciplining bodies and governing populations within the state, Barry Hindess (2000, 1495) argues that it has also always had an external dimension concerning the "international management of populations" (see also Walters 2002 on the "international police of populations"). As Hindess explains:

> I suggest that an understanding of the impact of citizenship in the modern world must focus on its role in dividing a global population of thousands of millions into the smaller subpopulations of territorial states; ... This involves consideration not just of the role of citizenship in bringing together members of particular subpopulations and promoting some of their interests, but also of the effects of rendering the larger population governable by dividing it into subpopulations consisting of the citizens of discrete, politically independent and competing states.
>
> (ibid., 1488)

By subdividing the world's population into subpopulations, citizenship serves to "facilitate or promote certain kinds of movement and interaction between its members and to penalise others" (ibid., 1495). Moreover, "because states are not self-contained, their existence as discrete political unities depends both on the maintenance of boundaries between them and on the continuing movement of people, ideas, goods and services across those boundaries" (ibid., 1488). In other words, in providing this governing rationale, citizenship hides the political artifice of the division of the world's population into distinct states, rendering it instead as "a natural, or at least an extrapolitical, division of humanity" rather than as a highly political exertion of power aimed at disciplining and fixing populations within space (ibid., 1491).

So citizenship is fundamentally about disciplining bodies both within and between states as an international disciplinary regime. However, as the rest of this chapter argues, citizenship has also become a more disciplinary regime, since it now operates in more pervasive forms of governing, with citizenship not only internationalized but also privatized and individualized to include new forms of surveillance, regulation, and even self-government. Together, these shifts in governing suggest that citizenship can no longer be assumed to be located within the state as simply an institution of the state, and thus regulated by state authorities.

Citizenship Post-9/11

As mentioned earlier, industrialized countries such as the UK, the United States, Canada, and members of the EU have turned towards citizenship policies that use border controls and travel regulations as a prominent part of their strategy for fighting the war on terror. Shifts in policy illustrate how citizenship is used to create a disciplinary regime of governing populations through internationalization and harmonization of policy on the one hand, and through privatization of policy on the other. Both engage other actors in the governing process, with the effect of decentering governing from state authorities and thereby downloading responsibility for governing to other authorities that remain less accountable to citizens. This shift towards allocating governing to other actors "above" and "below" the state has also been met by an internalization of governing. As a result, individuals participate in their own self-governing. Taken together, these changes make for a stronger disciplinary regime of governing populations.

Standardizing Border Controls and Travel Regulations

Scholars such as Jan Aart Scholte (2000) have noted that one of the principal effects of globalization is the creation of deterritorialized spaces alongside territorial spaces such that states are transformed in ways that create "supraterritoriality." States remain key economic and political assemblages; but where state authorities facilitate the globalization of capital, doing so often leads, paradoxically, to compromising state sovereignty in the process (ibid., 102). One of the primary ways that this supraterritoriality is created is through the standardization of regulations of new technologies and documents and procedures (ibid., chap. 6). State authorities, in conjunction with other actors, develop and implement a harmonized set of rules and regulations, but in doing so they create a level of standardization that contributes to supraterritoriality, which then weakens sovereignty and redistributes governing powers to substate, suprastate, and private-market actors (ibid., 103). This can be seen in the case of citizenship, where states remain key actors in implementing post-9/11 citizenship policies. However, they are also forced to compromise sovereignty over governing populations, as governing depends increasingly on the standardization and harmonization of border controls and travel regulations.

One example of this has been the way that travel regulations are being standardized through the ICAO. The ICAO, a UN agency, has come to play a greater role in overseeing and harmonizing policy concerning travel documentation, such as biometric passports, and the use of electronic data systems, such as the Advanced Passenger Information and Passenger Name Record (API/PNR) systems. In May 2003, for example, the ICAO adopted "a global, harmonized blueprint for integrating biometric information into passports and other Machine Readable Travel Documents (MRTDs)" (ICAO 2004, 1). This document has provided the basis for an international policy regarding the use of biometric identification, with facial recognition as the designated preferred form of biometrics. It recommended that a contactless integrated circuit chip, holding a minimum of 32 kilobytes, be used on all passports or other travel documents. In March 2004, the ICAO adopted a further set of recommendations to help states harmonize their policies on air travel and security according to specific international standards, including issuing machine-readable passports by 2010 (ibid., 1). Also recommended was the development of a standardized approach to using API/PNR systems to collect and forward personal travel details to immigration and customs authorities to verify identity and to expedite airport clearance (ibid., 1).[4] By compiling a variety of information and cross-checking this against different databases of information (e.g., immigration databases), these programs propose to detect trends in travel patterns, thus helping to identify individuals who pose security risks. The ICAO also outlined regulations to standardize programming language for data storage, all with the purpose of ensuring "global interoperability" (ibid., 2). These examples show the clear intentions of the ICAO and the international community to increasingly harmonize and eventually standardize policies between countries in order to create an international regime regarding travel documents.

However, while states have pushed for such policy harmonization, they have also been subject to pressures to increase the standardization of travel regulations and documentation (e.g., passports and passenger registration systems) through the ICAO. While states have used the ICAO's call for increased standardization as a way of implementing and justifying their own domestic policies, they have also been forced to implement similar policies in response to growing international pressure. In both cases, the ICAO has increasingly become the agency responsible for ensuring that standardization occurs. Consequently, states have found themselves compromising sovereignty in order to comply with international standards. Evidence of this can be seen by looking at responses taken by the United States, the EU, and the UK regarding the standardization of biometric travel identification.

In the case of the United States, the George W. Bush administration has pushed for standardized biometric travel documentation by appealing to the ICAO. In a letter dated October 26, 2001, to European Commission president Romano Prodi, President Bush called on the EU to help fight the war on terror by supporting ICAO recommendations and "encourag[ing] other nations to utilize secure, machine-readable passports and visas and explore further use of biometrics" (Foster 2001). Yet the United States has also supported ICAO recommendations as a way to bolster compliance with its own 9/11 policies. The USA PATRIOT Act and the 2002 Enhanced Border Security and Visa Entry Reform Act (EBSVERA) demanded that by

October 2004, biometric identification on travel documents be a prerequisite for entry into the United States. As Privacy International, an NGO, has argued, by appealing to laws like the Patriot Act and the EBSVERA, the United States "gave momentum to the standards that were being considered at the ICAO by requiring visa waiver countries … to implement biometrics into their Machine-Readable Travel Documents (MRTDs), i.e. passports" (Privacy International 2004a). Moreover, "moving the decision to the ICAO pushes the policy well beyond the Visa Waiver Program countries" (ibid.). In other words, by appealing to the ICAO's calls for standardization, the United States was able to extend the requirements of biometric identification to a number of other countries outside of its visa waiver program and to thereby further international compliance with standardization of biometric travel documents.

Like the United States, the EU and the UK also justified the need for biometric travel documents by referring to the need to follow ICAO recommendations as well as to U.S. policies. For example, in an August 2003 European Community report, the European Commission called for a "coherent approach" to integrate biometric identifiers on all travel documents including visas, residence permits, and EU passports. It did so by noting that a harmonized policy was "even more necessary given the need to take a common approach towards new U.S. legislation, which requires biometric elements in passports of citizens of countries granted a visa waiver as from 26 October 2004" (Commission 2003a, 2). The Commission then suggested that such a "coherent approach" could be achieved by adopting ICAO standards and "integrating biometric identifiers into the visa and the residence permit for third country nationals, in a harmonized way, thus ensuring interoperability" (ibid., 3–4). Similarly, the UK also justified its plans for biometric passports by citing both U.S. policy and the need for international harmonization. The United Kingdom Passport Service (UKPS), for example, explained its support for biometric passports by arguing that it was necessary in order to "support the UK's continued participation in the U.S. visa waiver programme" (UKPS 2004). Former home secretary David Blunkett further explained that the introduction of a "national compulsory identity cards scheme" with biometrics was necessary because of the U.S. visa waiver program, but also because of the "near universal support internationally" for biometric identification (Blunkett 2003).

Such examples show how, on the one hand, countries like the United States push for greater standardization and do so by handing over responsibility to international organizations like the ICAO. However, they also do so as a means of furthering their own domestic policies. On the other hand, countries like those of the EU and the UK find themselves in the position of supporting ICAO calls for increased standardization as a way of implementing desired policies that might otherwise be hard to sell domestically. Alternatively, governments that might choose otherwise find themselves pressured to implement such policies as a result of increased international pressure. As Privacy International (2004a) has argued, while in some cases policy changes are adopted "due to perceived 'international obligations' and efforts at harmonization," in others, they are evidence of "policy laundering." This is where "governments gain the benefits of policies by adopting international standards, without having consulted and deliberated, and often circumventing any such processes" (ibid.).

Like biometric passports, API/PNR systems are another example of travel policies being harmonized sometimes bilaterally, and also multilaterally through the ICAO. Several countries, including Canada, the United States, Australia, and members of the EU, have been working to adopt and harmonize API/PNR systems. To take Canada as an example, API/PNR systems were implemented in October 2002 as part of a joint initiative between the Canadian Customs Revenue Agency (CCRA) and Citizenship and Immigration Canada (CIC) and authorized under the Customs Act (Section 107) and the Immigration and Refugee Protection Act (IRPA). The Canadian government explains the adoption of API/PNR systems as enabling Canada "to identify and intercept persons posing security risks as early and as far away from our borders as possible" and to "intercept those who may pose a concern" (CIC 2004). Under the Customs Act, the CCRA is entitled to hold the information for as long as six years (Canadian Border Services Agency [CBSA] 2002). It is also entitled to share the information with other government departments and agencies for a variety of reasons, ranging from fighting terrorism to the broader goal of "protecting the health and safety of Canadians" (CBSA 2002). But Canada has also agreed to adopt API/PNR systems as part of a process to harmonize border controls between Canada and the United States through the Smart Border Action Plan, with the aim of coordinating actions to facilitate the "secure flow of people" (Government of Canada 2001, 1). The Smart Border Declaration views the harmonization of API/PNR systems between Canada and the United States as assisting in the achievement of three goals. API/PNR systems will help in collaborative efforts "[to identify] security risks while expediting the flow of low risk travelers"; to identify "security threats before they arrive in North America"; and, finally, to "establish a secure system to allow low risk frequent travelers between our countries to move efficiently across the border" (Government of Canada 2001, 1). Cooperation between the United States and Canada through the Smart Border Action Plan is just one example of how API/PNR systems are being internationalized through increased policy harmonization between countries.

However, API/PNR systems are also being harmonized by appealing to international organizations like the ICAO to ensure standardization (ICAO 2004, 1). As in the case of biometric travel documents, states have appealed to the ICAO to create greater harmonization between countries in their use of API/PNR systems. States have also used international calls for increased standardization as a way of either pressuring other countries to adopt these systems or justifying their own domestic policies. Negotiations between the United States and the EU concerning API/PNR systems illustrate these complexities.

In November 2001, the United States passed a law requiring all airlines traveling into, through, or from the United States to make PNR information electronically available to U.S. Customs. As a result, the United States (and Canada, which has also signed an information-sharing agreement with the United States) has called upon other countries, like members of the EU, to implement API/PNR systems and to sign on to information-sharing agreements. For its part, the EU was initially reluctant to harmonize API/PNR systems with the United States (and Canada; see Data Protection Working Party 2004), citing concerns about the possible violation of EU privacy laws. However, in December 2003, after a year of negotiations, the European Commission finally agreed to have its airlines hand travel information over to the U.S. government, subject to a series of amendments (see Commission 2003b). In finding itself pressured to comply with U.S. domestic policies, however, the EU justified its decision to share information by appealing to the ICAO and claiming the need for increased standardization of PNR systems. In its report, the Commission called for "a global approach with regard to the transfer of [PNR] data" through "the creation of a multilateral framework for PNR Data Transfer within the [ICAO]" (ibid., 10, 5). The report explained that its negotiations with the United States should "accelerate work on developing an international arrangement for PNR data transfers within the ICAO" and that "the transfer of PNR data is a truly international, and not only bilateral problem. Therefore the Commission has taken the view that the best solution would be a multilateral one and that the ICAO would be the most appropriate framework to bring forward a multilateral initiative" (ibid., 9). As in the case of travel documentation like biometric passports, API/PNR systems provide an example of how countries such as the United States, may have supported greater standardization through the ICAO to further domestic policy, while other countries, such as those of the EU, have used the call for standardization to justify their own policy decisions that might otherwise be unpopular domestically.

From the perspective of governing populations, this type of internationalization of citizenship policies regarding travel regulations reveals how allocating governing authority to international organizations like the ICAO shifts responsibility for disciplinary measures to international authorities away from individual domestic governments as a way of circumventing public deliberation on such travel policy matters. This enables governments to treat policy changes as either a *fait accompli* or as simply a bureaucratic matter—in either case, as a matter beyond the need for public debate and input from their citizens. Moreover, as civil rights groups have warned, such harmonization and standardization of policies can lead to increasingly disciplinary and undemocratic regimes of governing. The European NGO Statewatch, for example, has argued that the U.S.-EU agreement regarding the sharing of passenger information is the start of a much more global initiative, and it has stated that it "heralds an EU-USA axis initiative seeking to impose the exchange of passenger data globally through the ICAO. This will be the first step to vetting all passengers before they get on a plane, boat or cross-border train—denying boarding to those considered an immigration or security risk" (Statewatch 2003).

These examples suggest that governments are able to work together more effectively, as Statewatch notes, to discipline the movement of individuals and groups by collecting and sharing personal travel details and monitoring movement according to travel profiles. Furthermore, civil rights groups such as Privacy International and the American Civil Liberties Union (ACLU) have argued that the harmonization and standardization of travel regulations, such as API/PNR systems and biometric passports, is part of a larger project of "enabling the creation of a global surveillance infrastructure" (Privacy International 2004a, 1). These groups have raised concerns that information obtained from these policies could be used to create national databases. Based on current passport and travel document statistics, the databases could potentially hold enormous amounts of information, with Privacy International predicting that "the biometric details of more than a billion people will be electronically stored by 2015" (Statewatch 2004). Moreover, the personal information contained in these national databases could eventually be shared between countries, creating, in effect, a centralized international database that could be used to monitor global movement between countries (Privacy International 2004a, 2; see also Privacy International 2004b). Clearly, this is a case of where citizenship policies have a large potential of being used to discipline individuals and populations, by monitoring their movement, but in less democratic ways, in that decisions are more likely to be made outside of the public eye, by unelected officials. Insofar as biometrics and API/PNR identification systems become an international standard, pushed through international bodies like the ICAO, the potential for surveillance of movement globally becomes increasingly likely.[5]

Privatization of Border Controls and Travel Regulations

If governing populations through citizenship is decentered from state authorities to international actors like the ICAO and through greater policy harmonization between states in the areas of border controls and travel regulations, it is also being privatized as governments increasingly allocate governing responsibilities to private companies like airlines—especially in the areas of identifying travelers and monitoring and regulating populations and their mobility more generally.

As I have discussed elsewhere, one example of this is the increased reliance on data aggregators or companies, such as Acxiom and ChoicePoint, that are in the business of compiling and selling databases of consumer and personal information (Rygiel forthcoming). Governments rely on data aggregators as part of passenger prescreening programs that use API/PNR systems such as the Computer Assisted Passenger Pre-Screening System (CAPPS II), which has now been replaced with a scaled-back version called Secure Flight in the United States. These programs displace power away from state authorities to private companies. The latter take on much of the surveillance and data-gathering work required in the monitoring of populations that was formerly done by state government authorities. Civil and privacy rights organizations like the ACLU warn of the problems that could arise as governments increasingly cooperate with private companies in the monitoring and control of mobility. In addition to issues concerning information access and ownership, the real problem, some suggest, occurs when companies sell this information to governments, because only governments have the authority to centralize private-sector data and to curtail civil liberties (Stanley and Steinhardt 2003, 7). As an example of the potential problems likely to emerge with API/PNR systems and their reliance on private companies, the ACLU points to the U.S. Department of Justice's $8 million contract with ChoicePoint to use its databases. The ACLU notes, "Although the Privacy Act of 1974 banned the government from maintaining information on citizens who are not targets of investigations, the [Federal Bureau of Investigation (FBI)] can now evade that requirement by simply purchasing information that has been collected by the private sector" (ibid., 8). Unlike governments, private companies are neither representative nor responsible to citizens. Their growing involvement in monitoring the movements and habits of individuals can be used by governments to circumvent legal restrictions on the surveillance of populations.

However, data aggregators are just one example of greater private-sector involvement in API/PNR systems. Private airline companies also play a greater role now that they are legally required to hand over passenger information to governments (e.g., the U.S. government). Evidence of the sort of problems likely to emerge from this growing government dependency on private companies to provide personal information can be seen in the case of America's Northwest Airlines. From October through December 2001, Northwest violated its own privacy policy (along with that of Dutch airline KLM, with which it has a flying partnership) by sharing undisclosed passenger information with the U.S. government's National Aeronautics and Space Administration (NASA) (Steindhardt 2004; Northwest Airlines 2004). This was at the same time that CAPPS II was initiated and when, "according to the *Washington Times*, NASA's Aviation Systems Division obtained more than 15 million private passenger records from Northwest Airlines after a secret meeting between officials from the two organizations" (Blumenthal 2003). However, this illegal distribution of personal records by a private company to the government is not a unique case. In 2002 JetBlue Airways handed over its data on 5 million customers to another private data-mining company, Torch Concepts, which had been hired by the U.S. Defense Department with the Transportation Security Administration (TSA) brokering the exchange (ibid.). Torch Concepts' company documents show that a test resembling CAPPS II was conducted with the data. The test correlated "JetBlue customers' records with their Social Security numbers, income levels and home ownership statuses to group customers into one of three categories based on their perceived threat level: young, middle-income homeowners; older upper-income homeowners; and a group of passengers with 'anomalous' records" (ibid.).

The fact that private companies, like airlines, that collect personal information on their consumers are now legally obliged to turn over this information to U.S. government authorities raises similar concerns about how this information will be used when compiled or cross-checked with government databases. For example, the ACLU warned that programs like CAPPS II "would reportedly draw on enormous stores of personal information from data aggregators and other sources, including travel records, real estate histories, personal associations, credit card records and telephone records" (Stanley and Steinhardt 2003, 12). This information could then be used to conduct surveillance "not where there is evidence of wrongdoing" but by "monitoring *everyone* for signs of wrongdoing" (ibid., 12). This represents a significant shift in thinking, with criminality associated not with actions committed, but simply with certain types of behaviors, activities, or intentions to act—the result being an enormous potential to discipline individuals' ways of living and being.

Self-government

The examples above show how responsibility for governing populations and their mobility has been allocated to actors "above" and "below" the state through the increased standardization of policies on the one hand, and through privatization on the other. At the same time, there has also been an internalization of disciplinary power as individuals take on more *self-governing* in the areas of border controls and travel regulations.

In *Discipline and Punish*, Foucault notes that disciplinary power works through a "new micro-physics of power" designed to produce "subjected and practiced bodies, 'docile' bodies" (1979, 138). It does so, in part, because it is "exercised through its invisibility," yet simultaneously "imposes on those whom it subjects a principle of compulsory visibility" (ibid., 187). Foucault (1980) illustrates this aspect of disciplinary power in greater detail in his discussion of the Panopticon. The Panopticon works through the formula of "power through transparency" (ibid., 154). A watchtower rises in the center of a circular building that has glass windows all around, both inside and outside. The building houses the prisoners in sunlit cells, which are visible to the prison guard in the watchtower all the time (ibid.). This design allows the powers of surveillance to be transferred from the responsibility of the prison warden to that of the prisoners, such that the prisoners eventually internalize the watchful gaze of surveillance and become self-regulating or self-disciplining (ibid.).[6] In other words, disciplinary power works by making individuals feel the gaze of surveillance. They begin to modify their thoughts and actions, becoming self-governing. Citizenship makes use of this aspect of disciplinary power through policies that encourage us to govern ourselves, and thus it regulates our movements, behaviors, and actions. For example, travel and identification regulations that require biometric information (e.g., biometric passports or travel passes) make us feel that we are under scrutiny. So, we begin to regulate our own behavior, appearance, and thoughts. Similarly, border controls and travel regulations (e.g., API/PNR systems) requiring that personal data be collected to create travel profiles work through self-government by getting us to identify ourselves as objects to be governed. This happens, for example, when we "voluntarily" self-identify as a "low-risk" traveler and apply for a registered or trusted traveler pass. (Programs like CANPASS and NEXUS require travelers to "voluntarily" undergo a security check during which biometric and other forms of personal information are gathered.) Not only do such policies encourage us to participate in our own self-governing, but they also encourage us to become involved in the governing of our co-citizens in the process—as, for example, when we engage in distinguishing between members of the political community and nonmembers or when we vigilantly report "suspect" people. The last section of this chapter looks at some further examples of how populations are increasingly disciplined post-9/11 through policies that encourage self-government.

In his 2002 State of the Union address, President Bush exclaimed, "as government works to better secure our homeland, America will continue to depend on the eyes and ears of alert citizens" (Bush 2002). Self-governing enlists the help of citizens as "overseers" in a number of surveillance programs. These include government-run hotlines for citizens to report suspicious terrorist-like activities and behaviors; terrorism education and training programs; and programs like President Bush's Citizen Corps initiative, which is part of his larger USA Freedom Corps program.

The U.S. government implemented a hotline immediately after 9/11 and invited citizens to report anyone or any activity that they thought looked suspicious—although the government had to shut down the hotline soon after it began because it led to too many false reports (435,000) (Berkowitz 2003). However, other hotlines—like the FBI's "Report It" (www.reportit.com/terrorism.htm)—are still in operation and encourage individuals to report their suspicions to the FBI (https://www.ifccfbi.gov/complaint/terrorist.asp).

Programs have been established to educate and train citizens in terrorism detection and reporting. One program is run by the Community Anti-Terrorism Training Institute (C.A.T. Eyes). Developed by U.S. military and law enforcement officers, the program assists "local communities [in their] fight against domestic terrorism and racial profiling" and "enhances neighborhood security, heightens the community's power of observation, and encourages mutual assistance and concern among neighbors" (http://www.cateyesprogram.com). According to its website, C.A.T Eyes "will be a passive surveillance program. People will just be educated observers on their way to market, work, or school. The main objective of the C.A.T. Eyes program is to educate the Neighborhood." Several police departments, including those in New Jersey, Pennsylvania, Massachusetts, and Ohio, have been trained in the program, as have various communities in cities and towns in Florida, Nevada, and California (Ridgeway 2003). Some "1,000 agencies throughout Virginia, Ohio, New Jersey, Pennsylvania, Maryland and Washington DC" have been trained, as have "over 5,000 citizens" in the city of Pittsburgh alone (the "first trained city") (www.cateyesprogram.com).

As part of the training, citizens learn about terrorism and how to report it, and about signs to look for that are "out of the ordinary," such as suspicious packages, car bombs, and strange-smelling odors or chemicals. Citizens are also educated about what signs to look for such as "what a person doing preattack surveillance would be doing. (Taking pictures, measuring, watching, etc. ...)" (http://www.cateyesprogram.com). Citizens are trained to report those who simply look suspicious or who look like they do not belong in the neighborhood (Beale 2003). As one media report explained, citizens are trained to look for "inconsistencies," such as "Does that 'construction worker' really look like one? Is that 'police' uniform the real thing? Could a business really support a person's lifestyle?" (Booker 2003). Moreover, citizens are instructed, "When you see somebody who looks out of place hanging around for no apparent reason, size him up. Note a basic description: size, sex, age, apparent ethnicity and any distinguishing characteristics" (ibid.). By training citizens to be vigilantly on the lookout for signs considered to be suspicious or abnormal, the program necessarily relies on the preconceptions citizens bring to the behaviors, dress, activities, and appearances they consider normal and belonging to their community. By engaging citizens in constructing notions of what constitutes "normal" behavior and looks, programs like these use disciplinary power as part of the process of disciplining populations (see chap. 1 in this volume).

In addition to hotlines and training programs, there is also the U.S. Freedom Corps initiative, introduced in Bush's 2002 State of the Union address. Under the direction of the Department of Homeland Security, the initiative is designed to get American citizens involved through their local communities to help fight terrorism (White House 2002a). Through this program, Bush called on all citizens to dedicate two years, or 4,000 hours over their lifetime, to community service to help fight the war on terror (ibid.). As part of this initiative, Bush launched the Citizen Corps program, which included plans for the Terrorism Information and Prevention System (Operation TIPS), a system designed to engage millions of workers employed in the postal, trucking, and public utility sectors in identifying and reporting any so-called suspicious terrorist activity (White House 2002a, 2002b). Due to concerns expressed by civil liberty and privacy watch groups, Operation TIPS was eventually prohibited under Section 808 of the Homeland Security Act. However, similar programs have been initiated outside the parameters of the Citizen Corps by enlisting the services of companies and their workers. For example, FedEx is setting up a special computer system so that some of its 250,000 employees can report suspicious activity while on the job directly to the Department of Homeland

Security (Block 2005). Other companies such as Time Warner's America Online, Western Union, and Wal-Mart have made similar offers of citizen service (ibid.).

All of these examples (hotlines, C.A.T. Eyes, Citizen Corps) are of interest because of the way they train American citizens about how to play the role of "comrade" as "overseer" (Foucault 1980, 157). Through such programs, citizens learn how to carefully watch and monitor not only the actions and behaviors of their neighbors in relation to terrorism, but also their own behavior so as not to appear suspicious to others. With the aim of identifying those activities and behaviors that look different from whatever constitutes the "normal" in a particular community, such programs have a highly disciplining and regulative effect, ensuring that local populations adhere to whatever is considered the norm of a particular community. These types of examples reveal how citizenship policies and practices are used in governing, and specifically how they are operationalized as technologies of self-government.

In addition to these types of citizen initiatives designed to encourage citizens to do the disciplining work of government themselves, there is also support for greater use of technologies like biometrics, which work at a bodily level of control to create more "subjected and practiced bodies" (Foucault 1979, 138). Since 9/11, citizenship policies have increasingly integrated biometric technology into programs such as the EBSVERA and the US-VISIT (United States Visitor and Immigrant Status Indicator Technology) entry/exit program that require that all travelers to the United States carry identification with biometric identifiers by October 2004 and that most foreign visitors traveling on a visa be fingerprinted and photographed upon entry. In addition, registered and trusted traveler programs, such as the Canadian and American NEXUS, Free and Secure Trade (FAST), and CANPASS Air programs use biometrics. While NEXUS and FAST require fingerprint and security checks, CANPASS Air uses iris scans to enable "low-risk" air travelers to pass quickly through customs. Finally, in addition to these types of border controls and travel initiatives, plans for new biometric travel documents are also under way in many countries, including the United States, the UK, the Netherlands, Australia, New Zealand, the Philippines, and Canada (see Lyon 2005, 2003, 72–76).

Biometric technology works by using a characteristic of the body, something unique to the individual (e.g., finger print, iris pattern in the eye, voice) as a means of identification. As Simon Davies explains, while other conventional forms of identification include "something you have, such as a card" and "something you know, such as a password or [personal identification number (PIN)]," biometrics is based on "*something you are*, such as a pattern of ridges on a fingertip" (1994, emphasis added). It is a much more invasive form of identification. Unlike other types of identification, biometric identification is not something that can be acquired; instead, it reduces one's identity to the fixed attributes of the physical body. Disciplinary power is enacted at the very level of the individual body. Some scholars, such as Irma van der Ploeg, have argued that we need to consider the ways in which this "'informatization of the body' may eventually affect embodiment and identity" (2003, 58; see also Muller 2004).

Travel and identification documents that use biometrics subject individuals to disciplinary power in a highly individualizing way. This is because biometric technology involves managing individuals through practices that establish a form of control at the level of the individual and the physical body. From the gathering of flight and payment details to biometric cataloging, the core idea behind biometric travel arrangements and identification is that, as individuals, we are always (at least potentially) being watched and monitored and are thus, ultimately, knowable.

A common argument put forth to justify the use of biometric technology for identity cards explicates this very idea. Originally argued by Alan Dershowitz (2001), and now circulating within government circles (e.g., Coderre 2003), is the argument that "individuals have the right to privacy but not anonymity" (see also website "On the Identity Trail" for more on this). The argument is that, as individuals, we no longer have the right to not disclose who we are. Rather, we must make ourselves knowable to governing powers in the name of security. The intention of such surveillance, however, is to discipline individuals into being "good citizens," meaning citizens who will avoid political or criminal activity that challenges governing powers for fear of being known to authorities. More specifically, such forms of border control also seem to be about governing through division by attempting to divide the "good" Muslim and Arab citizens from the "bad" (meaning anyone suspected of terrorist involvement or anyone who presents a political challenge to governing authorities (Mamdani, n.d.). In other words, Dershowitz's argument suggests that the good citizens (but also more specifically, the "good" Muslims) with nothing to hide would want to be the proud carriers of biometric identity cards as a symbol of their status as good citizens and members of the community, thus separating them out from those who present a threat. More than being just about mobility rights, these forms of border control force certain groups to regulate their own behavior, travel, and political voice and thus provide for a much more disciplinary regime of governing populations that extends beyond simply the regulation of mobility.

Finally, it is not just that biometrics governs by engaging us to regulate our own actions, behaviors, and political activities. Biometrics also disciplines by making us more visible as objects for governing. However, it does so, as Foucault suggests, in ways that potentially make disciplinary power invisible by turning the highly contentious issue of gathering biometric information into a routine and administrative procedure. Moreover, where travel identification is said to be "voluntary," those choosing not to carry biometric identification will likely be regarded as suspicious—that is, as having something to hide, and therefore be subject to greater scrutiny. This leads, in and of itself, to greater pressure on all of us to participate in identification programs. Insofar as we then opt "voluntarily" for identity cards, we participate in processes of self-regulation, becoming in some sense, as Foucault suggests, "principles of our own subjection" (see endnote 6).

Conclusion

The preceding discussion of how citizenship functions, especially after 9/11, as a disciplinary regime of governing populations shows that citizenship, like other forms of global politics, can no longer (if it ever could) be understood simply according to the nation-state system. Rather, as the discussion and examples of 9/11 citizenship policies demonstrate, citizenship's disciplinary power depends on the way that governing is displaced from the level of the state to other actors and systems. These include international and private actors and networks, as well as the way that power disciplines both at the level of the individual body and by engaging us as citizens to share in our own self-governing and in the governing of co-citizens. Claims that, with the weakening of the nation-state system, citizenship is also somehow weakened or in crisis are premature and ignore the way that citizenship now operates through disciplinary power at a variety of interconnected levels. As I have argued in this chapter, post-9/11 examples of border controls and travel regulations reveal how, in its transformation as a globalizing regime, citizenship is also becoming a more disciplinary regime.

In conjunction with the state, citizenship depends increasingly on governing by other actors such as international and private-market actors and even individuals themselves through practices of self-government. As border controls and travel initiatives are increasingly harmonized between countries and standardized across the international community, civil rights organizations are right to warn of the potential dangers that may accompany what they see as a growing international—or even global—infrastructure that is designed to discipline the mobility of people. As these initiatives are also privatized at the same time through increased dependence by governments on private companies (e.g., data aggregators and airlines), this too raises new concerns about accountability and the protection of civil rights. Finally, the increased role that these initiatives give to forms of self-government—from surveillance programs that enlist the services of citizens to travel and identification passes using biometrics—means that disciplinary power is enacted in even more insidious ways by engaging us as citizens to govern ourselves and other co-citizens and by exercising power over and through the individual body and its physical attributes. Together, these interconnected levels of governing illustrate that citizenship is in fact anything but weakened; rather it has been strengthened as a more disciplinary governing regime, even as it has been dislocated from the state and state system.

Notes

1. Since the 1990s there has been a resurgence of interest in citizenship (Isin and Turner 2002). Renewed study of citizenship has occurred, in large part, in response to debates about globalization and what has been referred to as a "crisis of citizenship" (Scobey 2001). Despite a large body of diverse literature, much scholarship shares the assumption that globalization and its deterritorialization of the state has weakened citizenship, leading to a "decline of citizenship" (e.g., Falk 2000; Turner 2000; Hettne 2000; and Jacobson 1996. This assumption is common across scholarship despite diverging opinions between scholars who see the erosion of the nation-state as having a negative impact on citizenship (Hettne 2000; Jacobson 1996; and Miller 2000) and those who see it as an opportunity to rethink citizenship along the lines of more inclusive models such as post-national (Soysal 1994), cosmopolitan (Archibugi and Held 1995), and transnational (Faist 2000) forms of citizenship.

2. The theoretical approach of viewing citizenship as a form of government is based on Michel Foucault's broader notion of government as the "conduct of conducts" (1994, 138). As Foucault explains:

> Basically, power is less a confrontation between two adversaries or their mutual engagement than a question of 'government'. This word must be allowed the very broad meaning it had in the sixteenth century. 'Government' did not refer only to the political structures or to the management of states; rather, it designated the way in which the conduct of individuals or of groups might be directed—the government of children, of souls, of communities, of families, of the sick. It covered not only the legitimately constituted forms of political or economic subjection but also modes of action, more or less considered and calculated, that were destined to act upon the possibilities of others. To govern, in this sense, is to structure the possible field of action of others.
>
> (1994, 138)

3. On this point, see Knight and Smith in chapter 9, where they discuss how transnational activists attempt to challenge the effects of neoliberalism and the growth of corporate power.
4. API systems gather basic passenger information (name, citizenship, passport number, and date of birth), while PNR systems provides more detailed information (reservation date, itinerary, and method of payment).
5. As Knight and Smith argue in chapter 9, threats to or abuse of rights that are not manifest through dramatic events make it difficult to articulate grievances and frame and mobilize resistance, thus effecting activists' power to hold governments and corporate actors accountable.
6. Foucault argues that the Panopticon system functions effectively because the chief inspector and his staff, as well as the prisoners, internalize the gaze of surveillance and discipline themselves according to the general principle that "each comrade becomes an overseer" (1980, 157). As Foucault explains, "each person, depending on his place, is watched by all or certain of the others. You have an apparatus of total and circulating mistrust, because there is no absolute point. The perfect form of surveillance consists in a summation of malveillance" (1980, 158). Foucault concludes that this form of disciplinary power leads to the subject becoming the agents of their own subjection. He writes, "[h]e who is subjected to a field of visibility, and who knows it, assumes responsibility for the constraints of power; he makes them play spontaneously upon himself; he inscribes in himself the power relation in which he simultaneously plays both roles; he becomes the principle of his own subjection" (1979, 202).

Bibliography

Anderson, Benedict. 1983. *Imagined Communities: Reflections on the Origin and Spread of Nationalism*. New York: Verso.

Anthias, Floya, and Nira Yuval-Davis. 1992. *Racialized Boundaries: Race, Nation, Gender, Colour and Class and the Anti-Racist Struggle*. London: Routledge.

Arat-Koc, Sedef. 2005. "The Disciplinary Boundaries of Canadian Identity after September 11: Civilizational Identity, Multiculturalism and the Challenge of Anti-Imperialist Feminism." *Social Justice* 32, no. 4: 32–49.

Archibugi, Daniele, and David Held, eds. 1995. *Cosmopolitan Democracy: An Agenda for a New World Order*. Cambridge: Polity Press.

Beale, Lewis. 2003. "Trying to Avoid Another Sept. 11: Spurred by Tragedy, a Former Colonel Offers Antiterrorism Training." *New York Times*, September 7.

Berkowitz, Bill. 2003. "Citizen Tipsters or Deputy Dawgs." *Working Assets* online. http://workingforchange.com (accessed January 13, 2006).

Biemann, Ursula. 2000. "Performing the Border." In *Been There and Back to Nowhere: Gender in Transnational Spaces*, xx. Berlin and New York: B Books and Autonomedia.

Block, Robert. 2005. "In Terrorism Fight, Government Finds a Surprising Ally: FedEx." *Wall Street Journal*, May 26.

Blumenthal, Max. 2003. "Data Debase." *American Prospect* online. http://www. prospect.org/print-friendly/webfeatures/2003/12/blumenthal-m-12-19.html.

Blunkett, David. 2003. "ID Cards Statement." November 11, 2003, statement by the Home Secretary in the House of Commons. http://ips.gov.uk/identity/news-publications-legislative.asp.

Booker, Betty. 2003. "Counter-Terrorism Training for Us Ordinary Citizens." *Richmond Times-Dispatch*, September 15. http://www.cateyesprogram.com/pdf/richmond.pdf.

Bush, George W. 2002. "State of the Union Address." The White House, Washington, D.C. http://www.whitehouse.gov/news/releases/2002/01/20020129-11.html.

Campbell, David. 1998. *Writing Security*. Minneapolis: University of Minnesota Press.

C. A. T. (Community Anti-Terrorism Training Institute) Eyes. "Goals of the C. A. T. Eye Program." http://www.cateyesprogram.com (accessed January 15, 2006).

CBSA (Canada Border Services Agency). 2002. "Advanced Passenger Information/ Passenger Name Record (API/PNR)." February 2. http://www.cbsa_asfc.gc.ca/newsroom/factsheets/2002/oct/api-e.html.

Chrétien, Jean. 2001. "Address by the Former Canadian Prime Minister on the Occasion of a Special House of Commons 'Take Note' Debate on the International Campaign against Terror." Ottawa, Canada, October 15.

CIC (Citizenship and Immigration Canada). 2004. "The Advanced Passenger Information/Passenger Name Record Program (API/PNR)." January 12. http://www.cic.gc.ca/english/visit/api.html.

Coderre, Denis. 2003. "Notes for an Address by the Honorable Denis Coderre, Minister of Citizenship and Immigration, to a Forum on Biometrics: Applications and Implications for Citizenship and Immigration." National Arts Centre, Ottawa, Canada, October 8. http://www.cic.gc.ca/english/press/speech/bio-forum.html.

Commission of the European Communities. 2003a. "Proposal for a Council Regulation Amending Regulation (EC) 1683/95 Laying Down a Uniform Format for Visas; Proposal for a Council Regulation Amending Regulations EC 1030/2002 Laying Down a Uniform Format for Residence Permits for Third-country Nationals." COM (2003) 558 final, 2003/0217 (CNS), 2003/0218 (CNS), Brussels, September 24.

———. 2003b. "Transfer of Air Passenger Name Record (PNR) Data: A Global EU Approach." COM (2003) 826 final, Communication from the Commission to the Council and the Parliament, Brussels, December 16.

Data Protection Working Party. 2004. "Opinion 3/2004 on the Level of Protection Ensured in Canada for the Transmission of Passenger Name Records and Advanced Passenger Information from Airlines." 10037/04/EN WP 88, European Commission, Brussels, February 11. http://www.europa.eu.int/comm/privacy.

Davies, Simon. 1994. "Touching Big Brother: How Biometric Technology Will Fuse Flesh and Machine." *Information Technology & People* 7, no. 4: 38–47. http://www.privacy.org/pi/reports/biometric.html.

Deleuze, Gilles, and Félix Guattari. 1987. *A Thousand Plateaus: Capitalism and Schizophrenia*. Minneapolis: University of Minnesota Press.

Dershowitz, Alan M. 2001. "Why Fear National ID Cards?" *New York Times*, October 13.

Faist, Thomas. 2000. "Transnationalization in International Migration: Implications for the Study of Citizenship and Culture." *Ethnic and Racial Studies* 23, no. 2: 189–222.

Falk, R. 2000. "The Decline of Citizenship in an Era of Globalization." *Citizenship Studies* 4, no. 1: 5–17.

Foster, James. 2001. "United States Mission to the European Union. US Letter from James J. Foster, Deputy Chief of Mission, on Behalf of President George Bush, to Mr. Romano Prodi, President of the Commission of the European Communities, with Demands for EU Cooperation." October 16. http://www.statewatch.org/news/2001/nov/06Ausalet.htm.

Foucault, Michel. 1979. *Discipline and Punish: The Birth of the Prison*. New York: Vintage Books.

———. 1980. "The Eye of Power." In *Power/Knowledge: Selected Interviews and Other Writings 1972–1977*, edited by Colin Gordon, 146–65. New York: Pantheon Books.

———. 1994. "The Subject and Power." In *The Essential Foucault: Selections from Essential Works of Foucault 1954–1984*, edited by Paul Rabinow and Nikolas Rose, 126–45. New York and London: New Press.

Government of Canada. 2001. "The Smart Border Declaration: Building a Smart Border for the 21st Century on the Foundation of a North American Zone of Confidence." Ottawa, Canada, December 12.

Hardt, Michael, and Antonio Negri. 2000. *Empire*. Cambridge: Harvard University Press.

Held, David, and Anthony McGrew, eds. 1999. *The Global Transformation Reader*. Malden, MA: Blackwell Publishers.

———. 2002. *Globalization/Anti-Globalization*. Cambridge, UK, and Malden, MA: Polity Press and Blackwell Publishers.

Hettne, B. 2000. "The Fate of Citizenship in Post-Westphalia." *Citizenship Studies* 4, no. 1: 35–46.

Hindess, Barry. 2000. "Citizenship in the International Management of Populations." *American Behavioural Scientist* 43, no. 9: 1486–97.

Hollifield, James. 2004. "The Emerging Migration State." *International Migration Review* 38, no. 3 (Fall): 885–912.

International Civil Aviation Organization (ICAO). 2004. "ICAO Facilitation (FAL) Division – Twelfth Session." FAL/12-WP/4 (5/11/03), Cairo, Egypt, March 22–April 2.

Isin, Engin F., and Bryan S. Turner, eds. 2002. *Handbook of Citizenship Studies*. London: Sage.

Jacobson, David. 1996. *Rights across Borders: Immigration and the Decline of Citizenship*. Baltimore and London: Johns Hopkins University Press.

Lyon, David. 2003. *Surveillance after September 11*. Cambridge: Polity Press.

———. 2005. "The Border is Everywhere: ID Cards, Surveillance and the Other." In *Global Surveillance and Policing: Borders, Security, Identity*, edited by Elia Zureik and Mark B. Salter, 66–82. Portland, OR: Willan Publishing.

Mamdani, Mahmood. "Good Muslim, Bad Muslim: An African Perspective." Social Science Research Council. After Sept. 11 (essays). http://www/ssrc.org/sept11/essays/mamdani_text_only.htm.

Manley, John. 2001. "Address by Former Minister of Foreign Affairs to the U.S. Foreign Policy Association." New York, November 5.

Massey, Doreen. 1994. *Space, Place and Gender*. Minneapolis: University of Minnesota Press.

Miller, David. 2000. *Citizenship and National Identity*. Cambridge, UK, and Malden, MA: Polity Press and Blackwell Publishers.

Muller, Benjamin. 2004. "(Dis)Qualified Bodies: Securitization, Citizenship and 'Identity Management.'" *Citizenship Studies* 8, no. 3: 279–94.

Northwest Airlines. 2004. "Northwest Airlines Statement on Media Reports Regarding NASA Aviation Security Research Study." January 18. http://www.nwa.com/corpinfo/newsc/2004/pr011820041268.html.

On the Identity Trail. http://idtrail.org/.

Pettman, Jan Jindy. 2005. "Questions of Identity: Australia and Asia." In *Critical Security Studies and World Politics*, edited by Ken Booth, 159–77. London and Boulder: Lynne Rienner.

Privacy International. 2004a. "About the Open Letter to the ICAO: A Second Report on 'Towards an International Infrastructure for Surveillance of Movement.'" March. http://www.privacyinternational.org/issues/terrorism/rpt/icaobackground.html.

———. 2004b. "Transferring Privacy: The Transfer of Passenger Records and the Abdication of Privacy Protection; The First Report on 'Towards an International Infrastructure for Surveillance Movement.'" Written in cooperation with European Digital Rights Initiative, the Foundation for Information Policy Research, and Statewatch with a Commentary from the American Civil Liberties Union on *A Perspective from America*, February.

Ridgeway, James. 2003. "An Informed Citizenry: Telling Trend Takes Hold." *Village Voice*, June 11–17.

Rygiel, Kim. Forthcoming. "The Securitized Citizen." In *Recasting the Social in Citizenship*, edited by Engin Isin, 268–300. Toronto: University of Toronto Press.

Salter, Mark. 2003. *Rights of Passage: The Passport in International Relations*. Boulder and London: Lynne Rienner.

Scholte, Jan Aart. 2000. *Globalization: A Critical Introduction*. New York: St. Martin's Press.

Scobey, David. 2001. "The Specter of Citizenship." *Citizenship Studies* 5, no. 1: 11–26.

Soysal, Yasemin Nuhoglu. 1994. *Limits of Citizenship: Migrants and Postnational Membership in Europe*. Chicago: University of Chicago Press.

Stanley, Jay, and Barry Steinhardt. 2003. *Bigger Monster, Weaker Chains: The Growth of an American Surveillance Society.* New York: American Civil Liberties Union.

Statewatch. 2003. "EU: Commission 'Compromises' and Agrees on Handing over Passenger Data to USA." *Statewatch News* online, December. http://www.statewatch.org/news/2003/dec/11cuuspassengerdeal.htm.

———. 2004. "Civil Rights Groups Warn of Dangers in International Biometric Passport System." *Statewatch News* online, March 29. http://www.statewatch.org/news/2004/mar/25icao.htm.

Steinhardt, Barry. 2004. "Letter from Barry Steinhardt, Director, Technology and Liberty Program of the American Civil Liberties Union to EU Commissioner Bolkestein." January 21. http://statewatch.org/news/2004/jan/18aclu-pnr-eu.htm.

Thobani, Sunera. 2004. "Exception as Rule: Profile of Exclusion (September 11: Canada)." *Signs: Journal of Women in Culture and Society* 29, no. 12: 597.

Torpey, John. 1998. "Coming and Going: On the State Monopolization of the Legitimate 'Means of Movement.'" *Sociological Theory* 16, no. 3: 239–59.

———. 2000. *The Invention of the Passport: Surveillance, Citizenship and the State.* Cambridge: Cambridge University Press.

Turner, Bryan. 2000. "Review Essay: Citizenship and Globalization." *Citizenship Studies* 4, no. 1: 81–6.

United Kingdom Passport Service (UKPS). 2004. "UKPS News. Entry to the USA: New Requirements from October 26, 2004." January 9. http://www.passport.gov.uk/news.asp?mode=print&intElement=695.

van der Ploeg, Irma. 2003. "Biometrics and the Body as Information: Normative Issues of the Socio-Technical Coding of the Body." In *Surveillance as Social Sorting: Privacy, Risk and Digital Discrimination,* edited by David Lyon, 57–73. London and New York: Routledge.

Walker, R. B. J. 1993. *Inside/Outside: International Relations as Political Theory.* Cambridge Studies in International Relations. Newcastle: Cambridge University Press.

Walters, William. 2002. "Deportation, Expulsion and the International Police of Aliens." *Citizenship Studies* 6, no. 3: 265–92.

White House. 2002a. "President to Discuss New Citizen Corps Initiative." http://www.whitehouse.gov/news/releases/2002/01/20020130.html (accessed January 13, 2002).

———. 2002b. "Citizen Corps Grows Strong in America's Communities." April 8. http://www.whitehouse.gov/news/releases/2002/04/20020408.html.

CHAPTER 6

The Nation-State, the Global Media, and the Regime of Supervision

Ali Riaz and Anthony DiMaggio

> Borders, knowledge, categories, power—rarely have these things been so at
> stake as at the present time. A time of sovereignty asserted and diffused, of
> borders transgressed, questioned and enforced, of violence that is exercised
> with uncertain justice and legal foundation, but is exercised nonetheless.
> A time, a world where states assert their own law, criminalise [*sic*], deter and
> detain, and in so doing infringe international law and universal human rights.
> A world where capital flows across borders with rapidity and impunity but
> the flow of people is the subject of increasing anxiety and control.
>
> (Burke 2002)

Since late last century, we have witnessed a "change of guard" in the
global political arena and a reconfiguration of political power. A set of
actors is being replaced by another set, making the conflict and confrontation between "dominant" and "emerging" actors the central characteristic of international relations. The uncertainty, the chaos, and the confusion,
succinctly described by Burke above, are the most compelling evidence of
this ongoing transformation. The nation-state, one of the most critical actors
in the global political arena and a central institution of the international
system for more than two centuries, is being challenged by a number of
competing systems—both from the inside and the outside. Subnational,
transnational, and supranational forces are undermining the authority,
power, and legitimacy of the nation-state, which used to enjoy a monopoly
of power over citizens residing within clearly defined boundaries.

In this chapter, we look into one of the forces challenging the nation-
state—the global electronic media, and the responses of nation-states to that

challenge. We argue that international television networks, such as the Cable News Network (CNN), the British Broadcasting Corporation (BBC), the Satellite Television Asian Region Ltd. (STAR), and Al Jazeera, to varying degrees, have challenged the state's capacity to follow independent policies within domestic and international contexts and that they have undermined the authority and legitimacy of the state. National "boundaries" and "sovereignty" are being violated. The states have also reacted sharply, with limited success. However, the erosion of the state's ability to control has not created a void wherein the media are acting without "supervision." The logic of capitalism has been one such means of "disciplining" the media, but the media have also become "instruments of discipline"—participants in an emerging "regime of supervision." This chapter argues that the regime of supervision is neither bound by space nor structured institutionally, but is intended to increase the "docility of the subjects" and to multiply the "asymmetry of power" (Foucault 1984).

This chapter, therefore, addresses three questions: first, how do the media challenge the power and authority of the nation-state? Second, how are nation-states responding to these challenges and how are the media subverting the steps taken by the nation-states? Third, in the absence of "supervision" by the nation-states, what mechanisms have evolved to "discipline" the media?

Responses to these questions require a background—an understanding of the position of the nation-state in evolving global politics. We will begin with a brief discussion on this issue. Throughout the chapter, the roles of various global media, especially radio and television, will be assessed to illustrate the nature and scope of the challenges posed by the global media. The nation-states' responses to these challenges and to subversive media techniques will be illustrated with an in-depth case study of Qatar-based television channel Al Jazeera. These discussions lead us to the concluding section of the chapter, where we respond to the third question posed above.

The Nation-State—Dead or Alive?

Efforts to analyze the dramatic changes in international politics and to understand the future of nation-states have intensified since the beginning of the 1990s, resulting in a number of studies and generating intense debate in scholarly and popular discourses. There are two tendencies in these analyses, supporters of which are described as either "globalists" or "skeptics" (Held and McGrew 2000, 10). The first insists that the nation-state has become an obsolete institution, and thus an obituary of the nation-state is long overdue. Ohmae (1995) and Guehenno (1995), for example, proclaimed the death of the nation-state more than a decade ago. Ohmae contends that four forces—capital, corporations, consumers, and communication—have combined to seize the economic power once held by the nation-state. Holton (1998, 106) argues that the global economy, transnational bodies, international law, and hegemonic powers and power blocs are undermining the authority of the nation-state. In short, those who argue that we are witnessing "the withering away of the nation-state" maintain that the nation-state has been

> reduced to a managerial role in which it strives to cope with economic constraints that are beyond its control, it watches helplessly as the balance of forces swings towards the global markets. Within its historical borders it has ceased to be the locus of political action and identity, of social cohesion and the general interest. Beyond its frontiers it often retains only the formal attributes of sovereignty.
>
> (Burgi and Golub 2000)

The essential point of the globalists is that the exclusive link between territory and power is broken; thus a realignment of power and institutions has taken place in favor of institutions not anchored in a specific territory.

The second tendency, in contrast, insists that the nation-state remains the central institution, although its role has changed. Within this tradition, the state has been called "a true survivor" (Drucker 1997). Neorealist international relations (IR) theorists of the Keohane and Waltz tradition reject the idea altogether. Although the phenomenal development of communication technologies is often described as the nemesis of nation-states, some scholars in the field of communications (e.g., Morris and Waisbord 2001; Price 2002) maintain that "the state matters," even in the context of global media operations. Economists such as Helleiner (1995) go further and argue that states have played a critical role in the globalization of financial markets and that present trends are beneficial to the nation-state. Underscoring the resilience of the nation-state, the skeptics argue that "so far, at least there is no other institution capable of political integration and effective membership in the world's political community. In all probability, therefore, the nation-state will survive the globalization of the economy and the information revolution that accompanies it" (Drucker 1997, 159). The nation-state, we are told, has remained the main framework for political expression and the passage and enforcement of laws; therefore, proclaiming its demise is exaggerated and premature. Besides, "the ground reality" contradicts the assertion that the nation-state is a dying entity: since the debate on the demise of the nation-state began, more new states have emerged.

What is obvious from the arguments above is that the "rationalist" thinking that a well-defined prism is necessary to understand the world around us influences those who see the continued salience of the nation-state in the lives of people and its extraordinary permanence. Their understanding of global politics is based on the analytical primacy of national boundaries and the ontological primacy of the nation-state. Evidently, both of these can be questioned. For example, national security,[1] which by definition has been the exclusive terrain of the nation-state, is no longer, especially after 9/11. However, interestingly, it is the same post-9/11 global situation that demonstrates that the arguments dismissive of nation-states' power and their relevance, staples of the globalists, are in many ways overstated. The reemergence of the notion of *empire* in recent years, and especially after 9/11, shows that the nation-state has remained a powerful instrument in international relations and global affairs.

The debate on the nation-state's obsolescence has been prompted by the unprecedented growth of interconnectedness between societies, cultures, institutions, and individuals described as "globalization."[2] The process has resulted in "interpenetration and interdependency of relations on a world-scale, relationships in which time and space are 'compressed'" (Webster 2002a, 113). This process has unleashed two forces that challenge the nation-state: one from within the boundaries of nation-states in the form of ethnoreligious identity, demands for self-determination, and mobilization across national boundaries to draw more extensively on transnational bases of material and symbolic support (or, in other words, a force of *fragmentation*); and the other from the outside, as a result of the increasingly integrated nature of markets, the emergence of regional institutions to govern these markets, and the activities of multilateral institutions such as the International Monetary Fund (IMF) and the World Bank (or, in other words, *globalization* per se).[3]

These challenges can be classified into three forces: subnational, transnational, and supranational (Levine 1996). The subnational forces grow out of the assertions of identity based on "primordial" ties such as race, language, religion, tradition, and so forth. These forces, in essence, arise from local concerns and are often particularistic in nature. Transnational forces include transnational corporations (TNCs) and international nongovernmental organizations (INGOs) that do not require the approval of the nation-state and can easily circumvent any pressures placed upon them by governments. The supranational level consists of organizations such as the IMF, the World Bank, and the World Trade Organization (WTO)—and in the European context, the European Union (EU)—that have amassed enormous power and exercise that power over nation-states in various forms largely without any direct accountability.

These challenges, whether coming from within the boundaries of the state or from the outside, essentially undermine the validity of the twin pillars of the nation-state: the socio-political-economic organizations that allow the state to operate and the "national identity" that provides legitimacy to these organizations. The idea of national identity, an integral element of nationalism, swept the world in the nineteenth century with religious fervor and popularized the notion that diversities of any kind are a threat to nation building. Therefore, plural identities were sacrificed at the altar of the nation-state. The ethnic/religious loyalties of the individual were meant to be replaced with loyalties to the nation-state. An arbitrary cultural identity, "imagined" and based upon the control of artificial borders, was enforced as a sign of unity and strength. A homogenous national identity—constructed, articulated, and reproduced by the nation-state through legends, literature, customs, traditions, and celebrations—once considered to be the central element of "being" of modern citizens, is now fraught with problems and considered suspect. The growing assertions of "ethnic identities" all around the world demonstrate that no longer can all the citizens of a nation-state subscribe to a contrived and hegemonic identity.[4] Simultaneously, globalization, a phenomenon that produces a state of culture in transnational motion—flows of people, trade, communication, ideas, technologies, finance, social movements, and cross-border movements (Shome and Hedge 2002)—has unsettled the question of identity by producing "dis-location" of culture (Abbas 1997). The separateness between the "self" and the "different/other" is in flux, and new identities are forged, articulated, and rearticulated in a different fashion than they used to be. In the reformulation of identities, two forces play a pivotal role: global capital and the global media. They undermine the socio-political-economic organizations of the nation-state by subverting their authority and by operating largely outside their control.

Media Challenges to the Nation-State

What is at stake here are the two basic tenets of the nation-state: sovereignty and territorial boundary. Since the Treaty of Westphalia (1648), the nation-state has been understood to be comprised of sovereign territories with clearly defined boundaries within which routine and systematic surveillance is possible.[5] But the contemporary reality shows that the global media have often subverted both with impunity.

Sovereignty

The concept of sovereignty is intrinsically linked to the existence of nation-states. Although the definition of the term varies,[6] fundamentally it means that a state monopolizes the supreme and exclusive rights to control overall affairs in a given territory. Krasner (1988, 4) identifies four kinds of sovereignty: (1) international legal sovereignty ("territorial entities that have formal juridical independence"); (2) Westphalian sovereignty ("exclusion of external factors, whether *de facto* or *de jure*, from the territory of the state"); (3) domestic sovereignty (specification and exercise of legitimate authority within a polity); and (4) interdependence sovereignty (capacity of the state to control movement across its borders). Thus, although they are not mutually exclusive, two kinds of sovereignty—internal and external—can be identified. According to Williams (1996), internal sovereignty means that the state has command over its subjects, while external sovereignty means that the state is subject to no higher authority. From either point of view, encroachment into the jurisdiction of the state and any weakening of its power are deemed/considered violations of the sovereignty of the state.

Now, the question is, how do the global media, an integral part of the globalization process, undermine sovereign states? In what ways do media institutions affect the sovereignty of nation-states? The most obvious example of intrusion into national sovereignty is the Internet and the creation of "cyberspace" where the laws of the nation-state are often ignored and remain ineffective. Although some states are able to enforce strict limitations on online content and citizen access to select information and websites, the Internet has often remained outside the direct field of government censorship and restriction. The statement of John Perry Barlow, co-founder of the Electronic Frontier Foundation (EFF), in 1999 is the best-articulated evidence of the defiance of national sovereignty in cyberspace: "Governments of the Industrial World, you weary giants of flesh and steel, I come from Cyberspace, the new home of the Mind. On behalf of the future, I ask you of the past to leave us alone. You are not welcome among us. You have no sovereignty where we gather" (Barlow, n.d.).

The global broadcast media have been trying to emulate the Internet and to operate without controls imposed on them by nation-states. In many respects, CNN and the other global media have already succeeded in doing so. The events in Serbia in the winter of 1996–97 mark the high points in this regard. In December 1996, the Serbian authorities cracked down on the independent media. Their actions included switching off transmissions from Radio B92 and Radio Index, a Belgrade student station. Various global media outlets immediately increased their transmissions to the audience inside the country. The Voice of America (VOA), for example, increased its Serbian-language daily broadcasts to two and a half hours (VOA 2004). The BBC played a more significant role, enabling a radio station from Serbia—B92—to broadcast to the whole country and to the world. During the 1996–97 antigovernment demonstrations, transmissions of the independent radio station Radio B92, with broadcast license limited to Belgrade, were banned by the authorities. However, the station was allowed to communicate with its Internet service provider (ISP) in Amsterdam via a dedicated telephone line. B92 immediately redirected its feed and began live broadcasts over the Internet. News items were downloaded from the Net and distributed widely within the country and throughout the world. Within three days, the government succumbed and revoked its ban on radio broadcasts.

The successful distribution of radio programs on the Internet gave new life to the old idea of extending B92's coverage to the whole of Serbia. By the middle of 1997, B92 had established a network of independent radio and television stations, the Association of Independent Electronic Media (ANEM), consisting of more than thirty local radio stations from all areas of Serbia and Montenegro. With the assistance of the BBC, they set up a unique rebroadcasting scheme: every day, four hours of B92 and ANEM news programs were sent via the Internet from Belgrade to Amsterdam and then to London. The BBC then uplinked the B92 and ANEM transmissions to its satellite. Local ANEM radio stations downloaded them and put the programs on the air.

During the North Atlantic Treaty Organization's (NATO) bombing of Yugoslavia in 1999, control over the media space of the country was ensured—first, by bombing the Radio Television Serbia (RTS) building, and second, by creating "a ring around Serbia," a ring of FM transmitters from which the VOA and Radio Free Europe (RFE) launched round-the-clock programming into Yugoslavia.[7] These actions are blatant examples of the violation of the media space of a country and were undertaken in unusual circumstances. But they demonstrate that the technology is available to the media to defy the state's power. The availability of global television stations via satellite to citizens of countries where the authorities are unwilling to allow the stations to telecast displays the power of the independent media. It is now such a common occurrence that we tend to see it as "normal," but it constitutes, nevertheless, a violation of sovereignty both in the "Westphalian sense" ("exclusion of external factors, whether *de facto* or *de jure*, from the territory of the state") and in the sense of domestic sovereignty (specification and exercise of legitimate authority within a polity) of the nation-state.

Territoriality

The most tangible expression of the sovereignty of a nation-state is its territorial integrity—that is, its monopolistic jurisdiction over a particular territorial unit. It is through territorial control that a nation-state claims two kinds of sovereignty: Westphalian sovereignty and domestic sovereignty. The issue of territorial integrity is deeply rooted in the genesis of the nation-state. The historical evidence suggests that the "overwhelming majority of nation-states have been created in conditions of war and are sustained by possession of credible defence" (Webster 2002b, 211). A clearly defined and enforceable boundary has always remained at the heart of the existence of the nation-states. That is why the refinement of mapmaking and the emergence of cartography as a distinct discipline are closely tied to the emergence of nation-state, although, as Anderson (1983) noted, it grew out of the needs of military conquerors. The boundary delimits the power not only of the authority that remains within the demarcated lines but also of that which remains outside. It projects the political power of the state and draws a line of separation, however arbitrary it may be.

To nation-states, borders mean classification of the areas to be guarded, watched, suspected, dominated, released, and gazed at, and the goal of such markers is to accentuate the territorialist consciousness. Borders are markers in two ways. First, they reveal the territorial consolidation of states, and second, they reveal the actual power the states wield over their own societies. Clearly, there is a tension between two distinctly different functions of the borders: as "meeting places" and as "cut-off lines." These represent the conjunction and separation of national laws. Furthermore, the national borders have enormous symbolic significance: they create a dichotomous division—"us" and "them"—and they contribute to the construction of the "self" and of "the other." It is because of these physical, political, and symbolic significances that the national border has remained a significant element of the nation-state for more than two centuries.

But increasingly we are experiencing a world where political and geographical boundaries are being negated. People, money, images, and ideas now travel beyond political boundaries. This is not to say that national borders are disappearing; instead, one can argue that new borders are being created, but that the importance and efficacy of those borders is fading rapidly in the sense that they are no longer the focus of organization (Rosenau 1999). In the words of Dalby (1996, 39), "states may no longer be the neat containers of political community that international relations and political geography have for so long assumed." He feels that "more nuanced political cartographies" are necessary and that these new cartographies will consist of "multiple and overlapping maps ... which pay less attention to the boundaries of states and more to the flows and fractures that run across these boundaries" (39).

This new porosity of borders is largely a contribution of the new communication technologies. On the one hand, these technologies have given people the ability to obtain information, communicate, organize, conduct economic transactions, and politicize with little or no regard for national borders; on the other hand, they have weakened states. And governments are finding it increasingly difficult, almost impossible, to control this trend. The capacity of the state to control movement across its borders—what Krasner described as the interdependence sovereignty of the state—is also diminishing.

To appreciate the situation, we need to reconceptualize the notions of place and space, for the objective of the media is often to colonize space and thus make the control over place ineffective. Place is a geographical entity—clearly defined and physically located—while space is not fixed; it is uncontrollable and can be transformed.

In the context of the media, satellite transmissions demonstrate how space can be controlled and manipulated. Communication satellites, located in geostationary orbit, beam media content to certain areas of the earth's surface, areas that do not correspond to specific political boundaries.[8] Although political entities—nation-states for example—have complete control over the location (i.e., place) of the footprint, they have little control over the space in which satellite messages can be harnessed. Add to these the "spillover" areas, located within or on the border of the satellite footprints of the major media. The owners of the satellite cannot be blamed, as these are unintended areas of coverage, although the impact of the media is similar. Thus the geographic borders of a satellite's footprint remain a space where the direct control of the nation-state is minimal at its best, and nonexistent at its worst. An Australian judge acknowledged this when he insisted that "the capacity of local laws to control such media and to insist upon local public policy in matters such as culture, language and morality is reduced accordingly" (Kirby 1996). The Indian experience is similar. The information minister described the presence of satellites over the Indian sky as "an invasion." P. Unedra described his experience saying, "A file was put up in the Ministry as to how to counter the satellite invasion. What steps should be taken to stop it? I wrote back saying you cannot stop the sun shining by holding an umbrella. The more you try, the more you encourage people to watch" (quoted in Page and Crawley 2001, 266).

What we have seen in the Yugoslavian case is that while the state had unbridled control over its territory in 1999, the media space came under the control of NATO. This experience has bolstered the idea that any war should be preceded with a "telecom assault."[9] Accordingly, the U.S. military targeted the Taliban-controlled radio station and replaced it with U.S.-controlled broadcasts from aircraft at an early stage of the military operations in Afghanistan in October 2001 (Eykyn 2001).[10]

By identifying the modes of encroachment of the global media into the exclusive domains of nation-states, sovereignty, and territoriality, we are not suggesting that the nation-states have already lost the battle. On the contrary, our contention is that the nation-states are fighting back vigorously. What the nation-states want, and had been enjoying until the emergence of the global media, is a monopoly over place and space allowing them to control information and images and, therefore, possess supreme power. Whether such unrestrained power of the nation-state, in regard to information and imagery, is good or bad is a separate matter. But the changes that we have described thus far show that this power is now under threat and is facing challenges from, among other forces, the global media. Here it would be wrong to assume that, under these circumstances, nation-states are accepting this as inevitable. Instead, they are devising ways and means by which to maintain their control and power. There are ample examples of nation-states' efforts to reestablish control.

China, for example, has been at the forefront of attempts to control the seemingly uncontrollable medium—the Internet. They are using various methods, from filtering websites to forcing the providers to pledge to censor certain kinds of items. Amnesty International (AI) reports that "in mid-September 2002, China introduced new filtering systems based on key words, regardless of site or context. Filtering software has reportedly been installed on the four main public access networks in China. Prohibited words or strings of words on websites, e-mail, foreign news sites and search engines are affected" (AI 2002). Furthermore, in March 2002, the Internet Society of China issued *The Public Pledge on Self-Regulation and Professional Ethics* (2002), which went into force in August 2002; the signatories agree to "refrain from producing, posting or disseminating pernicious information that may jeopardise state security and disrupt social stability, contravene laws and regulations and spread superstition and obscenity" (Internet Society of China 2002). Similar efforts have been seen with respect to the broadcasting media. The STAR satellite television channels, which are owned by Rupert Murdoch, clinched a deal with a state-run television channel in China in 2003 when Murdoch agreed to drop the BBC from STAR broadcasts.

India, despite its policies of economic liberalization since the early 1990s, is yet to allow foreign investment in the media market and has placed certain restrictions on the media. For example, until 2000 India allowed only those media companies that were completely owned by Indians to uplink programs from within its territory. Leading satellite TV broadcasters like Zee and Star TV have had to send prerecorded tapes to Hong Kong or Singapore for uplinking. In mid-2000 when the policies were changed to allow foreign channels to uplink from India, the government insisted that "these channels will have to comply with India's broadcasting codes" (BBC News 2000).

These examples illustrate the steps taken by nation-states. However, the experience of Al Jazeera, a Qatar-based satellite television station that is described in the following section, documents the ferocity of the battle between the nation-states and the emerging threat to their power posed by the global media.

Al Jazeera and Media Activism—Discipline and Punishment in Application

Among the Arab media, Al Jazeera stands out as an institution dedicated to challenging state sovereignty. In a region where most of the media are owned or controlled by central authorities and autocratic political institutions, the station represents a major deviation from the status quo of media reporting and organizational structure. Those following the power struggle between Al Jazeera and Middle Eastern Arab regimes are well aware of the ways in which the station has disciplined—and been the subject of the attempted discipline of—state authorities. In challenging official statements and government propaganda, Al Jazeera has become a de facto enemy of governments that do not consider open and critical discourse a necessary component of media content and commentary. Through its critical reporting, it has been expelled from a number of countries that deem its reporting and content to be a threat to their legitimacy and stability. Before exploring the conflict between state and media however, it is important to provide a brief history of Al Jazeera's genesis and its evolution as an institution dedicated to questioning official misinformation, half-truths, and distortion.

Al Jazeera—A Brief Background

Al Jazeera does not fit the stereotype common in the United States and the West of complicit Arab media outlets, which are considered unofficial propaganda arms of the states in which they reside. The view of the Arab media as disseminators of state propaganda is perhaps best seen in the rhetoric of the *New York Times*, which speaks critically of Arab newspapers that "publish at the pleasure of their governments" (Sachs 2003). Formed in 1996, Al Jazeera stands out as a voice of dissent against state censorship; it is a lone voice in a sea of voices repeating the positions and doctrines of government officials. The network gained much of its staff from the now defunct BBC Arabic TV network, which trained employees to promote traditional

Western notions of professional journalism. Since its inception, Al Jazeera has relied primarily on funding from the government of Qatar, specifically from Sheik Hamid bin Khalifa al Thani. Thani took power from his father in a bloodless coup in 1995, and he committed the small Gulf nation to limited democratic and liberal reforms, the creation of an independent satellite network being a major part of his vision for modernizing Qatar. Thani was, and is, reluctant to intervene in the internal affairs of Al Jazeera, citing the outlet's professional integrity and independence from state censorship as factors that prohibit him from influencing its news content and editorial stances.

Through its critical reporting on events throughout the Middle East and the world, Al Jazeera has developed into a vibrant institution in its promotion of public awareness, Pan-Arabism, and democracy in countries where the individual is often subordinated to state authority, rather than the other way around. In this sense, the network arguably makes an important contribution to "disciplining" Arab regimes, which are more aware than ever of the role Al Jazeera plays in inciting resistance to government power and repression. By more closely examining the relationship between Al Jazeera and the Arab masses, the various governments in the region, and the United States, one gains a better understanding of how the station became a significant political player in major affairs of the day.

Al Jazeera's Challenge to the Regime of Supervision

Al Jazeera's editors claim that they are committed to the "objective" reporting of international and regional affairs. The station prides itself in presenting "the opinion, and the other opinion." Objectivity, according to the station's editors, encompasses more than just repeating official statements. Samir Khader, program editor for the station, summarizes its mission as follows: "The message of Al Jazeera is to educate the Arab masses on democracy, respect the other opinion, [with] free debate, no taboos. Everything should be dealt with with openness" (Noujaim 2004). Such debate often encompasses open confrontation and hostility between those espousing contrasting points of view. Programs such as the *Opposite Direction*, hosted by Faisal al-Hakim, became well known for presenting a wide diversity of opinions, while Hakim himself is often successful in inciting intense discussion and argumentation among guests espousing polar opposite views. Some have likened the *Opposite Direction* to the U.S. debate program *Crossfire* (formerly on CNN), at least in terms of its tendency to promote a tabloid form of shock TV in which guests shout back and forth over controversial political issues.

It is important to point out that, contrary to American corporate media institutions—which are typically hesitant, due to standards of "objective" reporting, to challenge official government statements as false—Al Jazeera has made questioning the official motives of Arab governments and the United States a mainstay of its coverage, editorials, and dialogue. It is here that one sees Al Jazeera in its role as a pioneer in promoting a sort of media activism in which reporting is often antagonistic to official motives that drive such developments as "the war on terror," among other government initiatives and actions. Al Jazeera became so popular throughout the Middle East in large part because of its willingness to promote critical commentary directed toward governments seen as resistant to popular protests and challenges to authority. The station, with approximately 35 to 40 million regular viewers, has not only disciplined Arab viewers to become more critical of government, but has also itself been disciplined by audiences expecting the station to continue its ten-year trend of holding regional and global political leaders' feet to the fire. The strong relationship between Al Jazeera and its audience is acknowledged in commentary by other media, although not always in a positive or supportive fashion. Saudi journalist Jamal Khashoggi, for example, lambasts the station for "being led by the [Arab] masses," rather than "lead[ing] the masses" (Iskandar and El-Nawawy 2003, 54).

Al Jazeera's independence from political censorship has not come without a price. Time and time again, the network has become the target of punishment by governments that view its adversarial style of journalism as unacceptably aggressive and antagonistic. Take for example Al Jazeera's reporting of the Israeli-Palestinian conflict. Israeli officials attacked the outlet for fueling Palestinian demonstrations and discontent against Israel, as the station often provided graphic imagery of Palestinians killed throughout the Israeli occupation. Conversely, Al Jazeera's editors maintained that they were simply showing viewers the reality of a brutal occupation and that "objective" reporting means no less than the broadcast of the reality on the ground in full. Strong emphasis on civilian casualties also contributed to an escalation of hostility between Al Jazeera and the George W. Bush administration, which viewed the station's reporting as a flagrant example of anti-American propaganda. Former secretary of defense Donald Rumsfeld was incredibly hostile to media outlets that he claimed "exaggerated the number of civilian casualties in the [Iraqi] conflict" (Brubaker 2006). Rumsfeld argued that outlets reporting casualty counts estimating tens of thousands of deaths in Iraq [sometimes estimating more] are guilty of deceiving the world about the nature of the conflict in Iraq: "The steady stream of errors all seem to be of a nature to inflame the situation and to give heart to the terrorists and to discourage those who hope for success in Iraq" (ibid.). Al Jazeera, however, responded to suggestions that journalists throughout Iraq were working with or supporting terrorists in an extremely skeptical fashion. Al Jazeera spokesperson Jihad Ballout denied Rumsfeld's "innuendo" that journalists benefit from "tip-offs" from terrorists regarding planned attacks throughout Iraq, and claimed that such charges "unduly obstruct freedom of the press" to report on controversial issues such as the growing number of Iraqi civilian casualties (Al Jazeera 2004b). Ballout considers Rumsfeld's comments "to be potential safety risks to all journalists who put their lives on the line in pursuit of the truth" in their reporting on the Iraq conflict (ibid.).

Punishment of the Arab World's most popular satellite network is not limited to rhetorical reprimand. The satellite network was thrown out of the Occupied Palestinian Territories by the Palestinian Authority (PA) during the Second Intifada after it ran a number of critical stories about PA corruption. Al Jazeera was also expelled from Iraq for its critical coverage of the U.S. occupation. A brief review of the network's critical coverage demonstrates the antagonistic relationship between the United States and Al Jazeera's editors and reporters. Concerning the 2005 Iraqi elections, Mohammed al-Obaidi editorialized on Al Jazeera that the U.S. occupation "is a violation of all international law. International charters that regulate the relationship between occupier and occupied do not give occupying authorities the mandate to instigate a change in the country's social, economic, and political structure" (Al-Obaidi 2004). Al Jazeera is critical of the war on terrorism in general, portraying the effort as a "so-called War on Terror." This represents a serious departure from American mainstream media coverage, which assumes without question that the conflict is a war directed against terrorism, rather than a war driven by other motivations such as power politics or domination of Middle Eastern oil.

Al Jazeera has been punished by governments in the region that view its unique brand of media activism as controversial and dangerous. In 2004, Al Jazeera's staff was withdrawn from Iraq after its coverage of the U.S. assault on Fallujah portrayed the United States in a critical light. Initially, two correspondents, Divar al-Omari and Tayseer Alouni, were expelled from the country, although the government gave no official justification, according to Al Jazeera. In response, Al Jazeera announced that in protest of the expulsions, it would no longer be reporting from Iraq.

The strong level of tension between Iraqi officials and the network's journalists and editors has been discernable throughout the conflict. Iraq's interim foreign minister Hoshyar Zibari attacked the network for "incitement" of violence and for reliance on "one-sided" and "distorted" framing of the news in relation to the war in Iraq (Al Jazeera 2004a). Al Jazeera's editors replied in a similarly confrontational manner, classifying Zibari's comments as "tantamount to incitement against the channel and its staff working in

Iraq" (ibid.). In the end, the Iraqi interim government was to have the last say in its attempts to discipline and punish the station for stepping out of the bounds of "acceptable" discourse regarding the U.S. occupation, the growing "insurgency," and the general state of post-Saddam Iraq. In 2004, an official ban was put in place against Al Jazeera, preventing it from reporting in Iraq. Regardless of the ban, the news outlet continues its critical reporting of the Iraq war. Continued commitment to adversarial reporting is recognized in the statements of the channel's editors, which acknowledge that the attacks of Iraqi and American officials "will not prevent the channel from pursuing its long cherished editorial independence." Despite the complaints of Western leaders, Al Jazeera "reiterat[ed] its adherence to its professional principles and internationally recognized media practices" (ibid.).

Al Jazeera and the United States—An Emerging Market for Activist Media?

In opposition to American and Iraqi attempts to censure Iraqi reporters and limit their skeptical coverage of the war on terror, Al Jazeera announced its own plans to establish an English-language network that was supposed to reach American and other English-speaking audiences by late 2006. This effort arguably represents an attempt on the part of the network to "discipline" American audiences, at least in the sense that Al Jazeera sought to introduce Americans to more critical perspectives and reporting regarding American actions in Iraq and U.S. foreign policy in the Middle East and elsewhere. The planned network, however, is marketed as an international media network rather than as network exclusively targeted toward the American public. Plans for an English-language extension to Al Jazeera put the network in a unique situation in that it is attempting to position itself as a major competitor of other television news outlets in the United States, such as CNN, Fox News, and MSNBC (Microsoft/National Broadcasting Company). While the American networks have traditionally been more sympathetic to the official war aims of the Bush administration, Al Jazeera's reporting brings with it the potential to open up a new paradigm of critical, activist journalism— one that is committed to challenging the administration's justification for war on a bedrock level. This new paradigm is about more than just questioning the United States and its foreign policy. The establishment of such a channel carries with it major potential in terms of challenging existing regimes in which media sources traditionally flow from the first world to developing countries. Nigel Parsons, managing director for Al Jazeera's international news outlet, explains: "We see ourselves as reversing the flow of information. This is the first English channel of its kind—broadcast from the developing world" (Sabbagh 2005).

A major question concerning the network's introduction relates to its ability to reach viewers on a large scale, as well as its potential for gaining new advertisers that are able to sustain the network and its critical perspectives. Gaining secure access to advertising revenue represents a major potential problem for the network in a country where corporate sponsors are often reluctant to be affiliated with institutions promoting major challenges to U.S. foreign policy objectives and initiatives. Al Jazeera's reporting model stands out from corporate media reporting in the United States, particularly when one looks at its financial backing. While the American media have traditionally been funded with advertising dollars and dominated by private owners, Al Jazeera is financed by the royal family of Qatar. Whereas American media networks and newspapers are primarily concerned with earning ever-increasing quarterly profits, Al Jazeera has historically lost money in its reporting over the past ten years. Still, many remain optimistic about the channel's prospects for success in this new market. Abdallah Schleifer of the Adham Center for Television Journalism in Cairo argues that "if done right, and I think it's going to be done right, this [network] could be a great boost to Al Jazeera itself because it could establish their credibility in certain areas where it's a bit speckled" (Whitaker 2004). One BBC News executive, wishing to remain anonymous, explains that Al Jazeera "bring[s] something different" to the American media market. "We welcome them. During the Iraq war, Al Jazeera's coverage demonstrated that the Western coverage of the conflict was too sanitized" (Sabbagh 2005). Al Jazeera's coverage, on the other hand, often focused more on the unpleasantness of war and occupation, highlighting gory images of civilian casualties and violence that have generally been absent in American mainstream media coverage.

Western officials remain deeply skeptical about the possibility that Al Jazeera will become a major American news network. American officials have long tried to exert pressure on the emir of Qatar to put the station up for sale to a private buyer. Success in selling Al Jazeera would also symbolize success in the reinforcement of the existing global capitalist regime of media power, whereby news outlets are run primarily with a profit motive, rather than by nonprofit media institutions. Private ownership of Al Jazeera would place great pressure on the news outlet to conform to the doctrines driving mainstream reporting throughout the corporate-owned media. Market pressures would likely fuel a curtailment of the channel's opposition to U.S. policy in the Middle East in two ways: (1) by threatening the station's funding, should corporate advertisers decide to boycott Al Jazeera in retaliation for controversial reporting, and (2) by reinforcing the neoliberal ideology stating that media reporting, like other vital public services, exists *not* primarily to educate the public, but for profit.

There remains much uncertainty in regard to Al Jazeera's potential for making a successful debut before American audiences. Hugh Miles, author of *Al-Jazeera: The Inside Story of the Arab News Channel That is Challenging the West*, speculates on the channel's ability to succeed in the United States: "The new channel will strive incredibly hard to prove its credibility ... The first year will probably be something of a test period. They'll [Al Jazeera's editors] see what works and then play to that" (Brandon 2006).

Although the English-language Al Jazeera network technically debuted in the United States in November 2006, the channel was boycotted by all American television carriers and satellite providers. As a result, access to Al Jazeera's news content has been available only via the Internet. The reluctance of cable and satellite providers to provide access to Al Jazeera most certainly has to do with the channel's controversial content. As Brendan Bernhard of the *New York Sun* argues, widespread American access to Al Jazeera's style of reporting may spotlight the deficiencies of American television news outlets. Most specifically, the "global range and scope of [Al Jazeera's] reportage" may very well "prove an embarrassment to the relative parochialism of CNN, MSNBC, [and] Fox News" (Bernhard 2006), as these media outlets often focus disproportionately on domestic news and celebrity gossip at the expense of global coverage. As a distinct voice in the American media market, Al Jazeera clearly stands out among a number of cable news competitors that have generally been hesitant to level substantive criticisms of the Bush administration in a time of war.

Discipline, the Regime of Supervision, and the Media

The preceding discussion clearly shows that the relationship between the nation-state and the media is far from fixed, and never a static event. Their relationship is being redefined through a complex web of events. Nonetheless, an absolute control of the nation-state over the media and media space is increasingly becoming a thing of the past. The erosion of the state's ability to control, as well as the underlying legitimacy of its right to do so, implies that the state is no longer in a position to impose the logic of supervision on the content and extent of the media. This, therefore, raises the question, Does there exist a void or have the media become the masters of their own domain? Our response is negative, an unequivocal "no" for three reasons.

First, "in geopolitics, a vacuum is not an option" (Saul 2004), because vacuum suggests a lack of a dominant ideology and/or power and an absence of a structure of power. In the present context, the ideology of globalization has already assumed the dominant position and is determined to establish its hegemony. Besides, the unipolar nature of the global structure indicates that an "order" is in place, however chaotic it may look. Thus, any suggestion of a void runs counter to the existing reality. Second, as the experiences of Al Jazeera reveal, the media are often subjected to harsh penalties, ranging from physical attacks to verbal abuse. Meaning, the media are "held responsible" by powers outside the realm of the media world, more often than not—the nation-states. Third, a close examination of the structure of ownership of the global media points to cross-ownership (that is, ownership and/or interests in other industries), which influences the contents of the media. Thus, media institutions, despite their enormous power to challenge the authority of the nation-state, are not free agents.

One can easily detect an apparent paradox here: while the global media are not supervised by the nation-states, neither are they completely on their own. Such a paradox can be resolved through an examination of the conditions underlying the emergence of global media institutions and their current role. The emergence of the global media is directly linked to the dramatic technological advancement of telecommunications, which in turn is a result of the restructuring of capitalism. The unprecedented higher level of interconnectedness that grew in the late 1960s—owing to the internationalization of production, the internationalization of financial transactions, and the internationalization of services—had created a demand for a constant exchange of information between and among the participants in the process, making information a necessary input into every aspect of economic decision making (Riaz 1997a, b). As Neuberger, at a very early stage of this process noted, "The larger the number of participants in the economic process, the greater the division of labor, the more complex the technological processes, and wider the assortment of goods and economic services an economic system produces, the more information intensive the economic process becomes" (Neuberger 1966, 132–33).

Interconnectedness brought recognition of information both as a commodity and as a resource—"a catalytic resource which acts as a powerful agent of change" (Jussawalla 1993, 128). To tap this resource and trade it as a commodity, it became crucial to have a system of enhanced capacity to store, retrieve, and analyze information, as well as a reliable, faster, and constant mode of communication. The development of the microprocessor in 1971 and the spectacular growth of telecommunications in the 1970s have been the logical advances in this direction. As Henderson (1989, 3) noted,

"The emergence of the global option (expansion of production overseas) ... would have been inconceivable without the development of information technologies, and particularly telecommunications. These technologies have been a major material condition for the emergence of the global option in as far as they have enabled particular labor processes, or sometimes entire production facilities, to be dispersed across the globe, while allowing managerial control ... to remain centralized in the 'world cities' of the core cities. So central have been these new microelectronics in the recent development of the international economy, that elsewhere Castells and I have suggested that global restructuring, at root, must be considered as a 'techno-economic process.'"

Thus, the global media are catalysts for and conduits of the global capitalist order and are subject to their logic of operation. While this logic allows them to defy the supervision of the nation-state, it also prevents them from operating on their own.

Although we point out that the logic of global capitalism is one of the means of supervision, we are not suggesting a deterministic position to the effect that the media lack any autonomy. Contrary to the deterministic explanation that "the contents of the media and the meanings carried by their messages are ... primarily determined by the economic base of the organizations in which they are produced" (Curran, Gurevitch, and Woollacott 1982, 18), we contend, in agreement with Foucault, that the media have become the instruments of disciplinary power. Discipline, to Foucault, is a technique of power: "'Discipline' may be identified neither with an institution nor with an apparatus; it is a type of power, a modality for its exercise, comprising a whole set of instruments, techniques, procedures, levels of application, targets; it is a 'physics' or an 'anatomy' of power, a technology" (Foucault 1984, 206).

Foucault reminded us that all modern societies are disciplinary societies. The concept does not refer to a program for a disciplined society, "but to the diffusion of disciplinary mechanisms throughout the social body, to the process by which the disciplines eventually [constitute] a general formula of domination" (Smart 1988, 91). Foucault has discussed the role that diffusion and disciplinary techniques have played in accelerating the "accumulation of capital" (Foucault 1979, 154). But he insisted that it is "the minute discipline, the panopticisms of the everyday" (Foucault 1984, 212) that reproduces and perpetuates domination. Foucault presents two images of discipline: "enclosed disciplines" ("a sort of social quarantine," referring to enclosed institutions with negative, constraining power) and "panopticism" (an "indefinitely generalizable" disciplining mechanism). The second, drawn from Bentham's idea of Panopticon—a program for the efficient exercise of power through the spatial arrangement of subjects according to a diagram of visibility so as to ensure that at each and every moment any subject might be exposed to "invisible" observation (Smart 1988, 88)—suggests that observation is essential to the disciplining mechanism. Foucault, highlighting a particular historical conjuncture, informed us that penitentiaries, schools, hospitals, administrations, and the police are the institutions whose "function is to assure that discipline reigns" either within a limited area or over the society as a whole. This objective is attained through three instruments: hierarchical observation, normalizing judgment, and examination (Smart 1988, 85).

Now that the society is no longer attached to a specific location, thanks to the globalization process, a new kind of Panopticon is needed, one with a larger gaze but that will perform similar functions. It is somewhat similar to the movement from "enclosed disciplines" to "panopticism." It is here that the global media enter: as a Panopticon of the new global order—for the purpose of continuous and functional surveillance, to be able to be the eyes of the authority, to provide the "disciplinary gaze." But the most significant role of the global media is to normalize "judgment." Foucault suggested that central to the disciplinary system of power is "infra-penalty"—to punish nonconformity, to correct it. Punishment, in this context, is not expiation or repression, but normalization (Smith 1988, 86). To tell what is important and what deserves to be known, and conversely what needs to be marginalized. The news agenda of the global media, especially the global media's coverage of war, is illustrative in this regard. Even a cursory glance at the coverage of war since 1991 reveals that media institutions cover what Castells (1996) identified as "instant wars"—those fought in short, decisive bursts by the power that commands the most advanced technologies—and present a sanitized version of them while other brutal wars, being fought without the involvement of these powers, remain unknown to the audiences.

The global media not only make decisions on their own coverage, but also take on the responsibility of ensuring conformity in the coverage of others. This is best reflected in an exchange between a CNN anchor and the editor in chief of Al Jazeera television on April 12, 2004, about civilian casualties in the Iraqi city of Fallujah. Following the brutal killing and mutilation of four American civilians on March 31, the U.S. military seized the city and began an operation against the militants in the city. An armed resistance ensued, leading to a bloody battle between the insurgents and U.S. forces. Over the following two weeks, U.S. forces continued bombing various parts of the city, causing high casualties. Al Jazeera, the only news network broadcasting from inside the city, relayed images of civilian causalities, including women and children. U.S. officials continuously denied any civilian casualties, although other sources (e.g., the Associated Press,)[11] reported that at least 600 civilians had died. In its coverage of the siege, CNN decidedly underplayed the civilian casualties, broadcasting U.S. claims that 95 percent of casualties were "military-age males" and U.S. allegations that any other accounts of the siege were untruthful. It was in this context that Daran Kagan interviewed Ahmed Al-Sheik of Al Jazeera. The following is part of their conversation, as reported by the media-watch organization Fairness and Accuracy in Reporting (FAIR): Kagan began the interview by asking Al-Sheik to respond to those accusations, citing U.S. officials as "saying the pictures and the reporting that Al Jazeera put on the air only adds to the sense of frustration and anger and adds to the problems in Iraq, rather than helping to solve them." After Al-Sheik defended Al Jazeera's work as "accurate" and the images as representative of "what takes place on the ground," Kagan pressed on:

> Isn't the story, though, bigger than just the simple numbers, with all due respect to the Iraqi civilians who have lost their lives—the story bigger than just the numbers of people who were killed or the fact that they might have been killed by the U.S. military, that the insurgents, the people trying to cause problems within Fallujah, are mixing in among the civilians, making it actually possible that even more civilians would be killed, that the story is what the Iraqi insurgents are doing, in addition to what is the response from the U.S. military?
>
> (FAIR 2004)

What CNN had been trying to do was to discipline Al-Jazeera for its non-conformity. In CNN's view, the "bigger story" ("what Iraqi insurgents [were] doing to provoke a U.S. response") needed to seen as normal and not be questioned. Those who question the validity of this judgment must be confronted and made docile; otherwise, anarchy will ensue. The nation-states, too, once employed the same argument in creating a regime of supervision that would allow them to have a monopoly over place and space and control over information and images. Events have come full circle; the subjects of the supervision have now become the participants.[12]

Future Prospects for Media Independence

This chapter has sought to analyze and address a number of ways in which the global media have challenged the authority and power of the nation-state. While such challenges to the nation-state are reflected in channels such as Al Jazeera and others discussed above, it is also imperative not to lose sight of the structural constraints that limit media outlets and prevent their full independence from the state and national governments. As long as media outlets are chartered by governments, their independence from elected officials and state power will never be completely fulfilled. American media corporations, for example, are granted charters to operate, as is true of any other U.S. corporation. Ultimately, this means that government leaders, as well as the American public, may leverage serious control over, and present serious obstacles to, total media independence and insularity. When it comes to radio and television, past restrictions on media content such as the fairness doctrine, as well as current government-imposed limits on how large a media corporation can grow and how large the markets it may control can be, demonstrate that the nation-state is still a major player when it comes to "disciplining" media organizations. While media outlets may move further and further toward challenging state sovereignty with the development of new technologies such as the Internet, the role of government in interfering in the affairs of the media should never be neglected or deemphasized. As long as media corporations (public and private) are funded or chartered by government, there will always be a place for the nation-state in the affairs of national and global media.

Notes

1. The term "national security," in this context, implies the nation's ability to defend its territory and its interests and the nation's ability to maintain geographic separation between itself and other nation-states.
2. Globalization has been described in various ways, and has come to mean different things to different scholars in different fields. Thus, a definition covering all aspects and meanings of globalization is impossible to find. In this chapter we have put aside the debate on definition, and focused on the impact of the process in regard to the nation-state and the global media.
3. On these forces below and above the state, see also Rygiel in chapter 5, and Knight and Smith in chapter 9.
4. This trend runs counter to the proliferation of the virtual community in cyberspace. Castells noted that new information technologies are integrating the world in global networks of instrumentality. Computer-mediated communication begets a vast array of virtual communities. Yet the distinctive social and political trend of the 1990s is the construction of social action and politics around primary identities either ascribed, rooted in history and geography, or newly built in an anxious search for meaning and spirituality. The first historical steps of informational societies seem to characterize them by the preeminence

of identity as their organizing principle (Castells 1996, 22). Michael Mann, however, disagrees with this line of argument. He suggests that social movements based on identity politics on balance strengthen the nation-state (Mann 2000, 144).

5. There are various definitions of the state, and the study of states has produced a voluminous literature. For the purpose of this chapter, I have used the above definition.

6. Sovereignty is one of the most ambiguous and contentious concepts in political science, and until the beginning of the 1990s remained a matter of peripheral interest to American academics. Hannum (1990, 14) underscored the contentious nature of the term saying that there is no universally agreed upon meaning of the term. Stephen Krasner, in 1988, noted the lack of interest of political scientists, saying that "sovereignty is a term that makes the eyes of most American political scientists glaze over" (Krasner 1988, 86). Kenneth Waltz, a neorealist, considered it as a "bothersome concept" (Waltz 1986, 90). But, of late, there has been a remarkable interest in studies of sovereignty.

7. "U.S. Launches 24-hour Broadcasts to Serbia," http://www.freeserbia.net/Documents/Kosovo/Broadcasts.html (accessed June 20, 2004). On March 25, the day after the first NATO bomb was dropped, the government shut down *Radio B92*. One week later, the government took over the Web address of the radio station and used it for government propaganda. In Amsterdam a new website was set up to provide whatever information the activists of the radio station could send outside the country.

8. The area that the satellite message is beamed to is called a footprint. The footprint of a satellite is the area of the Earth's surface where its signals can be received by satellite dishes of normal size, usually not more than nine meters (satellite dishes are measured in metrics, but that is almost 28 feet across).

9. Julian Borger, 1999. "Cyberwar could spare bombs; NATO Commander Wesley Clarke boosts the case for telecom assaults with a vision of how they might have been used in Kosovo," *Guardian*, November 5, p. 17.

10. The developments were as follows: during the night of October 8/9 the U.S. obliterated Asmaii Mountain—popularly called TV Mountain—in northeast Kabul. The target was the Taliban's *Radio Shariat* central studio and transmitting facility that was knocked off the air. Subsequently, some 20 other or so Taliban-run Voice of Shariat regional centers were similarly closed down. *Radio Shariat* had been the foreign media's main source of information from the Taliban government. (For details on Radio Shariat see "The Rise and Fall of the Taliban Controlled Stations 1996–2001," Radio Netherlands Media Network's Afghanistan Media Dossier 2002, www.rnw.nl/realradio/html/afghan_taliban.html.) These bombings cleared the airwaves for unopposed U.S. *psyops* broadcasts. On October 9, U.S. warplanes destroyed the long-abandoned shortwave tower on a hill in northeastern Kabul. The next day, U.S. Army psyops EC-130E planes began over-flying Afghanistan, broadcasting U.S. propaganda 10 hours a day. The psyops radio programming used the frequencies previously

employed by *Radio Shariat*. Another psyops component involved dropping leaflets.

11. For the AP's account see, "Tense Quiet in Fallujah." http://www.cbsnews.com/stories/2004/04/12/iraq/main611401.shtml (accessed July 12, 2004).

12. For a similar point on the participants of surveillance disciplining themselves, see Rygiel's conclusion in chapter 5, and Dartnell in chapter 7, who argues that the media coverage of the Iraq war is aimed at describing the war's impact on a "collective Euro-Americaland ('us') rather than a catastrophe for the Iraqis" to create docile bodies in the West, and vigilance against the other.

Bibliography

Abbas, Ackbar. 1997. *Hong Kong: Culture and Politics of Disappearance*. Minneapolis: University of Minnesota Press.

Al Jazeera. 2004a. "Al Jazeera Outraged at Iraq Criticism." July 26. http://english. aljazeera.net/NR/exeres/A3BF4F15-97CC-4B0BBAFE55A1CB3D859F.htm (accessed July 26, 2004).

———. 2004b. "Al Jazeera Slams Rumsfeld Terror Slur." August 18. http://english. aljazeera.net/NR/exeres/27A64DA6-E89F-4CD9-93700B224A801E89.htm (accessed August 18, 2004).

Al-Obaidi, M. 2004. "Why Iraqis Should Boycott Elections." *Al Jazeera*, December 3. http://english.aljazeera.net/english.DialogBox/PrintReview.aspx? NRORIGINALURL (accessed December 3, 2004).

Amnesty International (AI). 2002. "People's Republic of China: State Control of the Internet in China." August 17. http://web.amnesty.org/library/pdf/ASA170072002ENGLISH/$File/ASA1700702.pdf (accessed August 17, 2004).

Anderson, Benedict. 1983. *Imagined Communities: Reflections on the Origin and Spread of Nationalism*. 2nd ed. London: Verso.

Barlow, John Perry. n.d. "A Declaration of the Independence of Cyberspace." http://www.eff.org/pub/Publications/John_Perry_Barlow/barlow_0296.declaration. In "Cyberspace Regulation and the Discourse of State Sovereignty," *Harvard Law Review*. http://www.harvardlawreview.org/issues/112/7_1680.htm (accessed July 10, 2004).

BBC News. 2000. "Indian Boost for Broadcasters." *BBC*, July 26. http://news.bbc.co.uk/1/hi/world/south_asia/852409.stm (accessed August 17, 2004).

Bernhard, Brendan. 2006. "Is It Al-Jazeera or CNN International?" *New York Sun*, November 21. http://www.nysun.com/article/43884 (accessed June 15, 2006).

Borger, Julian. 1999. "Cyberwar Could Spare Bombs: NATO Commander Wesley Clarke Boosts the Case for Telecom Assaults with a Vision of How They Might Have Been Used in Kosovo." *Guardian*, November 5, 17.

Brandon, J. 2006. "Al Jazeera Aims to Go Global—in English." *Christian Science Monitor*, March 14. http://www.csmonitor.com/2006/0314/p07s02-wome.html (accessed March 14, 2006).

Brubaker, B. 2006. "Rumsfeld Says Media Exaggerating Iraqi Civilian Deaths." *Washington Post,* May 7. http://www.washingtonpost.com/wpdyn/content/article/2006/03/07/AR2006030700792.html (accessed May 7, 2006).

Burgi, Noëlle, and Philip S. Golub. 2000. "Has Globalisation Really Made Nations Redundant?" *Le Monde Diplomatique,* April. http://www.globalpolicy.org/nations/global.htm (accessed July 2, 2004).

Burke, Anthony. 2002. "Borderphobias: The Politics of Insecurity Post–9/11." *Borderlands* 1, no. 1 (August). http://www.borderlandsejournal.adelaide.edu.au/vol1no1_2002/burke_phobias.html (accessed July 2, 2004).

Castells, Manuel. 1996. *The Rise of the Network Society, the Information Age: Economy, Society and Culture.* Vol. 1. Cambridge, MA, and Oxford, UK: Blackwell.

Curran, James, Michael Gurevitch, and Janet Woollacott. 1982. "The Study of the Media: Theoretical Approaches." In *Culture, Society and the Media,* edited by Michael Gurevitch, Tony Bennett, James Curran and Janet Woollacott, xx. London: Methuen.

Dalby, Simon. 1996. "Crossing Disciplinary Boundaries: Political Geography and International Relations after the Cold War." In *Globalization Theory and Practice,* edited by Eleonore Kofman and Gillian Youngs. London: Pinter.

Drucker, Peter F. 1997. "The Global Economy and the Nation-State." *Foreign Affairs* 76, no. 5: 159–71.

Eykyn, George. 2001. "The US War of Minds." BBC, October 16. http://news.bbc.co.uk/1/hi/world/americas/1601463.stm (accessed October 16, 2001).

Fairness and Accuracy in Reporting (FAIR). 2004. "CNN to Al Jazeera: Why Report Civilian Deaths?" *Action Alert,* April 15. http://www.fair.org/activism/cnn-aljazeera.html (accessed August 20, 2004).

Foucault, Michel. 1979. *The History of Sexuality.* Vol. 1, *An Introduction.* London: Penguin.

———. 1984. "Panopticism." In *Foucault Reader,* edited by Paul Rabinow, 206–13. New York: Pantheon.

Guehenno, Jean Marie. 1995. *The End of the Nation-State.* Translated by Victoria Elliot. Minneapolis: University of Minnesota Press.

Hannum, Hurst. 1990. *Autonomy, Sovereignty and Self-Determination: The Accommodation of Conflicting Rights.* Philadelphia: University of Pennsylvania Press.

Held, David, and Anthony McGrew. 2000. "The Great Globalization Debate: An Introduction." In *The Global Transformations Reader,* edited by David Held and Anthony McGrew. Cambridge: Polity Press.

Helleiner, Eric.1995. "Explaining the Globalization of Financial Markets: Bringing States Back In." *Review of International Political Economy* 7, no. 2 (Spring): 164–85.

Henderson, Jeffrey. 1989. *Globalization of High Technology Production.* London: Routledge.

Holton, Robert. 1998. *Globalization and the Nation State.* London: Macmillan.

Internet Society of China. 2002. "Public Pledge of Self-Regulation and Professional Ethics for China Internet Industry." Revised July 19. http://www.isc.org.cn/20020417/ca102762.htm (accessed October 10, 2007).

Iskandar, Adel, and Mohammed El-Nawawy. 2003. *Al Jazeera: The Story of the Network That Is Rattling Governments and Redefining Modern Journalism.* Cambridge: Westview.

Jussawalla, Meheroo S. 1993. "Information Technology and Economic Development in the Asia Pacific." *Media Asia* 20, no. 3: 127–32.

Kirby, Michael. 1996. "Globalisation of the Media and Judicial Independence." Paper presented at a seminar of the International Commission of Jurists concerning media and the judiciary in Spain. http://www.austlii.edu.au/au/other/media/8744.html.

Krasner, Stephen. 1988. "Sovereignty: An Institutional Perspective." *Comparative Political Studies* 21, no. 1: 66–94.

Levine, Donald N. 1996. "Sociology and the Nation-State in the Era of Shifting Boundaries." *Sociological Inquiry* 66, no. 3: 253–66.

Mann, Michael. 2000. "Has Globalization Ended the Rise and Rise of the Nation-State?" In *The Global Transformations Reader*, edited by David Held and Anthony McGrew, 136–47. Cambridge: Polity Press.

Morris, Nance, and Silvio Waisbord, eds. 2001. *Media and Globalization: Why the State Matters.* Lanham, MD: Rowman and Littlefield.

Noujaim, Jehane. 2004. *Control Room.* Magnolia Pictures, distributed by Lions Gate Home Entertainment.

Neuberger, E. 1966. "Libermenia, Computia and Visible Hand: The Question of International Efficiency." *American Economic Review*, 56: 131–44.

Ohmae, Keinichi. 1995. *The End of the Nation State: The Rise of Regional Economies.* New York: Free Press.

Page, David, and William Crawley. 2001. *Satellites over South Asia: Broadcasting Culture and the Public Interest.* New Delhi: Sage.

Price, Monroe, ed. 2002. *Media and Sovereignty: The Global Information Revolution and Its Challenge to State Power.* Cambridge: MIT Press.

Riaz, Ali. 1997a. "Telecommunications in Economic Growth of Malaysia." *Journal of Contemporary Asia* 27, no. 4 (December): 489–510.

———. 1997b. "Role of Telecommunications in Economic Growth: Proposal for an Alternative Framework of Analysis." *Media, Culture & Society* 19, no. 4 (October): 557–83.

Rosenau, James N. 1999. "States, Sovereignty, and Diplomacy in the Information Age." Virtual Diplomacy Report, United States Institute of Peace, Washington, D.C. www.usip.org/oc/vd/vdr/jrosenauISA99.html.

Sabbagh, Dan. 2005. "Al-Jazeera Sets Up Service in English." *Times,* London, June 4. http://www.timesonline.co.uk/article/0,,251-1640725,00.html (accessed June 4, 2005).

Sachs, Susan. 2003. "Arab Media Portray War as Killing Field." *New York Times*, April 4, B1.

Saul, John Ralston. 2004. "The End of Globalism." *Financial Review,* February 20. http://afr.com/articles/2004/02/19/1077072774981.html (accessed July 1, 2004).

Shome, Raka, and Radha S. Hedge. 2002. "Culture, Communication, and the Challenge of Globalization." *Critical Studies in Media Communication* 19, no. 2: 172–89.

Smart, Barry. 1988. *Michel Foucault.* London: Routledge.

Voice of America (VOA). 2004. "VOA History." http://www.voa.gov/printerfr.cfm? tablename=tblVOAHistory&articleID=10008.

Waltz, Kenneth. 1986. "Political Structures." In *Neorealism and its Critics*, edited by Robert Keohane, 70–97. New York: Columbia University Press.

Webster, Frank. 2002a. "Global Challenges and National Answers in the Information Age." In *In Search of Boundaries: Communication, Nation-States, and Cultural Identities*, edited by Joseph M. Chan and Bryce T. McIntyre, 111–28. Westport, CT: Ablex.

———. 2002b. *Theories of the Information Society.* 2nd ed. London: Routledge.

Whitaker, Brian. 2004. "Al-Jazeera Has Made News in Arabic ... Now It Hopes to Make Its Mark in English." *Guardian*, September 2. http://www.guardian.co.uk/ international/story/0,,1295171,00.html (accessed September 2, 2004).

Williams, Marc. 1996. "Rethinking Sovereignty." In *Globalization: Theory and Practice*, edited by Elenore Kafman and Gillian Youngs, xx. London: Pinter.

CHAPTER 7

Disciplining Perceptions, Punishing Violations: Captivity in Televisual Narratives of the Iraq Conflict

Michael Dartnell

I mages and representations project and sustain the power to discipline and punish. The power to "evoke emotional responses, demand attention, threaten us, influence memories, and change ideas of what is natural" underlies the influence of images (Reeves and Nass 1998, 251). Transforming images into a simulacrum of experience, television projects fear, panic, despair, hope, moral indignation, outrage, and purpose, signaling that "the *conditions in which our beliefs are constituted* have entered into a phase of intense evolution" (Stiegler 2002, 149). By increasing the complexity, accelerating the appearance, intensifying the presence, and extending the reach of images and representation, the worldwide spread of television projects and sustains the power to discipline and punish. Television images shape identities and values that sustain global power by giving them stability, coherency, and intelligibility. However, the complexity, speed, intensity, and extent of televisual image production often masks the fact that "reality is always lost in the acts of picturing and describing" (Taylor 1998, 4). The disjuncture between lived experience and representation can be glimpsed through the notion of "global presence"—that is, a sense of planetwide immediacy and "nowness," of seeing and knowing, which characterizes globalized television practices. To discuss how television blurs distinctions between representation and lived experience, I examine select images from the Iraq conflict in 2003–2004 and relate them to literary narratives of captivity that appeared in colonial North America. The chapter argues that, like earlier preelectronic storylines, televised captivity narratives discipline and punish those who veer from particular gender, racial, and sexual roles.

Representations of conflict portray power, weakness, inhumanity, and the horror of war. Certain images

> take on iconic significance. A group of US marines raising the flag over Iwo Jima, for example, remains one of the abiding images of World War Two, while a (then) unknown girl running burned, scared and naked down a Vietnamese road speaks with equal eloquence of the conflict in Indo China … Images … somehow concentrate so many feelings about the conflicts they represent.
>
> (Howells 2003, 3)

Television networks have produced a wide variety of images of the Iraq conflict. The images represent the individuals, groups, and nations that structure international affairs. Stable and coherent images and identities are critical in a world buffeted by population movements, pandemics, economic and technological change, and the ideological-political consequences of 1989 and 9/11. While Allied authorities in World War II could censor and shape images, the Iraq conflict has seen the distribution of images that are antagonistic to power. Does this distribution transform representations of war when images are perceived in relation to Western identities, narratives, and values? To illustrate the deep integration of Western-centered representations of global politics, I will "read" a selection of images televised by the Euro-American media.

This discussion focuses on television, a powerful and discrete[1] device due to satellite and cable transmission, corporate concentration, and technological innovations that increasingly blend communicative platforms. Alongside radio and the Internet, television is often described as qualitatively transforming human communication. The Internet, radio, and television are all practices that *claim* to provide immediate and authentic communication. While the Internet supports transnational organizations, and radio was used by Rwanda's Hutu extremists in 1994, for example, to trigger genocide,[2] television's impact was evident in the Kennedy-Nixon debates, satellite transmission of the 1968 Tet offensive in Vietnam, heavy-handed censorship in the 1991 Gulf War, and images of Kosovars fleeing the Serb army in 1999. Images from the Iraq conflict thus join a genealogy of televisual images. The issue is whether the transformation of television news information provides "global presence" or sustains existing powers to discipline and punish.

Approaches to the Analysis of Televisual Images

Several approaches to interpreting television are relevant to the quagmire in Iraq. *Manufacturing consent theory*, well known because of its connection to Noam Chomsky, is an influential method for analyzing television. The approach[3] generally argues that governments decisively set news agendas. The resulting media products serve "to amuse, entertain, and inform, and to inculcate individuals with the values, beliefs, and codes of behaviour that will integrate them into the institutional structures of the larger society" (Herman and Chomsky 1988, 1). Manufacturing consent theorists contend that international news reporting in the United States in particular conforms to the frames of reference set by elites (see Bennett 1990). Some analysts contend, moreover, that the U.S. media ensure public acceptance and/or indifference to government actions abroad. Ben Bagdikian links television ownership to that of newspapers, radio, the Internet, and magazines. He argues that liberal press theories no longer apply because U.S. media ownership fell from fifty to five corporations in the past 25 years. Individual corporate media "jointly conform to the periodic ratings that presume to show what kinds of programs have fractionally larger audiences, after which 'the competitors' then imitate the winners and take slightly varying shares of the total profits" (2004, 6).

In contrast, CNN *effect theory* argues that the media do influence government policies. These analysts contend that the 1991 Kurdish refugee crisis in northern Iraq and the 1993 Somali crisis show how the media influence policymaking (Kennan 1993). Supporters of this view point to the media's impact in certain critical policy and humanitarian decisions. At the end of the 1990s, British and American supporters of intervention in Kosovo argued that the media could provoke intervention. More recent analyses acknowledge that the media have specific and limited influence, and in some cases only facilitate government action (see Freedman 2000 and Wheeler 2000).

The *media-policy interaction model* balances CNN effect theory with an approach adapted to specific circumstances. Piers Robinson argues that influence depends on the type of crisis and specific government policies. If elites agree on an issue, the "news media are unlikely to produce coverage that challenges that consensus" and "government will draw upon both its substantial resources and credibility as an information source in order to influence news media output" (Robinson 2002, 30). Conversely, if elites do not agree, "conditions exist under which the CNN effect might occur." In other words, with greater "uncertainty over policy within the executive, the . . . policy process is [more vulnerable] to the influence of negative media coverage" (ibid., 31–32). Robinson's approach applies the insights of manufacturing consent to specific situations and evaluates the extent of actual government influence on the media.

Interview-based research generally has no explicit theoretical framework for examining television, and claims to allow participants to "speak for themselves." The results are studies that do not precisely measure media influence,[4] since they do not account for subjects who distort or do not precisely remember events, or for subjective perceptions of significance. An insightful interview-based study is Adatto's *Picture Perfect*, which examines how "realistic" television, film, and photographic images deceive by tapping into deeply rooted ideals and myths. In North America, where "traditional notions of fixed selves, defined by character or soul, give way to the modern notion of a centreless self, always in the process of forming or reforming itself" (Adatto 1993, 18), these deceptive qualities are enhanced.

Unlike interview-based methods, *global television studies* link television to a globalization process that, in the last twenty years, has "transformed the televisual landscape and [has] contributed to the globalization of television as a medium and as an industry" (Held 1999, 357). James Rosenau says that television

> serves to provoke analyses, evoke emotions, and expand imaginations in ways and to an extent that have no parallel in prior history. People experience the diminution of time and distance by seeing the actions and reactions, the conflicts and collaborations, the sights and sounds—indeed, the whole range of past and present human experiences—that unfold elsewhere in the world.
>
> (2003, 241)

There are two trends in global television studies. One sees globalization as (negatively or positively) complete and totalizing. Rosenau's view that television embodies one trajectory toward global civil society is certainly one example of this.

The second global television studies approach (Parks and Kumar, eds. 2003) sees globalization as complex and multilayered. This approach contends that the diversity of televisual practices makes it difficult to link it directly to power. Ramaswami Harindranath (2003) says that television is one context in which "the role played by the hybrid, Westernized 'local' elite" (166) is seen in the majority world. John Tomlinson argues that television is only an additional path for human interaction (Tomlinson 2003), does not influence morals, and is "a different *kind* of cultural experience which is probably not morally sustaining in the same way as proximate experiences and personal relations close to the core of the lifeworld are" (Tomlinson 1999, 2). Arjun Appadurai situates television in "*imagined worlds*—that is, the multiple worlds that are constituted by the historically situated imaginations of persons and groups spread around the globe" (2003, 41). This approach was developed on the basis of Raymond Williams's *Television: Technology and Cultural Form*, which examines what television "does" and interprets meaning. Setting television in a context reveals that "the effect of a technology is in fact a social complex of a new and central kind" (Williams 1974, 24–25). Williams notes that frequent use of images contributes to a sense of global presence, and he criticizes Marshall McLuhan's view of technology as "only a matter of some autonomous process directed by remote engineers. It is a matter of social and cultural definition, according to the ends sought" (ibid., 137). To discern such ends, he focuses on institutions, forms, programming, effects, and alternatives to television.

Case study approaches include examinations of censorship and community representation in British television treatments of Northern Ireland's "Troubles." A key issue in Northern Ireland was preventing "coverage on radio or television of political or social events from being itself the cause of further events" (A. Smith 1996, 27). Covering two mutually antagonistic communities, BBC television constantly faced charges of betraying national interests and of not accurately reporting social phenomena.[5] Issues of bias and community misrepresentation are also raised by treatments of loyalism that feature a

> limited number of programmes devoted to the loyalist agenda, which in each case was roughly half of that afforded to the nationalists. There was also a similarity in their negative presentation of loyalism, with many programmes featuring loyalist intransigence and intimidation, and loyalists being depicted, time after time, as the chief stumbling-block on the road to progress.
>
> (Parkinson 1998, 122)

Another case study, El-Nawawy and Iskandar's (2002) analysis of the Qatari network Al Jazeera, focuses on non-Western TV[6] and applies CNN effect theory to the Arab world. The authors focus on how global news broadcasting challenges an international hierarchy by facilitating the influence of a small country such as Qatar, validates the perceptions of an Arabic-speaking public, overcomes the opposition of conservative Arab regimes in Saudi Arabia and Egypt, and impugns Western perceptions of power and legitimacy. They believe television news bears values of free expression: "If we have any agenda, it is to support and promote free democratic expression in the Arab world" (ibid., x). The study monitored Al Jazeera's broadcasts and operations to determine their differences and similarities relative to those of the BBC and CNN.

Visual culture theory (Howells 2003) situates television in the Western tradition of representation, alongside painting, photography, film, and new media. It interprets images with references to icons, forms, art history, ideology, semiotics, and hermeneutics. Howells (2003, 199) notes that television is widely seen as "realistic," is "one of our most prevalent visual texts," and relies heavily on previous cultural/visual knowledge for its impact (ibid., 215). He argues that the high volume of TV production supplies a wide variety of images and allows concentration on many narratives: "While film today typically takes the form of one-off narrative drama, television also includes series, documentaries, new programmes, and game shows, all of which provide varied fertile ground for the text-based analysis of our own cultural values and symbolic way of life" (ibid., 217–18). Television images and narratives often repeat long-standing themes.[7] A visual culture approach highlights the image continuities between television and other visual forms.

Global Presence in Televisual Images

Global presence is a myth and a reality. It is experienced subjectively through the Internet, cell phones, mobile text messaging, digital photography, and television, and it is organized objectively by conglomerates that own and operate satellites and transmission equipment, cables, Internet service providers, technological patents, production facilities, and copyrights. Global presence throws realism into crisis, since "out of the chaos of moods, confused opinions, and popularizing views of the sort spread by the mass media, a public opinion is much more difficult to form than out of the rational controversy between great currents of opinion that struggled against one another in society" (Habermas 1989, 238). Manifest since at least 1968 (Tet on TV), the crisis of realism enjoins us to "forget Foucault"; that is, forget about disciplining public life through spatial-territorial models of Western government (Baudrillard 1988). As I listen to Web music, chat on the Internet,[8] and peruse amazon.com while I write, global presence connotes myth and reality. The myth places *portions* of the global population in touch with one another and with unmanageable volumes of information. The reality encases our perceptions of the world within this myth and, as such, is politically relevant. Myths structure our lived reality, lend coherence to events, allow us to speak, and give meaning to events. Global presence is a myth used to discipline and punish.

By linking television and globalization, McLuhan's "global village" anticipates global presence. Two key concepts in McLuhan's theory are the basis
of global presence. First, he argues that the media create a global reality:

> As long as our technologies were as slow as the wheel or the alphabet or
> money, the fact that they were separate, closed systems was socially and
> psychically supportive. This is not true when sight and sound and movement
> are simultaneous and global in extent.
>
> (McLuhan 1995a, 101)

In other words, the electronic media supplant an older social order and
restructure a new "collective conscious." The second concept is electronic
immediacy media, especially "the mosaic image of the TV screen [that]
generates a depth-involving *nowness* and simultaneity in the lives of children
that makes them scorn the distant visualized goals of traditional education
as unreal, irrelevant and puerile" (McLuhan 1995c, 251). For McLuhan,
television replaces traditional ways of perceiving and experiencing cultural
messages, and "permeates nearly every home in the country, extending the
central nervous system of every viewer as it works over and molds the entire
sensorium with the ultimate message" (ibid., 245). The influence of television is totalizing and immediate: "When the news team seeks to become
the news source by means of direct dialogue rather than by remote report
of the event," he believes that our understanding of events becomes more
important than the actual event (McLuhan 1995b, 295).

As a "media guru," McLuhan (like Walter Benjamin) understood the
importance of technologically innovative communication. The issue is the
nature and extent of change. McLuhan believed a profound transformation
of human society by electronic media was under way. After the 1960s and
1970s, another wave of information technology (IT) and the idea of globalization further transformed global power. Has this wave fulfilled
McLuhan's vision and "the promise of a technologically engendered state of
universal understanding and unity, a state of absorption in the logos that
could knit mankind into one family and create a perpetuity of collective
harmony and peace"? (McLuhan 1995c, 262). Has something else occurred?
Do elements of preelectronic realities persist? Do we experience events at a
distance through television, or is "nowness" a conceptual apparatus that
serves to discipline and punish through the electronic media?

There is widespread consensus that the "media, including television, are
especially significant for globalization theorists in that they have been historically constituted by processes of globalization, but are simultaneously
seen as constituting a global order" (Casey et al. 2002, 111). However, we

need not uncritically accept that television has an immediate, totalizing, and simultaneous influence around the globe. Images of captivity from the Iraq conflict illustrate how television actually recapitulates narratives of Euro-American relations with non-Europeans. The older narratives, like industrialization and spatial-territorial political models, discipline and punish by excluding the majority of humanity from power, participation, and a better life, and by juxtaposing "civilization" and "barbarism."

Art historians and some media theorists argue that a global "now" merely updates the truth claims in the Western history of representation (painting, photography, film).[9] Instead of authenticity and immediacy, a complex assembly of devices and social imaginaries characterizes social digitization. Disassembling the presentation of televised "live events" and participation at a distance[10] reveals, moreover, that "the concept of electronic presence dates back at least to the nineteenth century and has been variously described over the years as 'simultaneity,' 'instantaneity,' 'immediacy,' 'now-ness,' 'present-ness,' 'intimacy,' 'the time of now'" (Parks 2003, 75). Since television and news broadcasting in particular claim to be uniquely "real" and to present "realistic" events,[11] global presence is a springboard from which the connection of actual events to televisual production(s) can be critically evaluated.[12]

In the 1960s, BBC television's *Our World* used global presence in a satellite broadcast about the worldwide population crisis. Global presence projected viewers into various global contexts and projected those contexts into viewers' homes. Presented as spontaneous and immediate, the event in fact concealed a complex technical and operational organization. This included scheduled/canned liveness, and time zoning. The accompanying metaphors of global presence ("liveness," "nowness," "direct," etc.) were "used to reassert Western hegemony during a period of spatial flux, a period of decolonization, outer space exploration, and Cold War geopolitics" (Parks 2003, 79). *Our World* relied on a (then) new image of the Earth as a whole planet (made possible by satellite images) to show "television pushing its own limits—extending itself, technologically, ideologically, culturally, and economically as a global system of seeing and knowing" (ibid., 82). Attempting to make the global village a perceived reality, the producers pioneered techniques that are now widespread. For example, Al Jazeera uses them to produce a counternarrative of the Iraq conflict (see also chapter 6). Al Jazeera's storyline is subsequently rerepresented on Euro-American screens as a captivity saga.

I use a *culture and technology* approach to analyze television and power. The approach treats image projection as a practice that shapes perceptions and uses technology to circulate ideas, values, and beliefs.

It views values as motivating forces in human societies (Dartnell 2006, 6–11). I agree that

> a culture of power is a culture of representation. The intellectual, ethical, religious discourses of power may well tend towards high art (great representations), and their more economic, pragmatic ones towards industrialized art (mass representations), but both rely on their ability to produce representations of the world and, more importantly, of themselves in the world.
>
> (Fiske 2003, 277)

The analysis concentrates on what differentiates human beings from others species—culture and technology—and links television to older cultural-technological practices. The approach highlights how communication devices reshape perceptions by mixing value-laden cultural and practical-technological components. A basic tenet of my approach is that "objective" analysis of images is not realistic, since interpretation and methodological narration are by definition subjective. The focus of attention must be content as much as instrumentalities, since "representing the other is representing 'our' power in it, and is not just a semantic sleight of hand but is a material exercise of power. Representation is *really*, not symbolically, powerful" (ibid., 278). By examining the contents of captivity storylines, the analysis highlights the continuity of ideologies, identities, and values of discipline and punishment and their transformation by televisual practice.

The Context of Image—U.S. Invasion, Pocahontas, and Captivity

The Iraq conflict followed open disagreement between members of the UN Security Council over how to ensure that Iraq neither produced nor used weapons of mass destruction (WMD). The United States argued that a threat existed while Sadaam Hussein was Iraqi leader, and demanded his resignation.[13] The military "shock and awe" campaign began with air strikes and was followed by an invasion on March 20, 2003. In early April 2003, U.S. forces entered Baghdad, a U.S.-backed administration was set up, and economic sanctions were lifted. By August 2003, antioccupation violence intensified and security deteriorated. In spite of Hussein's capture on December 14, 2003, and the reestablishment of Iraqi sovereignty in June 2004, suicide attacks, fighting between U.S. forces and Sunni and Shi'a paramilitaries, prisoner abuse by American and British troops, and the assassination of Iraqi leaders in the U.S.-based administration ensued. The context of images is one of disagreement between great powers over how to address the Iraqi conflict, massive global protests, failure to ensure security, reconstruction and reconciliation in Iraq, the rise of powerful post-Sadaam social movements, and America's inability to manage the situation.[14]

By August 2004, ninety-three individuals from 23 countries in the U.S.-led coalition or working on reconstruction were being held captive. Sixteen captives were Turkish. Seven were from the United States, China, and Lebanon, respectively. Thirty-three captives were from six Middle Eastern countries (Turkey, Lebanon, Egypt, Jordan, Iraq, and Israel). The largest group, with 24 captives, was from eight countries in Europe and North America (the United States, Italy, Canada, the Czech Republic, Bulgaria, Russia, Poland, and France). Thirty-two captives came from seven Asian countries (Nepal, China, Japan, India, Pakistan, South Korea, and the Philippines). Four captives were from two African countries (Kenya and Somalia). By August 31, 2004, Iraqi insurgents had executed 22 captives from eight of the 23 countries (Nepal, Turkey, the United States, Lebanon, Italy, Pakistan, Bulgaria, and South Korea).[15] Twelve victims were Nepalese. The United States and Pakistan each had two citizens killed. Five executed captives were from North America and Europe (the United States, Italy, and Bulgaria), two were from the Middle East (Turkey and Lebanon), and three were from Asia (Pakistan and South Korea). Although two American and two Pakistani citizens were executed, Turkey had more than twice the number of captives (16) than either of the other two countries (7). Targeting countries involved in reconstruction or the occupation illustrates the political nature of the kidnappings (Collier 2004, A15).

Images of captivity are part of the Euro-American-majority world story-line marked, for example, by disastrous encounters between French, British, and (later) Americans with Native North Americans. As Europeans intruded into northeastern North America in the seventeenth century, colonists encountered Natives who took hostages in war so as to

> replace individuals who had died prematurely or who had been killed in accidents or skirmishes. Some captives were adopted to assuage the grief of a mother who had lost a child, but more often captives were taken out of practical labour considerations. Some captives were harshly used as forced labour or slaves, but many were adopted into Indian families and assumed the social prerogatives and duties of the deceased.
>
> (Ebersole 1995, 3)

The story of John Smith and Pocahontas is well known. Smith's claim that Pocahontas saved his life is probably a "culture-bound and self-serving interpretation of a series of Powhatan rituals designed to transform strangers into relatives, allies, and trading partners" (Strong 1999, 54).

Native women sometimes chose high-status European men, and Pocahontas might have wanted Smith as a politically advantageous ally. "Torture" was thus ritual transformation so he could join the community.

Pocahontas's later assimilation, a founding American myth, illustrates another transformative meaning of captivity: movement from paganism to Christianity, from darkness to light, and from barbarism to civilization. She illustrates "othering" in captivity narratives. She is the "other": a "savage," "barbarian," "heathen," "uncivilized," and, we might add, nonwhite, non-European non-male who is thus not fully human. Pocahontas's conversion to Christianity and marriage to an Englishman highlight her singularity. This particular route was not open to most Native Americans, who were exterminated, marginalized, or confined to reservations. Othering defines colonial contact with non-European cultures and has been a fulcrum for global discipline and punishment since the seventeenth century. Othering allows colonizers to disregard the values, interests, and practices of the colonized by placing them at a polar extreme in order to politically and economically subordinate them. Pocahontas was not alone in navigating between colonized and colonizer, but she was relatively rare and able to do so because she submitted to the colonizer.[16]

Like Pocahontas, Euro-American captives of Native Americans were transformed. They were "lost" and risked losing their identity by death and assimilation. They became goods traded between France and Britain. Some English captives were marched north to Sorel, near Montréal, traded for hatchets and beaver pelts, and ransomed back to the home colonies. The French were pivotal to the exchange, but their missionaries were also captured and killed by Native Americans. Since captivity was integral to contact between Native- and Euro-American culture and military practices, individuals were pawns in a ritual aimed at creating fear for political ends. As the forced migration of Africans and the extermination of villages and entire nations in a push to "civilize" the Americas illustrate, Euro-Americans made extensive use of captivity.

Images of Captivity in Iraq

When viewed as tales of Euro-American conquest and rise to global dominance, captivity narratives can be reframed as the "folklore" of imperialism. They reappear when non-Europeans must be called to order ("civilized," "managed," "disciplined," or "punished").[17] Their reincarnation as television images feature American and "allied" captives as well as Iraqi prisoners. The images represent American prisoners and the U.S. home front, Iraqi prisoners and prisoner abuse, insurgents who capture Americans and other allied personnel, the Iraqi home front, and other foreign prisoners held by Iraqis. Each set of images relates to particular individuals, cultures, and histories. They are narratives of cultural contact. They also illustrate how storylines are consistent, whether published memoirs of former captives (e.g., Mary Rowlandson 1997), historical novels (e.g., James Fenimore Cooper's *The Last of the Mohicans* and Herman Melville's *Moby Dick*), films (e.g., *Little Big Man*, *The Deer Hunter*, *Taxi Driver*, *Dances with Wolves*), or television reports. The images are intimately related to conflict, domination, and, ironically, a possibility of enhanced understanding.

> Every captivity narrative posits an uneasy relationship between cultural and racial identity, suggesting that cultural identity is to some extent racially determined. The hero in these narratives enforces boundaries between the two competing cultures, while the captive poses the threat as well as the possibility of mediation between them.
>
> (Mortimer 2000, 164–65)

The colonizer–colonized dynamic is represented on television, and power is based in the ability to define images. Captivity touches a basic level of identity, due to the seizure, confinement, and control of bodies. Captives lose control of their bodies; they are powerless and subject to the will of their captors. Since our physical appearance provides a sense of coherence and continuity that sustains self and nurtures community and connection, loss of control over the body and its signifiers is a crisis. Captivity is an

> ultimate boundary situation where human existence, identity, and ultimate meaning are called into question as the captive's world is turned topsy-turvy and his freedom and autonomy are stripped from him, along with his social status, clothes, and other cultural accoutrements and markers. Frequently the captive undergoes various forms of degradation, as he is reduced to abject poverty, subjected to great physical deprivation, extreme hunger, and psychological stress, and divested of all status and power.
>
> (Ebersole 1995, 7)

There are various television narratives of captive bodies in Iraq. Bodies are good, bad, corrupted, and pure. Narratives of "innocence," "scapegoat," and "victim" can be read onto televisual images of three captive female bodies: Jessica Lynch, Lynndie England, and Shoshana Johnson. Jessica Lynch is a good and pure body. Hospitalized and out of danger, Lynch became the foremost celebrity captive. She showed that U.S. forces protect young, female, and telegenic soldiers (Relph 2003).[18] Returning to the United States, she quickly took "offers that have come her way including that million-dollar publishing deal" (ibid.). Images of Lynch entered the contested terrain of representations of gender and sexuality in American society. Youth, blonde purity, and a staged rescue in which she was acted upon rather than acting encapsulate the fable of American innocence, the civilizing mission of subordinating and containing non-Euro-Americans, and the redemptive potentials of violence. Her innocence coincides with several storylines.

> As Westerners, we've put a lot of time, money, and denial into trying to rid the world of death and darkness. Dark and light war with each other every night on TV. We glorify the light and repress the dark. And that's why we love sun blondes. By putting sun blonde in her hair, a woman aligns herself with that light. She plants her feet surely on the side of understanding, of consciousness. She follows along behind Plato like a duckling behind a mallard.
>
> (Ilyin 2000, 133)

The images of Lynch are in stark contrast to those from Abu Ghraib prison. Pfc. Lynndie England regularly stole into the facility to meet her lover, Cpl. Charles Graner. She often remained where prisoners were held and posed, smiling, for photographs with nude inmates who were in sexually humiliating positions (Serrano 2004, A12). The sensational photos of gender, racial, and sexuality hierarchies among U.S. personnel, tolerated by military leaders,[19] can be read as a narrative of scapegoating.[20] The images of England oppose those of Lynch in good girl–bad girl fashion. While Lynch is a suitably submissive blonde "package," England's sexual dominance illustrates the danger of masculinizing women in warfare and the need to punish those who do not submit. The message is that gender equality and women's sexual empowerment unleash female masculinity and aggressive predatory behavior. The negative images of England and the positive portrayal of Lynch suggest that good women are captives who need protection or rescue by men. England, a female warrior, did not need protection, was transformed into a scapegoat, and was punished with a sentence of three years in prison and a dishonorable discharge from the U.S. military.

The images of a female African-American prisoner in Iraq, Shoshana Johnson, contrasted those of Lynch and England. Johnson's return to the United States was "free of big money offers and public adulation. Instead her focus ... [was] ... on fighting for more disability benefit to help her through her recovery" (Relph 2003). Despite her capture and injuries, the sparse coverage of Johnson's case follows narratives of American society in which "African-American women ... [were] ... denigrated by the same rhetoric that revered white women" (S. Smith 2004, 132). The storyline conformed to Anglo-American narratives on race and transformation since the colonial period in which African Americans such as Johnson are marginalized and whites such as Lynch are validated.

> Neither the French nor the Spanish church was averse to converting Indians, many of whom married Latin Catholics. Only the English refused to welcome unions … Intermarriage was not an issue for northeastern Indians. Tribes that adopted French, English, or other native peoples of rival tribes aimed at the full integration of those adoptees … In the English view, blackness and the African body were spoke of and viewed negatively.
>
> (Namias 1993, 87)

Televisual narratives articulate long-standing racial tensions in the United States with regard to the treatment of female captives. Identity and morality were joined as Lynch was cast as innocent while Johnson suffered in Iraq and at home. Likewise, in captivity literature, "white women were placed on a pedestal and at risk when black women and Indian women were experiencing sexual abuse at the hands of white males on the plantation and on the frontier" (ibid., 111). The narrative reads as fear of miscegenation when Lynch was seen as threatened because she embodied "innocence" and Johnson was not, since she embodied "victim."[21] While "black captives are relegated to the background in these narratives, often remaining unnamed" (Strong 1999, 184), Johnson is named; her release is recorded, even celebrated. However, a white female captive is a celebrity; she is sexually innocent, racially pure, and a symbol of the power and reach of the U.S. military.

Race and ethnicity did not impact only Shoshana Johnson. As one observer notes, "in the wake of post–September 11, 2001, anti-Asian violence, I am reluctant to claim that the rights of citizenship once challenged under Executive Order 9066[22] are now fairly locked into place" (Creef 2004, 174). For Iraqis, Nepalese, Turks, Japanese, Koreans, Filipinos, and captives from other states, a racial-ethnic hierarchy of captivity inhibits portrayal of individuals who live, suffer, and fear like Euro-Americans. The hierarchy of television images by race, ethnicity, and religion is especially evident for Arabs and Iraqis. Iraqi prisoners are represented as so many broccolis at a supermarket: undifferentiated, tied up, bagged, ready to process. The contrast with displays of white American prisoners as innocent, threatened, and "good" individuals is striking. When Americans and British behave incorrectly or abusively toward Iraqis, as in the case of Pfc. England, it is cast as individual aberration rather than as systemic fault (see Jehl and Schmitt 2004). Yet Iraqis captured by Coalition forces are depicted as nonpersons: acted upon and disposed of as seen fit, in order to tame a wild country. The case of U.S. Marine Cpl. Wassef Ali Hassoun, a Lebanese-American seized on June 21, 2004, and freed in July, shows the tension of ethnicity. In Hassoun's case, the tension was caused by fear of assimilating Arab-Americans into mainstream American society. Found to be in love with an Iraqi while he was stationed in Iraq, his captivity was constructed in terms of speculation over his possible defection and alleged relationship, illustrating the underlying anxieties over racialized loyalties and the power of sex among non-European Americans. These "others" do not receive the same treatment in the media that Euro-Americans do, since their innocence and loyalty is constantly at issue.[23] Historic attitudes toward African Americans also cast suspicion on their motives, morality, and potential behavior; "before the rise of the abolition movement, free blacks in the North as well as enslaved blacks in the South were seen as an alien population recognizably 'depraved,' 'vicious,' and, for the most part, incorrigible" (Andrews 1988, 3).

Images of four American prisoners from Johnson's unit early in the conflict contradicted the media's projection of U.S. power through horrifically spectacular air raids on Baghdad. Each prisoner's image has fear written on his face. The images are "distancing" due to poor color quality and framing in Arabic font, which explicitly removes them from a Euro-American environment. Distancing highlights the threat to identity through isolation, the loss of individuality through confinement, the loss of morality by being "unfree" and hence "un-American," and subordination to unknown captors. In one series, a prisoner responds nervously to questions. The relaxed attitude of an average U.S. citizen is gone, replaced by the demeanor of a violator, which in fact increases distancing and alarm. This treatment anticipates that of Keith Matthew Maupin, whose probable execution is rarely mentioned.

Disempowerment and loss of body control are linked to sexuality. While seventeenth- and eighteenth-century white male captives were sometimes of sexual interest to Native women, and "Englishmen found Indians irresistible" (Namias 1993, 86), the contemporary sexual anxieties of white America are fear of, or contempt for, homosexuality, and terror at the prospect of homosexual rape of heterosexual men. The image of voracious homosexuals is powerful and ambiguous in contemporary American culture. Gay men are feared as ultramasculine males whose powerful sexuality overwhelms common sexual practice, but they are despised as feminized men who desire other men. As President Bush advocated abstinence in response to AIDS,[24] homophobic anxiety crystallized in prisoner abuse at

Abu Ghraib prison. The images feature masculinized female sexuality and mock homosexual acts. These deeply homophobic images depict gay sex as, by definition, nonconsensual, as one of the worst things that could happen to any male. As such, they recapitulate the intense anxieties of particular groups of white heterosexual American men.

The Abu Ghraib images are homophobic in several ways. They portray a consummate humiliation for Iraqi prisoners, and by implication any male, as they lay naked beside each other. Homosexuality is posited as the emasculating threat behind military defeat. Defeated Iraqi prisoners became undifferentiated, sexually powerless yet sexualized "objects" available for viewing and use. Digitization of genitals supposedly protects victims, but it also dehumanizes them and protects viewer sensibilities.[25] By protecting viewers, the narrative again becomes something that is happening to "us" rather than to the prisoners. The storyline follows Euro-American captivity literature when the prisoners are transformed from individuals into objects that are available to manipulate, define, and control. The most humiliating fate for Iraqi prisoners is being forced to perform mock homosexual acts at the bidding of male (or masculinized female) American soldiers. Made by soldiers themselves, this captivity "folk art" was retransmitted by corporate media. The issue of homophobia in these images was not addressed in media commentary.

The captivity theme is widely present across history in such diverse circumstances as Troy, Babylon and Jonah, Richard the Lion-Hearted and Mary Queen of Scots, John Smith and Pocahontas, Mary Rowlandson and *The Last of the Mohicans*, Patty Hearst, Entebbe, the Achille Lauro, Tehran in 1979, the Tupac Amaru in 1997, and U.S. prisons. Instances such as the captivity of non-Moslem women in the Indo-Pakistani Partition tragedy are less well known (Chakrabarty 2002, 144). Captivity was painful for Africans captured and transported to the Americas,[26] yet important for Anglo-American identity as the

> product of struggles in and against the wild: struggles of a collective Self surrounded by a threatening but enticing wilderness, a Self that seeks to domesticate this wilderness as well as the savagery within itself, and that opposes itself to Others portrayed as savage, bestial, demonic, and seductive.
>
> (Strong 1999, 1)

Televisual images of captives in Iraq thus joined a "discourse of domination" (ibid., 7) about colonization and embodied a system of discipline and punishment that has pit Euro-Americans against most of the world since the seventeenth century. Iraq narratives feature Americans pushing back barbarians, just as the British, French, and Americans settled an "uninhab-ited" continent, made it safe for commerce, brought culture and morality to indigenous peoples, and harnessed resources for humanity's improvement.

Conclusions—Discipline, Punishment, Convergence, Continuity

Particular images privilege specific versions of events, singular anxieties, and a certain history of the world. Televisual event management uses lights, colors, and appealing narratives to draw viewers into specific inter-pretations of events, an approach repeated on corporate websites. In July 2004, the BBC website focused on the "Iraq Handover" with a dedicated graphic and Web pages. The CNN website featured "The Struggle for Iraq," which ignored international protests and the UN's refusal to con-done the unilateral attack of March 2003. BBC TV graphics of a black Earth surrounded by red arrows claim global presence, while the CNN "Your need to know network" avows comprehensive national and global information. Framing by both networks repeats claims to universality and "civilization."

Captivity narratives reflect the language and values of news corporations based in the powers that attacked Iraq. American narratives depict captives as threatened and surrounded by masked men, while reports from the ter-rified family members back home reaffirm the captive's identity (Maupin). The human interest takes precedence over bringing to light the military/security business ties of the captives (Thomas Hamel, kidnapped by a group in Fallujah, works for a company that provides fuel to the American army, while Paul Johnson, executed by an Al Qaeda cell in Saudi Arabia, was an engineer for the U.S. defense corporation Lockheed Martin). In other cases, executions are privatized, mentioned only in passing while governments declare that no compromise with the perpetrators is possible (Nicholas Berg). Corporal Wassef Ali Hassoun stands out as one member of an elite U.S. military unit who loves an Iraqi woman and whose loyalty is threat-ened by his origins and his choice of partner.

Beyond marketing, global presence embodies the promise of new infor-mation technologies (IT). The power of IT in contemporary imaginations is such that when watching TV news, we assume participation in and com-prehensive access to knowledge about events at a distance. In fact, television images more closely resemble photos from a Mars probe: glimpses of reality and impressions, but no immediate and authentic experience of distant events. Television images from the Iraq conflict speak more to cultural and political predispositions regarding identity, contact between cultures, and "others" than they do to technology or events. As such, the images are "active and socially negotiated, the content of messages is a matter of dispute and contention rather than simply being given" (Wilk 2002, 174). By revealing the mechanisms of discipline and punishment, the images focus critique and contestation.

Television images of captivity discipline and punish by what they represent and fail to represent. They reconfigure the Iraq conflict into something that is happening to a collective Euro-Americaland ("us") rather than as a catastrophe for the Iraqis. The Iraqi people are eclipsed by a narrative about suffering endured at the hand of "savages" in the name of a great "civilizing mission" that "reproduces the 'first' world in all that it represents" (Fiske 2003, 279). George Bush's candor about a civilizing mission is replayed by the discursive and material power of *one* part of the world to represent another (ibid., 278). Casting Euro-Americans as victims follows the approach of ABC News with its *America Held Hostage* storyline in Tehran during the 1979 hostage crisis.

> The dominant images were of uncontrollable Islamic fanaticism and hatred of the West. Rather than delve into the roots of US involvement in Iran and try to explain the hostility encountered, the bulk of television news coverage became a human interest story focused on the hostages, and showed complete incomprehension of the volatility and complexity of Iranian politics and religion.
>
> (Schlesinger 1998, 139)

Images of prisoners provide selective views of conflict. Many images of Iraqi suffering do not appear in the mainstream North American media, purportedly to avoid presenting extreme images; thus nonsensational reporting joins the power nexus. The omission edits out an important aspect of the conflict: the images are extreme because circumstances in Iraq are extreme.

Televisual images of captivity reinforce the message of a just, civilized, and "rightful" power doing its best in the face of a nameless barbarian horde. Even televisual exposure of real abuse validates white heterosexual male realities. The parallels with older captivity storylines throws the claim of authenticity into question: "authenticity in terms of the reliability of authors and narrators, authenticity in terms of identity (individual, cultural, sexual, and racial), authenticity in terms of the existential situation one assumes in the world" (Ebersole 1995, 239). The captivity storyline suggests what IT can and cannot do. The impact of IT on the *contents* of communication and the alteration of power is less than imagined, since televisual power to discipline and punish remains tied to intrusive Western conventions of visual communication:

> Photography supposedly finally got linear perspective right, but linear perspective had been defined centuries before by Renaissance painters. Film represents motion by recording a series of still photographs and playing them back at a rapid rate. Television depends on a similar trick, although in this case, it claims to surpass film because television images can be broadcast "live." In each case, techniques of earlier media were borrowed and reconfigured. Photography reconfigured elements of landscape and portrait painting; film reconfigured techniques of stage drama; television borrowed from conventions of vaudeville, stage drama, and film. Throughout the history of media, the context has been one of rivalry to create an "immediate" or "authentic" or "compelling" experience.
>
> (Bolter and Gromela 2003, 86)

Captivity, heroism, and redemptive violence articulate discipline and punishment at a time when "our enemies would be a threat to every nation and, eventually, to civilization itself."[27] Captivity is a tool to discipline and punish women who veer from gender roles, and a reminder that "civilization" is an infinite progression; "a new captivity, a new hunt, and a new ceremony of exorcism repeat the myth scenario on progressively deeper, more internal levels" (Slotkin 1973, 564). Televisual power is part of a cycle of violence and regeneration played out by Anglo-American power and their however reluctant European allies. Televisual images provide what Bataille calls "a perfect coincidence of images" (1987, 90), an intersection in which global presence disciplines perceptions along familiar storylines, but does not reduce communication gaps.[28] The ritual cleansing of war sets a context in which captivity focuses the viewer on cultural contact between "civilization" and "barbarians." Global presence sets the contours for a civilizing mission and highlights the need to protect women from war, men from homosexual contamination, and society from racial mixing.

Notes

1. Television is "discrete" because its influence in Euro-American societies is ubiquitous and banal.
2. See Metzl (1997, 628).
3. Variants of manufacturing consent theory include: Herman and Chomsky (1988), Bennett (1990), Entman (1991), and Hallin (1994).
4. Studies using an interview approach include: Adatto (1993), Gowing (1996), Minear, Scott and Weiss (1996), and Strobel (1997).

5. Ironically, Section 31 of the *Broadcasting Act of 1960* in the Irish Republic banned broadcasting likely to promote or incite crime or undermine government authority and removed much reporting about the troubles from TV. See Purcell (1996, 253–64).

6. For another example of a case study of a specific broadcaster see Crisell (2002).

7. In 2004, for example, the program *The Simple Life* expresses tensions, fragmentation, and contradictions between cosmopolitan urban elites and working classes in American society. The show echoes themes in American politics, culture and society since at least the 1830s. The themes were also present in the 1960s sitcom *Green Acres*.

8. See Gay.com and MSN Messenger.

9. They call it "offering a more immediate or authentic experience." See Bolter and Grusin (1999, 19).

10. See Lisa Parks, "*Our World*, Satellite Televisuality, and the Fantasy of Global Presence" in *Planet TV,* edited by Parks and Kumar (2003, 74–93).

11. Bolter and Grusin (1999, 189) argue that television news and information claim immediacy "based on the shared belief that they are presenting what 'really happened.'" Howells says "TV so often provides us with a reflection not of how life is but of how we would rather it might be. It works as a compensatory document, which represents what we lack rather than what we already have. The dreams may be real, but they should not be confused with reality itself" (2003, 210).

12. See Sconce (2001).

13. On March 17, 2003, the British UN ambassador said the search for a diplomatic solution was over. UN inspectors then left Iraq, and President Bush gave Hussein and his sons 48 hours to leave the country.

14. See Sadler (2004) and Ware (2004). For results of polls on American public attitudes toward the conflict and Bush administration policies, see http://www.pollingreport.com/iraq.htm.

15. They included: Fabrizio Quattrocchi, an Italian security guard shot on April 14; US businessman Nick Berg, beheaded on May 11; Kim Sun-il, a South Korean translator beheaded on June 22; US soldier Keith Maupin, whose death on June 29 has not been confirmed; Georgi Lazov, a Bulgarian truck driver beheaded on July 14; Pakistanis Azad Hussein Khan and Sajjad Naeem, whose dead bodies were shown on video on July 29; Italian journalist Enzo Baldoni was killed on August 26; and 12 Nepalese citizens, thought to be working as cooks and cleaners, were executed on August 31.

16. Captivity narratives depict colonists who had varying degrees of success at this. Some narratives relate experiences of captured slaves who learned native American languages and cultures, escaped, returned with colonists, and mediated between the two on behalf of the colonizers.

17. See also Mertus and Rawls' analysis of the use of torture by the U.S. in the war on terror in chapter 2 in the volume.

18. See also "Jessica Lynch Condemns Pentagon," *BBC News*, November 7, 2003, http://news.bbc.co.uk/2/hi/americas/3251731.stm.

19. "A high-level outside panel reviewing American military detention operations has concluded that leadership failures at the highest levels of the Pentagon, Joint Chiefs of Staff and military command in Iraq contributed to an environment in which detainees were abused at Abu Ghraib prison and other facilities" (Schmitt 2004).
20. For a discussion of narratives on white captives in Asia, see Dixon (1994).
21. As Namias (1993) notes, images of the feminine vary enormously from the seventeenth to the twentieth centuries.
22. Executive Order 9066 (February 19, 1942) by U.S. President Franklin Delano Roosevelt led to internment of 110,000 Japanese-Americans during World War II. See "Executive Order 9066: The Internment of 110,000 Japanese Americans," Asian American Studies Center, UCLA, http://www.sscnet.ucla.edu/aasc/ex9066/.
23. After his release, Hassoun emphasized his loyalty to the U.S. and stressed that he "did not desert." See "Missing Marine 'Did Not Desert,'" BBC News, July 20, 2004, http://news.bbc.co.uk/2/hi/middle_east/3908701.stm. See also Mertus and Rawls in chapter 2 (on torture), and Rygiel in chapter 4 (on border controls) for other examples in this volume of the racialized othering in the "war on terror."
24. On June 23, 2004, President Bush stated: "I think our country needs a practical, effective, moral message. In addition to other kinds of prevention, we need to tell our children that abstinence is the only certain way to avoid contacting HIV. It works every time." See "President Bush Discusses HIV/AIDS Initiatives in Philadelphia: Remarks by the President on Compassion and HIV/AIDS People for People," Philadelphia, Pennsylvania, http://www.whitehouse.gov/news/releases/2004/06/20040623-4.html.
25. For more on this point, see also Mertus and Rawls discussion of the role of the body in public spectacle in chapter 2 in this volume.
26. See Segal (1995), and Wright (2004).
27. See "No Nation Can Be Neutral in This Conflict," Remarks by the President to the Warsaw Conference on combating terrorism, November 6, 2001, http://www.whitehouse.gov/news/releases/2001/11/20011106-2.html. Condolezza Rice adds that "the reason terrorists are coming to Iraq is that they understand that a stable and prosperous Iraq in the center of the Middle East will be a serious blow to their efforts to bring down civilization." See "Global Message," From remarks by NSA Rice on FOX Special Report with Brit Hume, September 17, 2003, http://www.whitehouse.gov/news/releases/2003/09/20030917.html.
28. Attitudes toward IT are suggested by people's relationship with screens. See "People Feel Loyal to Computers," BBC News, April 24, 2004, http://news.bbc.co.uk/2/hi/technology/3625911.stm.

Bibliography

Adatto, Kiku. 1993. *Picture Perfect: The Art and Artifice of Public Image Making.* New York: Basic Books.
Andrews, William L. 1988. *To Tell a Free Story: The First Century of Afro-American Autobiography,* 1760–1865. Urbana: University of Illinois Press.

Appadurai, Arjun. 2003. "Disjuncture and Difference in the Global Cultural Economy." In *Planet TV: A Global Television Reader*, edited by Lisa Parks and Shanti Kumar, 40–52. New York: New York University Press.

Bagdikian, Ben. 2004. *The New Media Monopoly*. Boston: Beacon Hill.

Bataille, Georges. 1987. *Story of the Eye*. San Francisco: City Light Books.

Baudrillard, Jean. 1988. *Forget Foucault*. New York: Semiotext.

Benjamin, Walter. 1977. "The Work of Art in the Age of Mechanical Reproduction." In *Illuminations*, 219–53. London: Fontana.

Bennett, Lance. 1990. "Toward a Theory of Press State Relations in the United States." *Journal of Communication* 40, no. 2: 103–25.

Bolter, Jay David, and Diane Gromela. 2003. *Windows and Mirrors: Interaction Design, Digital Art, and the Myth of Transparency*. Cambridge, MA: MIT Press.

Bolter, Jay David, and Richard Grusin. 1999. *Remediation: Understanding New Media*. Cambridge, MA: MIT Press.

Casey, Bernadette, Neil Casey, Ben Calvert, Liam French, and Justin Lewis. 2002. *Television Studies: The Key Concepts*. London: Routledge.

Chakrabarty, Dipesh. 2002. *Habitations of Modernity: Essays in the Wake of Subaltern Studies*. Chicago: University of Chicago Press.

Collier, Robert. 2004. "Migrants Trade Poverty for Danger." *San Francisco Chronicle*, August 5, A15.

Creef, Elena Tajima. 2004. *Imaging Japanese America: The Visual Construction of Citizenship, Nation, and the Body*. New York: New York University Press.

Crisell, Andrew. 2002. *An Introductory History of British Broadcasting*. New York: Routledge.

Dartnell, Michael. 2006. *Insurgency Online: Web Activism and Global Conflict*. Toronto: University of Toronto Press.

Dixon, Robert. 1994. "The Unfinished Commonwealth: Boundaries of Civility in Popular Australian Fiction in the First Commonwealth Decade." In *De-scribing Empire: Post-Colonialism and Textuality*, edited by Chris Tiffin and Alan Lawson, 131–51. London: Routledge.

Ebersole, Gary. 1995. *Captured by Texts: Puritan to Post-Modern Images of Indian Captivity*. Charlottesville: University of Virginia Press.

El-Nawawy, Mohammed, and Adel Iskandar. 2002. *Al-Jazeera: How the Free Arab News Network Scooped the World and Changed the Middle East*. Boulder, CO: Westview.

Entman, Robert. 1991. "Framing US Coverage of International News: Contrasts in Narratives of the KAL and Iran Air Incidents." *Journal of Communication* 41, no. 4: 6–27.

Fiske, John. 2003. "Act Globally, Think Locally." In *Planet TV: A Global Television Reader*, edited by Lisa Parks and Shanti Kumar, 277–85. New York: New York University Press.

Freedman, Lawrence. 2000. "Victims and Victors: Reflections on the Kosovo War." *Review of International Studies* 26, no. 3: 335–58.

Gowing, Nik. 1996. "Real-Time TV Coverage from War." In *Bosnia by Television*, edited by James Gow, Richard Paterson and Alison Preston, 81–91. London: British Film Institute.

Habermas, Jürgen. 1989. *The Structural Transformation of the Public Sphere.* Cambridge, MA: MIT Press.

Hallin, Daniel. 1994. *We Keep America on Top of the World: Television Journalism and the Public Sphere.* London: Routledge.

Harindranath, Ramaswami. 2003. "Reviving 'Cultural Imperialism': International Audiences, Global Capitalism, and the Transnational Elite." *In Planet TV: A Global Television Reader,* edited by Lisa Parks and Shanti Kumar, 155–68. New York: New York University Press.

Held, David. 1999. *Global Transformations: Politics, Economics and Culture.* Palo Alto, CA: Stanford University Press.

Herman, Edward, and Noam Chomsky. 1988. *Manufacturing Consent.* New York: Pantheon.

Howells, Richard. 2003. *Visual Culture.* Malden, MA: Polity.

Ilyin, Natalia. 2000. *Blonde Like Me: The Roots of the Blonde Myth in Our Culture.* New York: Touchstone.

Jehl, Douglas, and Eric Schmitt. 2004. "Army's Report Faults General in Prison Abuse." *New York Times,* August 27. http://query.nytimes.com/gst/fullpage.html?res=9404E7DC113EF934A1575BC0A9629C8B63.

Kennan, George. 1993. "Somalia, through a Glass Darkly." *New York Times,* September 30. http://query.nytimes.com/gst/fullpage.html?res=9F0CE2DA113CF933A0575AC0A965958260&sec=&spon=&pagewanted=3.

McLuhan, Marshall. 1995a. "The Gutenberg Galaxy." In *Essential McLuhan,* edited by Eric McLuhan and Frank Zingrone, 97–148. Concord, Canada: Anansi.

———. 1995b. "A McLuhan Sourcebook: Key Quotations from the Writings of Marshall McLuhan." *In Essential McLuhan,* edited by Eric McLuhan and Frank Zingrone, 270–97. Concord, Canada: Anansi.

———. 1995c. "Playboy Interview: 'Marshall McLuhan—A Candid Conversation with the High Priest of Popcult and Metaphysician of Media.'" In *Essential McLuhan,* edited by Eric McLuhan and Frank Zingrone, 233–69. Concord, Canada: Anansi.

Metzl, Jamie Frederic. 1997. "Rwandan Genocide and the International Law of Radio Jamming." *American Journal of International Law* 91, no. 4: 628–51.

Minear, Larry, Colin Scott, and Thomas Weiss. 1996. *The News Media, Civil Wars and Humanitarian Action.* Boulder, CO: Lynne Rienner.

Mortimer, Barbara. 2000. *Hollywood's Frontier Captives: Cultural Anxiety and the Captivity Plot in American Film.* New York: Garland.

Namias, June. 1993. *White Captives: Gender and Ethnicity on the American Frontier.* Chapel Hill: University of North Carolina Press.

Parkinson, Alan. 1998. *Ulster Loyalism and the British Media.* Dublin: Four Courts Press.

Parks, Lisa. 2003. "*Our World,* Satellite Televisuality, and the Fantasy of Global Presence." In *Planet TV: A Global Television Reader,* edited by Lisa Parks and Shanti Kumar, 74–93. New York: New York University Press.

Parks, Lisa, and Shanti Kumar, eds. 2003. *Planet TV: A Global Television Reader.* New York: New York University Press.

Purcell, Betty. 1996. "The Silence in Irish Broadcasting." In *War and Words: The Northern Ireland Media Reader*, edited by Bill Rolston and David Millers, 253–64. Belfast: Beyond the Pale Publications.

Reeves, Byron, and Clifford Nass. 1998. *The Media Equation: How People Treat Computers, Television, and New Media like Real People and Places*. Palo Alto, CA: CSLI Publications.

Relph, Daniela. 2003. "Seeking the Full Lynch Story." *BBC News*, November 12. http://news.bbc.co.uk/2/hi/americas/3262529.stm.

Robinson, Piers. 2002. *The CNN Effect: The Myth of News, Foreign Policy and Intervention*. London: Routledge.

Rosenau, James. 2003. *Distant Proximities: Dynamics Beyond Globalization*. Princeton, NJ: Princeton University Press.

Rowlandson, Mary. 1997. *Sovereignty and Goodness of God, Together with the Faithfulness of His Promises Displayed: Being a Narrative of the Captivity and Restoration of Mrs. M. Mary Rowlandson and Related Documents*. Boston: Bedford/St. Martin's.

Sadler, Brent. 2004. "Reporter Gets inside Look at Insurgency." *CNN*, July 8. http://edition.cnn.com/2004/WORLD/meast/07/06/iraq.insurgent.videos/index.html.

Schlesinger, Philip. 1998. "Terrorism." In *Television: An International History*, edited by Anthony Smith, 132–43. Oxford: Oxford University Press.

Schmitt, Eric. 2004. "Defense Leaders Faulted by Panel in Prison Abuse." *New York Times*, August 24.

Sconce, Jeff. 2001. *Haunted Media: Electronic Presence from Telegraphy to Television*. Durham, NC: Duke University Press.

Segal, Ronald. 1995. *The Black Diaspora: Five Centuries of the Black Experience outside Africa*. New York: Farrar, Straus and Giroux.

Serrano, Richard. 2004. "GIs Decried Prison Abuse but Didn't Tell Superiors." *San Francisco Chronicle*, August 5, A12.

Slotkin, Richard. 1973. *Regeneration through Violence: The Mythology of the American Frontier, 1600–1860*. Middletown, CT: Wesleyan University Press.

Smith, Anthony. 1996. "Television Coverage of Northern Ireland." *In War and Words: The Northern Ireland Media Reader*, edited by Bill Rolston and David Millers, 22–37. Belfast: Beyond the Pale Publications.

Smith, Shawn Michelle. 2004. *Photography on the Color Line: W. E. B. Du Bois, Race, and Visual Culture*. Durham, NC: Duke University Press.

Stiegler, Bernard. 2002. "The Discrete Image." In *Echographies of Television*, edited by Jacques Derrida and Bernard Stiegler, 145–63. London: Polity.

Strobel, Warren. 1997. *Late Breaking Foreign Policy*. Washington, D.C.: U.S. Institute of Peace.

Strong, Pauline Turner. 1999. *Captive Selves, Captivating Others: The Politics and Poetics of Colonial American Captivity Narratives*. Boulder, CO: Westview.

Taylor, John. 1998. *Body Horror: Photojournalism, Catastrophe and War*. New York: New York University Press.

Tomlinson, John. 1999. *Globalization and Culture.* Chicago: University of Chicago Press.

———. 2003. "Media Imperialism." In *Planet TV: A Global Television Reader,* edited by Lisa Parks and Shanti Kumar, 113–34. New York: New York University Press.

Ware, Michael. 2004. "A Chilling Iraqi Terror Tape." *CNN,* July 4. http://www.time.com/time/world/article/0,8599,660926,00.html.

Wheeler, Nicholas J. 2000. *Saving Strangers: Humanitarian Intervention in International Society.* Oxford: Oxford University Press.

Wilk, Richard. 2002. "Television, Time, and the National Imaginary in Belize." In *Media Worlds: Anthropology on New Terrain,* edited by Faye Ginsburg, Lila Abu-Lughod and Brian Larkin, 171–88. Berkeley: University of California Press.

Williams, Raymond. 1974. *Television: Technology and Cultural Form.* London: Routledge.

Wright, Michelle. 2004. *Becoming Black: Creating Identity in the African Diaspora.* Durham, NC: Duke University Press.

CHAPTER 8

Discipline and Resistance in Diplomacy: Religion and the UN Declaration of Commitment on HIV/AIDS

Evelyn L. Bush

In recent years, religious groups have been increasingly assertive in their efforts to exert influence within international institutions (Buss and Herman 2003; Butler 2006; Casanova 2001; Jansen 2000; Tarrow 2005; Voye 1999). This chapter will examine the discursive tactics that both religious and secular actors use to assert competing claims at the United Nations (UN). Specifically, through an examination of debates over competing programmatic strategies for addressing Human Immunodeficiency Virus/Acquired Immune Deficiency Syndrome (HIV/AIDS) prevention, it will show how different forms of power elaborated by Foucault (1988) are exercised, challenged, and defended.

First, the chapter will show how diplomatic speech privileges a discourse of "rationalizing progress." This discourse expresses a purposive orientation, with attention to measurable goals, procedures, and effectiveness, and a commitment to progress similar to that which is embedded in the concept of "development" (Boli and Thomas 1999, 38; Ferguson 1994). It has been the object of considerable inquiry in the study of "world culture," particularly among those working from the world polity perspective, which demonstrates the proliferation of rationalist culture across a variety of transnational fields, ranging from environmental protection to education (Boli and Thomas 1999; Meyer 1980; Meyer et al. 1997). The rationalist organizing principles expressed in development discourse constitute an expansion of what Foucault describes as regulatory power—power that not only is intimately tied to the expanding power of the bureaucratic state (Ferguson 1994), but also threatens the sovereign power of states whose authority is legitimated in part through appeals to religious forms of identity. The privileged status of this discourse constrains all actors—regardless of the forms of power they have an interest in defending—to state claims in ways that, on the surface, tacitly reinforce a secular orientation toward the sources of, and solutions to, social problems. When religious groups advance agendas or interpretations of social problems that deviate from those of the UN mainstream, discursive attempts to shame them usually take the form of accusations of moralism, emotionalism, or some other nonrational quality that is implied to be associated with religion. Because of the public nature of these forums, this shaming, or the mere potential for it, functions as a technique of surveillance and a form of disciplinary power (Foucault 1991).

Second, however, this chapter will also illustrate how this uniform standard for speech does not preclude religious influence. As Foucault explains, techniques of power can be used by multiple agents across multiple contexts, and as such, can be subverted or otherwise used as tools of resistance (ibid.). Similar to the dynamics described by Knight and Smith (chapter 9, this volume), religious groups are as equally adept as their secular counterparts at using secular discourse to oppose challengers and to achieve their objectives. Furthermore, by disciplining language into a form that satisfies the rationalist terms of debate, religious groups can enact changes in UN documents in ways that render the influence of religious authorities barely perceptible to the casual observer—that is, surveillance disciplines the forms, but not necessarily the content, of competing claims.

Even when the religious dimensions of conflict are perceptible, press accounts are often sufficiently obscure as to give the impression that the given conflict is reducible to a simplistic "religious vs. secular" antagonism. As a result, the values-based agendas of both religious and secular actors, and the multiple intersecting dimensions of conflict to which they are relevant, are less subject to scrutiny than would be the case if the values and objectives underlying preferred courses of action were made explicit. One implication of this uniform, rationalist discourse, which will be illustrated in this chapter, is that issues pertaining to religion and human rights, which often lie at the heart of contentious debates, are sidestepped and therefore left unresolved.

This chapter will introduce the contours of this discursive terrain by exploring diplomatic conflicts over the prevention of HIV/AIDS. In particular, I analyze UN documents pertaining to the negotiations over the UN Declaration of Commitment on HIV/AIDS (the Declaration), which was drafted and signed in 2001 at the UN General Assembly Special Session on HIV/AIDS. Conflicts over the Declaration were ultimately conflicts over how the problem of HIV/AIDS was to be defined. This control over interpretation, or the power to problematize, is itself identified by Foucault as an important form of power, one function of which is the exclusion of alternative interpretations and solutions (Edelman 1992; Ferguson 1994; Leatherman, chap. 1, this volume). During the negotiations over the Declaration, states' representatives disagreed over whether the crisis was best defined in terms of rationalism or morality. Were solutions to the pandemic to be found in the expert application of specifically targeted surveillance techniques or in a strengthening of moral authority that prohibited risky behaviors? Thus, the opposing factions were advocating, or defending, the rights to two different forms of power, one regulatory and one simultaneously disciplinary and pastoral.[1]

Both religious and secular actors, however, debated the Declaration in terms of science and program effectiveness—that is, the same discourse that was used to shame religious actors into compliance with the dominant paradigm was also used as a basis for asserting counterclaims. What this discourse obscured, however, was the fact that debates over the Declaration involved conflicts that cut across multiple, intersecting dimensions: religious vs. secular, conservative vs. liberal, global North vs. global South, state vs. civil society, individualist vs. collectivist rights, women vs. patriarchy.

In fact, the entire session should be viewed as having meaning and implications that go beyond the global institutional response to HIV/AIDS. Its more fundamental meaning and function can also be understood as the ritual production, affirmation, and contestation of a unified moral order. In many ways, the session had the features of a ceremony of power (Foucault 1991)—one comprised of extremely repetitive, near-uniform speeches, presented in a tightly structured format, and amid the material symbols of national and global institutional authority. These ritual enactments were oriented not only toward producing conformity to principals of rationalizing progress, but also toward the affirmation of a unified world community, self-defined as "apolitical," in which exercises of asymmetrical power are absent, or at least ameliorated, through rational procedures for problem solving and debate. The public nature of the session—and the surveillance of diplomatic speeches by the media, which take for granted the dominant discursive paradigm—further facilitated the impression of a unified moral order opposed by a marginal set of rogue contenders. It accomplished this by shaming, or punishing, deviations from the dominant discursive model. By throwing the religious vs. secular dimension into sharpest relief, however, this disciplining technique obscured the complex, intersecting, and competing dimensions along which power was in fact being exercised and resisted. For Foucault, as Leatherman points out (chapter 1, this volume), it is this entire "grid" of relations that must be taken into account to understand the effects of various techniques of power in historical context.

Dimensions of Conflict

Conflicts over religion at the UN, by and large, are not conflicts between different religions. Instead, cleavages occur in more varied and interesting ways. First, conflicts that are simultaneously transcultural and intrareligious have been of tremendous importance in recent years. These conflicts have almost invariably been over issues having to do with women, sexual orientation, or reproductive freedom, with family planning and AIDS most frequently in the spotlight. Usually breaking down across "liberal" and "conservative" lines (by current American definitions), the alliances formed around these cleavages are internally quite diverse, at once cutting across religious and national identities while creating cleavages within religions and countries. In other words, the same issues that create intrareligious conflicts often serve as the basis for powerful interreligious alliances. On the conservative side, which to varying degrees opposes contraception, abortion, and equality with regard to sexual orientation, it is not uncommon to find states and nongovernmental organizations (NGOs) from the North and South working hand in hand along with conservative American evangelicals, the Vatican, and Islamic NGOs and states.[2] The same diversity is found in coalitions on the left, which favor freedom of sexual orientation, as well as women's control over decisions pertaining to the timing and spacing of children, including legal access to contraception and abortion. Supporters of this position are also found in the North and South, and among religious and secular advocates alike. At least when it comes to issues of sexuality, reproduction, and the human rights of women, transnational conflict is organized less along the lines of Samuel Huntington's *Clash of Civilizations* (1998) and more along those of James Davidson Hunter's *Culture Wars* (1992).

But this dimension of conflict is complicated by a second dimension that runs, albeit roughly, across North vs. South lines. Some will recognize in this dimension the controversial battle between universalism and relativism or, in human rights language, individual vs. collective/corporate rights (hereafter referred to as "collective" rights). In terms of religion, by and large, northern states assign priority to an individualist model of religious freedom that recognizes the rights of individuals to freely choose adherence, or non-adherence, to any given religion. In contrast, southern states, especially those in the Middle East, are more likely than their northern counterparts to assign priority to a collective rights framework that prioritizes religious rights as properties of groups. From the collectivist perspective, "outsiders" (often northern) who intervene on behalf of individuals (usually women), whose human rights are violated in the name of religion, are agents of "cultural imperialism." Charges of cultural imperialism are taken seriously enough in diplomatic circles that, in order to avoid them, speakers will avoid discussing contentious religious issues as religious issues in public forums. Instead, opposing positions are justified in terms of "program effectiveness," "compatibility with development objectives," and so on.

Nonetheless, through argumentation over "effectiveness," competing models of religious freedom are promoted and defended, as was the case during the negotiations over sexuality and the Declaration. The dominant position among states' representatives at the Special Session was that freedom of sexual orientation is a human right, one that requires protection regardless of religious or cultural context. That is, an individualist model of religious freedom is tacitly assumed, meaning that protection of a right to sexual orientation is not seen as violating the religious freedom of any individual. Furthermore, protection of that right is identified as essential to the identification and treatment of persons living with HIV/AIDS. At the session, this position conflicted with that of the representatives of many Muslim countries, as well as the Vatican,[3] who adhere to interpretations of religion that define homosexual relations, along with any sexual relations outside of marriage, as immoral. What is more, as I will demonstrate below, members of the Organization of the Islamic Conference (OIC) implicitly assign priority to religion as a collective right. Therefore, while individualists–universalists give priority to freedom of sexual orientation as an individual human right, the requirement that governments proactively protect that right is interpreted by collectivists–relativists as a violation of cultural rights.

The conflicts between North and South and over interpretations of religious freedom intersect with another dimension of conflict—conflict among states and NGOs. Southern governments have often made the accusation that northern transnational NGOs function as Trojan horses that carry not only Western values, including Christianity, but program objectives favoring northern states' economic interests (see, for example, "NGOs: Sins of the Secular Missionaries," 2000). From this perspective, support for NGOs that challenge a government's policies are viewed as illegitimate, "back-door" intrusions into the internal affairs of states.

These claims against northern NGOs take on added significance when we consider them in light of competing models of religion–state relations. In the context of the debate over HIV/AIDS and homosexuality, in countries where religion is viewed as a legitimate basis for law and government, nonmarital sexual relations may be deemed not only as sinful, but also as crimes against the state. Even if specific sexual practices are not prohibited by laws, states may nonetheless refrain from intervening in local, cultural enforcement of sexual norms. Thus, the requirement that states intervene to protect individuals who violate religious norms pertaining to sexuality would constitute a change in state behavior. Therefore, NGO insistence upon freedom of sexual orientation is not only viewed in light of the challenges NGOs pose to religious authorities, but also in light of international relations, and as one of many instruments through which northern governments exercise power over southern governments.

Finally, we can add to the "NGO vs. state" dimension of conflict the issue of competition within religious economies and how it has been impacted by the greatly expanded role of faith-based organizations (FBOs) within the NGO universe since the end of the Cold War (Hearn 2002). With religious missions increasingly taking the form of development NGOs (ibid.), what has occurred is a close marriage between the regulatory and pastoral forms of governmentality discussed by Knight and Smith (chapter 9, this volume). The expanded role that FBOs have come to play in HIV/AIDS prevention and care through the U.S. President's Emergency Plan for AIDS Relief (PEPFAR) is only a more recent manifestation of a symbiotic relationship between religion and development organizations that has been developing since the 1980s (ibid.). Given the political support it derives from conservative evangelicals, the Bush administration has had an interest in promoting and protecting conservative religion's place in the public sphere and as the preferred framework for interpreting and responding to HIV/AIDS. Thus, the PEPFAR guidelines' stipulation that two-thirds of programs focusing on prevention of the sexual transmission of AIDS endorse "Abstinence-Be Faithful" approaches (Cohen 2006) comes as little surprise.

At the same time, the very presence of U.S.-based Christian FBOs in foreign contexts requires an individualist model of religious freedom. If we consider the interests that religious groups have in evangelizing "emerging religious markets," not only does the individualist model legitimate, and indeed provide protection for, FBOs and Christian missions, to the extent that it constitutes a "free-market" model of religious competition, it will work to the advantage of the more powerful religious "entrepreneurs" in the religious field—those with abundant resources and ties to northern states, and those that programmatically support international development objectives and the economic agendas upon which they are based. Thus, at the time of this writing, the Bush administration's interests in the cultural rights debate were ambiguous.

Taken as a whole, then, the conflicts that ensue over HIV/AIDS at the UN are multilayered and complex, and have issues of religious freedom at their core. However, as the following cases will show, the rationalism of diplomatic language, along with assumptions embedded in journalism and public speech, obscure this complexity by reducing these various layers of conflict to a strictly dichotomous sacred vs. secular antagonism. This does not preclude, however, actors on all sides of the debate using rationalist reductionism to their advantage, whether to discipline and punish challengers or to resist authority.

Summary of the Debates

Two debates will be discussed in this chapter. The first debate was over the participation of an NGO called the International Gay and Lesbian Human Rights Commission (IGLHRC). During the months prior to the convening of the Special Session, 11 states raised objections to this NGO's participation in the session, culminating in its removal from the list of participants. Debates over the NGO's participation status ensued up until the first day of the session in the General Assembly. During the debate in the General Assembly, neither religion nor homosexuality was mentioned by the Islamic states that opposed the NGO's participation. Rather, the conflict played out on strictly procedural grounds.

A second controversy that emerged was over language used in the draft document of the Declaration of Commitment on HIV/AIDS. Specifically, the draft Declaration that was presented for negotiation prior to the session made explicit references to "men who have sex with men, sex workers and their partners, and injecting drug users and their sex partners" (Human Rights Watch 2001). Arguments both for and against the inclusion of this "explicit" language were made during the session, as well as during informal negotiations over the document that took place during the months prior to the session. By the end of the three-day session, the text had been revised in subtle ways. Rather than directly naming these vulnerable *groups*, the document referred to *behaviors* that increase vulnerability, including "risky and unsafe sexual behavior and injecting drug use" (UN General Assembly 2001c, 26, par. 62). The phrase "men who have sex with men" was no longer present in the document and was subsumed under a more ambiguous phrase, "vulnerable groups"; the reference to "sex workers" was rephrased as "all types of sexual exploitation of women, girls and boys, including for commercial purposes" (ibid. 27, par. 63). The changes in wording, though barely perceptible to the casual observer, and leaving no obvious trace of religious influence, were the culmination of heated debates that involved objections raised by members of the OIC, the Vatican, and the United States (Bosely 2001).

A close reading of the press releases, briefings, and session transcripts pertaining to these conflicts illustrates two things. First, session participants and observers (i.e., the press) make distinctions about discourse that define it as either "value-laden" and "cultural" on the one hand, or "factual" and "based in reality" on the other. In particular, claims made by religious organizations are vulnerable to being discredited as culturally determined, and therefore uninformed, while secular claims are more readily awarded the status of objectivity. However, when speakers' claims are evaluated as falling into one of these two categories, the evaluations are based less on the actual content of speakers' claims, and more on the status of the party making them. In essence, accusations of irrational motivation or logic are used to publicly shame religion-based parties to the debate that challenge dominant perspectives, while the status of "factual" is used to legitimate the speech of parties that endorse prevailing standards. This discursive reduction of the conflict to one of religion vs. science, or values vs. objectivity, not only disciplines diplomatic speech into the framework of rationalizing progress, but also obscures the complexity of the intersecting dimensions along which power is exercised in UN diplomacy.

Second, I will show two ways that religious actors skillfully use rationalizing tactics to negotiate this context and, in doing so, subvert this technology of power in order to serve their own interests.[4] First, they use procedural rationalism, by challenging controversial proposals and platforms on procedural grounds, or by exploiting certain procedural ground rules, rather than by attacking the actual substance or values promoted by dominant groups. Second, at other times, religious groups introduce "evidence" that they interpret as indicating religion's superiority as a practical solution to the prevention of HIV transmission. By "playing along" with fictions that (a) the UN is an apolitical institution whose rational procedures for debate ensure fairness and neutrality, and (b) the debates during the session really were only over program effectiveness, religious groups exerted influence over the drafting of the Declaration in ways that prevented the collectivist rights position—and its human rights implications—from becoming a focus of public debate.

Before proceeding with the analysis, it should be pointed out that religion is not marginal to HIV/AIDS prevention and care. The need for religious cooperation with international institutions is actually quite practical and has to do in large part with resources, such as hospitals, schools, and transnational networks that are under religious control. This is especially the case in Africa, where, due to the legacy of colonialism, religious institutions are among the only nongovernmental structures whose networks are broad and deep enough to reach most of the population in any given territory.

For instance, the Catholic Church alone, including agencies of the Catholic Church and Catholic NGOs, was providing 25 percent of care to HIV/AIDS victims globally at the time of the UN Special Session (Barragan 2001). Furthermore, by the time of the session in 2001, evidence had begun to emerge suggesting that, at least when condom use is incorporated, religion-based programs could be highly successful. For example, the "AIDS education through Imams" program was not only described in a Joint UN Program on HIV/AIDS (UNAIDS) study as "remarkably successful" at the time, but was referred to by several delegations at the session as a model for other countries to consider incorporating.[5] Arguably, mobilization of an effort as extensive as "AIDS education through Imams" would have been difficult to achieve without the preexisting networks of the religious communities. The resource-related characteristics (including cultural resources) of religious institutions and networks provide a core incentive for states and international institutions to include religious groups in the development and implementation of their programs. The analyses that follow should be read with these practical, along with the normative, matters in mind.[6]

The Debate over NGO Participation

Typically, NGOs that wish to participate in UN forums must first acquire consultative status, a process that begins with an application to the Committee on NGOs. This Committee is comprised of representatives from 19 member states and has the sole authority to approve or deny consultative status (ECOSOC 1996).[7] National NGOs from countries without membership on the Committee on NGOs can be admitted to consultative status only after consultation with the member state that hosts the NGO's secretariat (ibid., pt. 1, art. 8). Consistent with this policy, only organizations that are registered within the state out of which they operate are permitted to apply for accreditation (ibid.). Therefore, any NGO that is not recognized as legitimate by a state out of which it operates is likely to be denied accreditation. In other words, NGO accreditation is subject to the approval of states and is vulnerable to being influenced by political considerations from the outset.

The terms for participation in the Special Session stipulated that NGOs without consultative status could participate, but only on a nonobjection basis. This meant that any member state had the option to require that a non-accredited NGO be removed from the list. Prior to the session, on April 19, 2001, a list of participating NGOs was circulated. Subsequent to the list's circulation, the IGLHRC received 11 objections, and was subsequently stricken from the list (UN General Assembly 2001d). When the amended list (which did not include the IGLHRC) was distributed on

May 18, 2001, representatives from the European Union (EU) and Canada raised concerns about the changes, and more specifically about the anonymity and lack of transparency surrounding them. The representative from Norway, concurring with the EU's concerns, stated at a meeting of the General Assembly that:

> he found it very disquieting that the list had been changed from the list that had been circulated on April 19. He noted, in particular, that three [NGOs] had been stricken from the list with no explanation given from those that had a duty to explain. Transparency should be at the heart of the Assembly's work, he added. It was unacceptable that there was not at least an explanatory footnote in the document providing information about the changes. Whether or not the changes were legitimate, the reasoning needed to be highlighted for the membership at large.
>
> (UN General Assembly 2001a)

On June 22, the issue was again raised, when in a meeting of the General Assembly, Canada's representative proposed that the IGLHRC be included on the list of participants for the Human Rights Round Table (UN General Assembly 2001b). Egypt, Libya, Qatar, and Pakistan all made interventions in opposition to Canada's proposal. But the objections were not made in terms of the substantive issues surrounding the NGO's inclusion or exclusion. Rather, the objections were raised on issues of procedure (ibid.).

Procedural objections were raised again during the first day of the Special Session, when the Assembly turned its attention to a proposed amendment regarding the list of civil society actors that were permitted to participate in the round tables at the session (ibid.). The amendment proposed "that the list of participants for Round Table 2—the round table on human rights—include the name of Karyn Kaplan of the International Gay and Lesbian Human Rights Commission."[8]

Egypt was the first to raise an objection, stating, "It is not the issue of an organization that will participate or not participate in a round table. It is the issue of the right of Member States to use the rule of nonobjection basis. If we abolish this rule today, those countries that do not move in a group will be the countries that suffer the most. That is why I am proposing, on behalf of the Organization of the Islamic Conference (OIC)—which represents 56 countries—a motion of no action on this amendment."[9]

The next representative that the president of the Assembly called upon to speak was the representative of Canada, who explained the reasoning and purpose behind the amendment. He stated, in regard to the objections to the IGLHRC's participation, that "after lengthy informal discussions over the past few days, it has become apparent that your Office [the Office of the President of the General Assembly] is not at liberty to divulge the identities of the objecting delegations; nor is it able to enlighten the Assembly as to the nature or basis of the objections; nor, it seems, were any of the anonymous and objecting delegations able or willing to share any such information with other members of the Assembly."[10] He went on to say that excluding this NGO through these methods set a dangerous precedent, allowing for a system of "anonymous, arbitrary blackballing" that could have a severe chilling effect on all future NGO participation, regardless of the values held by any particular NGO.

When the representative of Sudan took the floor in response, he objected, but not to any of the points made by Canada. Instead, he objected on the basis of a point of order. He directed his comments to the president, stating that the president

> should have been advised properly ... that the first speaker to address this very important issue after you returned to the Chair was the representative of Egypt, on behalf of all the [OIC] member States, and that was in the of voting on the issue that we are addressing. I think that giving the floor to the representative of Canada was a grave mistake, because according to the rules of procedure, once a motion has been proposed it has to be seconded and voted on, and there should be no debate.[11]

Similar arguments over procedure and points of order ensued, taking several twists and turns as Islamic states retrospectively questioned the legitimacy of the vote due to various questions, especially about quorum. Although most of the procedural issues raised were technically legitimate, at times they bordered on ridiculous. For example, one representative challenged the president's conclusion that if a person had voted, they indeed had been present for the vote, the number of votes therefore counting as sufficient evidence of a quorum in the absence of an actual count prior to a vote.

In the end, Egypt's request for no motion was voted down (63 votes opposed, 46 votes in favor, 19 abstentions), and the amendment reinstating the IGLHRC was put favorably to a vote. At the end of the session, Islamic states, one by one, refused to vote on the final list of accredited NGOs, resulting in a final vote in favor of the amended list of NGOs, which included the IGLHRC. The Islamic states' refusal to vote was in protest of the fact that the Assembly was putting to vote, in public, an issue that was supposed to be resolved informally, with the option of anonymity, and by consensus (i.e., the nonobjection rule). Overall, these procedural debates went on for over two and one-half hours. Not once during the process were the issues of religion or homosexuality raised by any member of the OIC.

Press accounts of the event, however, painted a different picture of the proceedings, one that focused exclusively on the religious dimension of the objections to the IGLHRC's participation in the summit. Although there was an occasional vague reference to the objections being raised "on points of order and rules of procedure" (UN General Assembly 2001b), there was no discussion of what those procedures were, or the fact that the debate over the nonobjection basis for participation had political implications. In addition to the issue raised above about consensus vs. vote, the objections raised by the OIC states also spoke very directly to a controversial issue in UN politics—the issue of NGOs being viewed by some southern states as "secular missionaries" working on behalf of northern states' interests. Allowing NGOs that were not even accredited to participate in the session in spite of the objections raised by southern states could exacerbate concerns that NGOs are instruments of northern states' foreign policy objectives.

In the press, however, instead of addressing the complexity of the issues at stake, the debate was characterized as entirely religion-based, with one reporter claiming that the OIC states raised "moral objections" to the NGO's inclusion [quotation marks used in press report] (Riley 2001). In my reading of the transcript, however, I did not see the phrase "moral objection" used by any of the Islamic states' representatives during the meeting addressing the participation of the IGLHRC. The representative of Pakistan did describe his objection as "a matter of principle." But the principle he was referring to was not one of religion, as the article led the reader to believe. Rather, it was the principle of "fair play." Specifically, he was referring to a procedure (i.e., nonobjection) that had been agreed upon and documented in a formal resolution and then violated in a public forum, retrospectively abolishing the option of anonymity. According to his understanding, the principle of nonobjection meant that "the objection raised by any Member State is not a matter for discussion in the General Assembly ... We believe that it is not for the General Assembly to consider the merits or demerits of any objection. That is for the committee on NGOs to do."[12] By removing the anonymity that was guaranteed to all member states in determining the participation of nonaccredited NGOs, the northern states were using a technique of surveillance, and the potential for public shaming, to discipline the OIC into allowing for the IGLHRC's participation. It was an exercise of power that betrayed an unequal status among northern and southern states at the UN.

In terms of the OIC's use of rationalizing tactics to resist that exercise of power, the point is not that by arguing exclusively in terms of points of order, Islamic states were using a procedure that is novel in the world of politics. Obviously, it is not. The point, rather, is twofold. First, when conservative religious groups use procedural rationalism, they use it in a way that removes their obligation to publicly defend the religious bases of their claims. Though religion may be at the very core of a particular conflict, rather than being addressed in a public forum, it remains predominantly a backstage event. One reason for this backstage status of religious conflict is that religion's status in international institutions is still tenuous and contested. As the following section will illustrate, although diplomatic speech is carefully crafted to avoid giving any impression of bias, there are, nonetheless, subtle ways in which representatives, spokespersons, and the press discredit religion and reinforce secular viewpoints.

This brings me to the second point of the current section. In spite of the fact that religion was not explicitly mentioned during the session where NGO participation was debated, the press nonetheless reported it as a religious vs. secular conflict. As a result, other intersecting dimensions of the conflict—North vs. South and states vs. NGOs—were ignored, leaving readers uninformed about how the exercise of religious authority also intersects with conflicts over competing forms of authority. What is more, the underlying debate was constructed as one between rationalism and religion, when it might have more accurately been characterized as a debate over competing moral frameworks, as will be illustrated in the following section.

The Debate over Language

The main debate over language in the Declaration was over the explicit targeting of "men who have sex with men, sex workers and their clients, and injecting drug users" for intervention. Parties in favor of this language saw it as constituting a necessary statement against the denial, stigmatization, and discrimination that they described as severely impeding efforts to identify infected persons, provide treatment, and prevent the spread of the epidemic.

Parties who objected to the draft language countered that it implied tacit approval of behaviors that were not only morally contrary to the beliefs of their cultures, but also associated with the spread of the epidemic. They charged that, in the absence of a commitment to eradicating the behaviors themselves, explicit mention and, by implication, public approval of "men who have sex with men, sex workers and their clients, and injecting drug users" would hamper their attempts to prevent increases in the prevalence of HIV/AIDS in their countries. From their perspective, identifying prostitutes is not an adequate solution in the absence of concerted attempts to end the practice of prostitution; identifying injecting drug users would not be as effective as eradicating injecting drug use. Following this logic, and bringing us closest to the crux of the controversy, identifying "men who have sex with men" would be inadequate in the absence of a commitment to eradicating the behavior of "men having sex with men."

To begin, there were both values-based and instrumentally based arguments on each side of the language controversy. While the OIC was concerned with preserving what they described as the collective moral frameworks of their cultures, the dominant perspective was oriented toward upholding an individualist model of human rights, itself a conceptual framework that rests, in part, on its widely accepted moral authority. At one point, the representative of Norway, arguing in support of the IGLHRC's inclusion in the session, even described the debate as "a fight about the soul of the [UN]."[13] But the individualist model is also based on moral authority in another sense. The very act of distinguishing between behaviors that should or should not be regulated primarily through the moral authority of religious norms is to make a claim about what is and is not essential to religion and what does and does not affect freedom of religious belief. In effect, it is a religious claim (Asad 2003, 139–40). Nonetheless, the arguments were not consistently treated as such in UN spokespersons' interactions with the press. For example, during a press conference pertaining to the negotiations leading up to the Special Session, the following question was posed to the deputy secretary-general:

> Are you concerned that the final declaration may be watered down so much that it will not have the impact the [UN] would like because of serious differences remaining on issues such as homosexuality, prostitution and so forth?
>
> (UN Deputy Secretary General 2001)

First, it is worth noting that the question posed by the press is not in terms of a conflict between two or more subsets of actors within the UN, but between "what the [UN] would like" and what others who have disagreements about "homosexuality, prostitution and so forth" would like. The deputy secretary-general follows suit in her response. She begins by pointing out that there is much good faith and a strong desire among the delegations "to come to an agreement so that the session ends on a full consensus on a good, strong declaration." But she goes on to say, "I think that ways will be found to find words that take into account the cultural sensitivities without doing damage to the intent of the declaration" (ibid.). The dispute then, is framed as one between an entity called the UN community that is in agreement with "the intent of the declaration," and a set of presumably culturally sensitive outsiders who oppose it.

She then distinguishes among and subtly characterizes the types of concerns of each of these parties:

> Clearly, I sense that there is a very strong desire across Member States to find this compromise, which will mean that they will have to find the right words to deal with the reality, but not to offend the sensitivities of some cultures. It is a reality, and it has to be taken into account.
>
> (ibid.)

This statement implicitly creates and reinforces two assumptions. First, delegates in favor of the inclusion of explicit language are operating from the standpoint of "reality" (i.e., fact, science, objectivity), and second, delegates opposing it are operating from the standpoint of "sensitivity" (i.e., emotion, an absence of concern with "reality" or "facts"). And this was not merely an aberration wherein one spokesperson uttered some carelessly worded phrases. Rather, this characterization of "some cultures" as either ignorant or unconcerned with scientifically established mechanisms of HIV/AIDS transmission was also frequently evinced in delegates' speeches during the session. In spite of the polite "diplomatese" in which the speeches were delivered, the preference for naming behaviors, rather than groups, was variously and frequently described as "ancient taboos," "moral squeamishness," and "burying our heads in the sand."

Taken at face value, these characterizations might appear reasonable enough, especially if we take for granted a popular conception of religion as antithetical to reason or science. However, examination of the actual statements presented by the Islamic representatives during the Special Session reveals that this characterization is not accurate. While Islamic states made no attempt to hide the fact that they approached the issue of HIV/AIDS from a perspective that assigned priority to religion, they justified this approach on the basis of what they described as its proven effectiveness in stemming the tide of AIDS—that is, they did not argue in terms of religion per se, but through the observation that Islamic countries had, and continue to have, the lowest prevalence of HIV/AIDS globally.[14] What is more, in constructing their arguments, they made reference to the same "facts" as those referenced by their secular counterparts—that HIV/AIDS is especially prevalent among men who have sex with men, injecting drug users, and people with multiple sexual partners. But they foreground the fact that the relationship is not due to features that are inherent in the carriers, but to particular behaviors. Based on this distinction in emphasis, they arrived at programmatic solutions that differed from those of the majority.

The representative from Saudi Arabia, for example, drew explicit connections between the religion of Islam and the fight against HIV/AIDS. But, in addition to asserting the priority of Islam in policy and programmatic decisions, he justified his position through appeals to Islam's perceived effectiveness in preventing the spread of the disease:[15]

> The Kingdom is committed to the international recommendations and strategies that are in conformity with the teachings of Islam ... The number of patients infected with AIDS in the Kingdom of Saudi Arabia is small, not exceeding 440 cases since 1985. The reason for this is the adherence to the religion of Islam, which prohibits sexual relations outside the confines of marriage. In spite of this, an awareness campaign was established by using the media to all groups, especially the young, who are the highest risk group. The program emphasizes adherence to Islamic teachings and explaining the dangers of the disease, its complications, the way it spreads, and ways to avoid it.
>
> (Al-Masruwah 2001)

Iran's representative gave what was perhaps the most strongly worded statement on behalf of Islam and did make pointedly moral claims. But again, the Iranian representative justified his position in terms of the "reality" of the causes of HIV transmission and the effectiveness of their preferred course of action. The general point and tenor of the representative's statement are captured in the following excerpts:

> Let us not delude ourselves. The spread of the disease cannot be addressed in a vacuum. The moral aspect involved in and around the why and how of it all and the established fact that irresponsible sexual behavior, of different forms, has been among the key factors in the spread of the disease, cannot, and in fact, should not be brushed aside, under any pretext, even in the name and under the guise of empathy for the hapless infected ... The question, however, for all of us is whether the totality of the international community can bring itself to the point of addressing the real causes of the pandemic and coming up with what it takes to combat it, effectively and meaningfully, and certainly with empathy and compassion ...
>
> Care and treatment of the already infected is all but imperative and should be pursued with vigour as a matter of priority. Yet, it is our considered view that prevention, in the broadest sense of the word and most certainly based on elements of moral choice, responsible sexual behaviour and promotion and protection of family, provides a more effective shield against further spread of the pandemic.
>
> (Sayyari 2001)

This statement makes very strong moral claims against the behaviors that are associated with HIV/AIDS transmission. It also contains, however, a cause-and-effect argument about how the disease is spread—an argument that begins with the same facts as those used to defend the person-focused, as opposed to behaviorally focused, language. But in this case, the tables are turned, and it is the secularists who are accused of "burying their heads in the sand" and ignoring "the reality" surrounding the causes of HIV transmission and effective solutions.

Both sides are in agreement as to the multiple causes of HIV transmission, which they identify as including injecting drug use and risky sexual behaviors such as nonmonogamy and men having sex with men. However, they propose different solutions. The majority group claims, given the knowledge about how HIV is transmitted, that the best way to confront the epidemic is to specifically target for testing and treatment categories of individuals who engage in these behaviors. The minority group, given this same knowledge, along with the knowledge of the relatively low prevalence of HIV/AIDS in their countries, claims that the best way to confront the epidemic within their countries is to limit these behaviors at the outset.

In terms of these competing claims, let us assume, for the sake of argument, that both parties are correct.[16] That is, perhaps "what works best" varies by region and by current rates of HIV transmission. This brings us to the question of whose approach should be represented in a unified Declaration of Commitment.[17] What are the practical implications, from each perspective, of the various forms of language proposed to describe vulnerable groups?

From the standpoint of Islamic states' representatives, to explicitly give priority to—and, from their perspective, tacitly approve of—"men who have sex with men, sex workers and their clients, and injecting drug users" would be to compromise a cultural system that they view as an effective resource for preventing the transmission of HIV/AIDS. This claim is succinctly captured in the representative of Egypt's statement: "Moral and religious values have protected many countries and we should not omit these resources when it is now desperately needed" (Sallam 2001). Yet, it is difficult to support the claim that the mere mention of such groups as "men who have sex with men" in a declaration would seriously influence people's sexual orientations or, for that matter, erode long-standing shared beliefs and practices embedded in local cultures (unless, of course, the "shared" status of these beliefs and practices is more tenuous than is acknowledged by their proponents).

From the majority standpoint, use of the more abstract phrase "vulnerable groups" would "weaken the document" by failing to explicitly name those groups who are most vulnerable. It is not clear, however, why the use of the more general phrase "vulnerable groups" would weaken actual programs targeted toward them. As the executive director of the International Council of AIDS Service Organizations pointed out, he would have "preferred explicit language, but the absence of it would not slow the Council down. 'The entire world knows who the vulnerable groups are. Funders and donors in many countries who do not agree with this are still working with those populations'" (see "Press Conference by AIDS Service Organizations," 2001).

Given the arguably negligible practical difference between naming groups of people vs. behaviors, why the protracted debate? The reason is that the debate, as well as the debate over the IGLHRC, at its core, is not really about program effectiveness; it is about religion and human rights. What simmers beneath the surface of all of the discussion about what constitutes an effective response to HIV/AIDS is a more fundamental conflict about whether priority should be given to human rights as properties of individuals or properties of groups.

On the one hand, there is the desire of the majority to make a public, principled statement regarding openness toward the categories of people in question, and the rights of individuals to live their lives in ways that may or may not be congruent with the beliefs of religious authorities. This can mean the right to challenge authorities' religious interpretations, to reject predominant religions altogether, or even to openly identify with religious communities while engaging in contested practices. From this perspective, matters of sexual orientation and religious observances are left to the individual, and the freedom to choose among them is a universal right.

On the other hand, the individualist rights framework poses a threat to those who advocate for religious freedom as a property of groups—especially groups wherein religious meaning is interpreted solely through established "authorities." From this perspective, the requirement that authorities be signatories to public declarations that, in their view, tacitly condone non-marital sexual relations constitutes an infringement upon the rights of local cultures and, getting to the North–South dimension of the conflict, the rights of local authorities to maintain sovereign rights over their citizens or subjects. The North–South dimension of the conflict is alluded to in the statement given by the Iranian representative:

> The issues and concepts under discussion in the present conference involve long-established fundamental ethical principles and values, they simply cannot be subjected to a post-modern "laissez-fair, laisser passer" mentality and approach ...
>
> (Sayyari 2001)

The focus on protection of "established fundamental principles" in the face of "a post-modern '*laissez-fair, laissez passer*'" mentality and approach is, at its core, an endorsement of the collective model of cultural rights. In addition, this particular choice of words, with its allusion to market rationality, suggests a broader critique of global capitalism and the expansion of free-market logic not only territorially but into all spheres of social and private life, including those that encompass religion and sexuality. To criticize this critique leaves speakers vulnerable to charges of cultural imperialism.

The reluctance to risk such charges however, impedes progress toward the protection of human rights by leaving the really difficult questions essentially off the table, or at least divorcing them from public scrutiny. Consider, for example, the excerpt above wherein the representative of Saudi Arabia claimed that adherence to Islam is the reason for Saudi Arabia's low rate of HIV prevalence. What the representative's statement failed to address are the conditions of that adherence—that is, to what extent is "adherence to the religion of Islam" in Saudi Arabia freely chosen, as opposed to chosen in light of severe penalties imposed upon those who fail to conform to particular norms, especially those pertaining to sexuality? Neither does his statement take into account differential enforcement of religious norms or questions about how prohibitions against risky behaviors might suppress self-identification of infected persons.

Since the debate over HIV/AIDS is framed predominantly in the language of "rationalizing progress," and in terms of prevention and treatment effectiveness, more fundamental questions such as these about religious freedom are subordinated.[18] As a result, rather than precluding religious influence, the lack of explicit argumentation over religion can actually work to the advantage of authorities whose practices are not wholly consistent with prevailing human rights norms, by preventing them from being called upon to publicly account for their stances on religious freedom. In the end, the Declaration was modified in conformity with the preferences of the Vatican and the OIC. It is worth considering the counterfactual question of whether there might have been a different outcome if the debate had been framed in terms of competing models of religion and human rights, rather than terms of effectiveness.

Summary and Conclusion

Considered in combination, the debates covered in this chapter reveal how speech is constrained, or disciplined, for actors on both sides of the controversy over sexuality and the UN response to HIV/AIDS. For the OIC, speech is disciplined to conform to the framework of rationalizing progress.

To fail to conform is to risk punishment by having one's claims discredited as being based in "mere belief" or even "taboo." This risk is particularly acute when one expresses viewpoints that run contrary to those of the mainstream. Furthermore, the distinction been "rational" and "sensitive" is at times made less according to the content or form of any particular message, and more according to the identity of the messenger. In other words, religious groups, by virtue of their status as "religious," have less maneuverability than their secular counterparts in terms of the types of arguments they can make and still maintain legitimacy.

At the same time, for advocates of human rights as properties of individuals, speech is constrained by underlying North–South tensions and by the associated need to refrain from making claims that could be interpreted as "cultural imperialism." Interestingly, the concept of cultural imperialism, along with collectivist/cultural rights more generally, is itself a product of the "dialectics of rationalizing progress" (Boli and Thomas 1999, 38). As human rights law has expanded to encompass rights as the properties of groups, competing claims have emerged, both justified through rationalist discourse. It appears then, that no less than is the case with religion, rationalist discourse is extremely flexible, so much so that it can be adapted to opposing sets of principles and can be used as a tool to enforce, resist, and transform power. But the tendency of these "common languages," rational or religious, to obscure the complexity of controversial issues is problematic. In this case, conformity to a rationalist discourse obscured other struggles over power, such as those between men and women, states and civil society, and North and South.

How, then, do we think about the various actors that are party to these struggles? Are they forces of imposition or forces of resistance? The answers vary depending upon which axis within the grid of power relations we focus on. Beginning with Islam, in the context of the debate over HIV/AIDS, Islamic states and movements are forces of resistance to the secularization and marketization of societies and life-worlds. As with fundamentalisms (Riessebrodt 1993), in the context of widespread and rapid rationalization, Islam presents alternative frameworks for organizing society, all the while relying upon the same technologies that are used by the forces against which it resists. Yet, if we think in terms of gender and sexual relations, Islamic states and many Islamic movements are forces of domination. In fact, resistance to the regulatory power diffused through globalization and international institutions can be seen as, in part, an effort to maintain sovereign power over the bodies of men and, especially, women. To the extent that this sovereign power of the state over men's and women's bodies is seen as legitimate, it is further enforced through disciplinary techniques at the micro level, particularly within the family, and through pastoral agents that reinforce patriarchal family forms.

Likewise, the role and function of northern NGOs is ambiguous. In the context of HIV/AIDS, if we look locally at relations of power between women, gays, and lesbians on the one hand, and men and patriarchal institutions on the other, the disciplinary, regulatory, and pastoral power enacted through ideologically progressive NGOs is a tool for resistance to inegalitarian patriarchal orders, which AIDS researchers have identified as driving the AIDS pandemic in many contexts (Lawson 1999). Internationally, however, NGOs can also be seen as conduits for regulatory and pastoral power that extend global corporate hegemony by easing the process whereby social functions are removed from the state and privatized (Hearn 2002; Bornstein 2005). The large-scale incorporation of conservative FBOs and missionary organizations into NGO fields only complicates this picture, as the same techniques used by more liberal NGOs (religious and secular alike) to democratize rights (Knight and Smith, chapter 9, this volume) can be used to discipline local societies and bodies in conformity with, simultaneously, patriarchal and neoliberal values. Yet, within the framework of rationalizing progress, all of these considerations are discursively subordinated to the question of "program effectiveness."

In retrospect, conformity to the discourse of rationalizing progress, and especially the failure to risk attracting the label of "cultural imperialist," may have come at an unanticipated cost. For in the present, the collectivist cultural rights framework is no longer the sole domain of less powerful actors within the international system. Though at the time of this writing, the George W. Bush administration still ultimately endorses an individualist model of religious freedom (since that is where its international economic and religious market interests lie), it also draws heavily on a collective religious rights framework, one that is very thinly veiled behind a "secular" discourse about protection of the family. This "protection of the family" discourse not only legitimates the allocation of PEPFAR funding to conservative FBOs that oppose the use of condoms, but, more generally, legitimates the disciplining of bodies in conformity with patriarchal models of sexuality and reproduction. How the Christian Right will continue to negotiate the delicate balancing act between the two forms of religious freedom—since it has an interest in both—will be worth observing.

Notes

1. See Knight and Smith, this volume, for a discussion of Foucault's typology of power.
2. For a discussion of the strategies of actors within these alliances, see Butler (2006).

3. In the interest of brevity, this chapter will not discuss Vatican politics at the UN. This decision does not at all imply that the Holy See's position is less relevant than that of Muslim states to the conflicts discussed in this paper. Rather, it is because the Holy See's structural position vis-à-vis other states in the world system is sufficiently different from that of Muslim states that their diplomatic strategies can be expected to work in different ways, perhaps necessitating an entirely different chapter. All the same, the Vatican-Muslim alliance at the UN is certainly understudied and worthy of scholarly attention.

4. For a discussion of how these strategies have been used by the Religious Right in the U.S., see Wuthnow (1988), 207–14.

5. Through it, the Islamic Medical Association of Uganda (IMAU) mobilized 850 mosques and trained 6,800 community volunteers who visited 102,000 homes in Uganda over a period of five years to educate people about HIV and how to protect themselves from it (UNAIDS 1998, 13). By the end of this five-year period, Uganda Ministry of Health surveys showed a significant decline in HIV infection, with some urban health clinics reporting the percentage of mothers testing HIV-positive to have dropped by almost half (ibid. 8).

6. The documents that I used for this analysis include 13 UN press releases (released between February 1, 2001 and June 22, 2001), transcripts of 27 UN press briefings (delivered between May 2, 2001 and June 27, 2001), 10 independent press reports (given between July 20 and July 21, 2001), and the complete transcript from the proceedings of United Nations General Assembly Special Session on HIV/AIDS, which was held June 25–27, 2001. I also refer to a variety of supporting documents, including the UN Declaration of Commitment on HIV/AIDS, the United Nations "Reference Document" on civil society participation at UN conferences and special sessions, the "Action Guide" for the implementation of the Declaration of Commitment on HIV/AIDS, and similar types of documents that were referenced throughout the Special Session.

7. All information and quotes for my discussion of this meeting of the United Nations General Assembly, Special Session on HIV/AIDS are extracted from United Nations document A/S-26/PV.1. This document is an official record and transcript of the United Nations General Assembly, Twenty-sixth Special Session, 1st meeting, Monday, June 25, 2001, 9 a.m., New York.

8. Quoted from "Mr. Hynes," Representative of Canada.

9. Statement by Representative of Egypt, A/S-26/PV.1.

10. Statement by Representative of Canada, A/S-26/PV.1.

11. Statement by Representative of Sudan, A/S-26/PV.1.

12. Statement by Representative of Pakistan, A/S-26/PV.1.

13. Statement by Representative of Norway, A/S-26/PV.1.

14. According the most recent statistics compiled by UNAIDS, Middle Eastern and Northern African countries account for less than 1 percent of HIV cases globally. Within the region, it is still the case that approximately 0.2 percent of the adult population is infected. However, between 2004 and 2006, the prevalence rate increased by 12 percent (UNAIDS/WHO 2006, 3).

15. It is not my intent here to evaluate any of the claims to effectiveness made by any of the parties, only to establish the nature of such claims.
16. Again, it is not my intent here to evaluate the validity of either of these claims, only to point out that each set of claims exists and has instrumental as well as values-based dimensions.
17. Of course, from the Foucaultian perspective, the need for uniformity is itself something to be explained. As Knight and Smith point out (Ch. 9 in this volume), the establishment of a universal set of techniques closes off opportunities for both innovation and resistance in particular, local contexts.
18. It is worth noting that in other diplomatic and programmatic contexts, human rights issues are discussed in terms of their relevance toward "development" goals. For instance, it is common to read that improvements in human rights for women are desirable because they will lead to more successful development, as if some external justification is needed that is not self-evident in the concept of "rights" when applied to women.

Bibliography

Al-Masruwah, Yacoub bin Youssouf. 2001. "Statement by H. E. Dr. Yacoub bin Youssouf Al-Masruwah, Deputy Minister of Health for Preventive Medicine, Kingdom of Saudi Arabia." United Nations General Assembly Special Session on HIV/AIDS, June 27.

Asad, Talal. 2003. *Formations of the Secular: Christianity, Islam, Modernity*. Palo Alto, CA: Stanford University Press.

Barragan, Archbishop Javier Lozano. 2001. "Statement by H. E. Archbishop Javier Lozano Barragan, President of the Pontifical Council for Pastoral Assistance of Health Care Workers, Head of Holy See Delegation to the XXVI Special Session of the General Assembly on HIV/AIDS." New York, June 27.

Boli, John, and George Thomas. 1999. "INGOs and the Organization of World Culture." In *Constructing World Culture: International Nongovernmental Organizations since 1875*, edited by John Boli and George Thomas, 13–49. Palo Alto, CA: Stanford University Press.

Bornstein, Erica. 2005. *Spirit of Development: Protestant NGOs, Morality and Economics in Zimbabwe*. Palo Alto, CA: Stanford University Press.

Bosely, Sarah. 2001. "US-Islamic Alliance Hits Aids Hopes." *Guardian*, June 28. http://www.globalpolicy.org.

Buss, Doris, and Didi Herman, eds. 2003. *Globalizing Family Values: The Christian Right in International Politics*. Minneapolis: University of Minnesota Press.

Butler, Judith. 2006. *Born Again: The Christian Right Globalized*. London: Pluto Press.

Casanova, Jose. 2001. "Religion, the New Millennium, and Globalization." *Sociology of Religion* 62, no. 4: 415–41.

Cohen, Susan. 2006. "GAO Report: Global AIDS Law's 'Abstinence-until-Marriage' Earmark Shortchanges Other Key Prevention Strategies." *Guttmacher Policy Review* no. 9: 2. http://www.guttmacher.org/pubs/gpr/09/2/gpr090219.html.

Economist. 2000. "NGOs: Sins of the Secular Missionaries." 354, no. 8115 (January 29): 25–28.

ECOSOC (United Nations Economic and Social Council). 1996. "Consultative Relationship between the United Nations and Nongovernmental Organizations." Resolution 1996/31, 49th plenary meeting, July 25. http://www.un.org/documents/ecosoc/res/1996/eres1996-31.htm.

Edelman, Murray. 1992. "The Construction and Uses of Social Problems." In *Jean Baudrillard: The Disappearance of Art and Politics,* edited by William Stearns and William Choloupka, 263–80. New York: St. Martin's Press.

Ferguson, James. 1994. *The Anti-Politics Machine.* Minneapolis: University of Minnesota Press.

Foucault, Michel. 1988. "On Power." In *Michel Foucault: Politics, Philosophy, Culture; Interviews and Other Writings 1977–1984,* edited by Lawrence D. Kritzman and translated by Alan Sheridan. New York and London: Routledge.

———. 1991. *Discipline and Punish: The Birth of the Prison.* 2nd ed. Translated by Alan Sheridan. New York: Vintage Books.

Hearn, Julie. 2002. "The Invisible NGO: US Evangelical Missions in Kenya." *Journal of Religion in Africa* 32, no. 1: 32–60.

Human Rights Watch. 2001. "UN: AIDS Conference Whitewash; US, Vatican, Egypt Undermining Frank Language in Conference." June 20. http://www.igc.org/globalpolicy.

Hunter, James Davidson. 1992. *Culture Wars: The Struggle to Define America.* Jackson, TN: Basic Books.

Huntington, Samuel P. 1998. *The Clash of Civilizations and the Remaking of World Order.* London: Simon and Schuster.

Jansen, Thomas. 2000. "Europe and Religions: The Dialogue between the European Commission and Churches or Religious Communities." *Social Compass* 47, no. 1: 103–12.

Lawson, Agathe Latre-Gato. 1999. "Women and AIDS in Africa: Sociocultural Dimensions of the HIV/AIDS Epidemic." UNESCO, Oxford.

Meyer, John W. 1980. "The World Polity and the Authority of the Nation-State." In *Studies of the Modern World System,* edited by A. Bergesen, 41–70. New York, NY: Academic Press.

Meyer, John W., John Boli, George Thomas, and Francisco O. Ramirez. 1997. "World Society and the Nation-State." *American Journal of Sociology* 103: 144–81.

Riessebrodt, Martin. 1993. *Pious Passion: The Emergence of Modern Fundamentalism in the United States and Iran.* London: University of California Press.

Riley, Mark. 2001. "Islamic Nations Block AIDS Pact Again." *Age,* June 27. http://www.globalpolicy.org/socecon/develop/health/2001/islamicbloc0627.htm.

Sallam, Ismail. 2001. "Statement by H. E. Prof. Ismail Sallam, Minister of Health and Population, Egypt." United Nations General Assembly Special Session on HIV/AIDS, June 25–27. http://www.un.org/ga/aids/statements/docs/egyptE.html.

Sayyari, Ali-Akbar. 2001. "Statement by Dr. Ali-Akbar Sayyari, Deputy Minister of Health and Medical Education of the Islamic Republic of Iran." United Nations General Assembly Special Session on HIV/AIDS, June 26.

Tarrow, Sidney. 2005. *The New Transnational Activism.* New York and Cambridge: Cambridge University Press.

UNAIDS. 1998. "AIDS Education through Imams: A Spiritually Motivated Community Effort in Uganda." *UNAIDS Case Study,* UNAIDS/98.33.

UNAIDS/WHO. 2006. AIDS Epidemic Update. December. http://www.unaids.org/en/HIV_data/epi2006/.

United Nations. 2001. "Press Conference by AIDS Service Organizations." UN Press Briefing, June 27.

United Nations Deputy Secretary General. 2001. "Transcript of Press Conference by Deputy Secretary-General Louise Frechette." United Nations Press Release DSG/SM/134, June 20.

United Nations General Assembly. 2001a. "Assembly Approves NGOs for Participation in Special Assembly Session on HIV/AIDS." Press Release GA/9865, May 18.

————. 2001b. "Assembly Fine-Tunes Arrangements for Special Session on Children, Disagrees over NGO Participation in AIDS Roundtable." United Nations Press Release GA/9882, June 22.

————. 2001c. "Declaration of Commitment on HIV/AIDS." United Nations General Assembly Special Session on HIV/AIDS, June 25–17.

————. 2001d. "General Assembly Approves List of Civil Society Participants for June HIV/AIDS Special Session." United Nations Press Release GA/9857, June 25.

Voye, Liliane. 1999. "Secularization in the Context of Advanced Modernity." *Sociology of Religion* 60, no. 3: 275–88.

Wuthnow, Robert. 1988. *The Restructuring of American Religion.* Princeton, NJ: Princeton University Press.

CHAPTER 9

The Global Compact and Its Critics: Activism, Power Relations, and Corporate Social Responsibility

Graham Knight and Jackie Smith

The Global Compact and Corporate Social Responsibility: A Field of Contention

On June 23, 2004, a network of nongovernmental organizations (NGOs) and other civil society actors, many of them associated with the Alliance for a Corporate-Free United Nations (ACFUN), held a public symposium to discuss the relationship between the United Nations (UN) and the issue of corporate accountability. The occasion for the event was another, quite different gathering, the Global Compact Leaders Summit being held the same day at UN headquarters. The Global Compact Counter-Summit, as the symposium was billed, was devoted primarily to voicing concern and criticism that the UN, particularly through its Global Compact (GC) project, was becoming too closely tied to corporate interests and was compromising its neutrality and integrity as an instrument of global governance. The following month, representatives from ACFUN and other groups participating in the counter-summit issued a Joint Civil Society Statement on the Global Compact and Corporate Accountability, calling for effective measures to enforce corporate accountability in areas such as human rights and the environment (Joint Civil Society Statement 2004).

As social movement researchers have noted, the growth of corporate power that has accompanied neoliberal globalization has resulted in the development of a transnational social justice movement challenging corporate and government conduct around issues such as inequalities, rights, social exclusion, and the environment (della Porta, Anretta, and Reiter 2006). The participants in the counter-summit were part of this broad network of activists whose aim is to call corporate power to account, question the capitulation of governments to the interests of global capital, and contest the ideological monologue of market supremacy. Less often recognized by observers of social activism, however, is the growth of a kind of corporate countermovement that recognizes the social, as well as economic, impact of corporate behavior and the need to promote social responsibility on the part of corporations. While corporate social responsibility (CSR) has a long history, dating back to earlier forms of business philanthropy, it has recently taken a new lease on life as an attempt to respond to the concerns of neoliberalism's critics about the disruptive impact of market forces on civil society and social well-being. The GC represents what is, to date, the most ambitious attempt to institutionalize CSR as a dimension of global governance.

The GC was first mooted by then UN secretary-general Kofi Annan at the 1999 World Economic Forum. The GC itself was inaugurated the following year as a multilateral scheme involving the participation of individual businesses, business associations, civil society organizations such as NGOs and labor union federations, and UN agencies. The centerpiece of the initiative was a code that comprised nine principles to which the GC's participants were asked to commit themselves. The nine principles pertained to three areas of concern—human rights, labor rights, and environmental protection—and were drawn from three existing documents, the Universal Declaration of Human Rights, the International Labor Organization's Fundamental Principles on Rights at Work, and the Rio Earth Summit Agenda 21(UN Environmental Programme 2002). A tenth principle, relating to financial probity and anticorruption, was subsequently added to the code (Greenleaf Publishing 2004; UN Global Compact 2006). The rationale of the code was to establish commitment to, and consensus around, universal principles at a global, as opposed to a national or regional, level.

The GC was designed primarily as an instrument of socialization—that is, as a means to humanize and moralize the cold calculus of market rationality and its principal agents, transnational corporations (TNCs) (Williams 2004); hence, it was closely associated with another, contemporaneous UN initiative, the Millennium Development Goals. The GC is an instrument of socialization in the double sense. It is designed to encourage social learning based on the best practices model of corporate performance, and to incorporate its participants into networks of interdependency and cooperation realized chiefly through communicative action. As is true of CSR generally, dialogue plays a central role in how the GC represents itself to the world. The GC set out to achieve its goals in three ways. The first is the establishment of learning networks in which participating corporations report on their progress in promoting the ten principles. The second is through policy discussions among participants about appropriate corporate responses to problematic situations, such as operating in conflict zones. Both of these seem, in practice, to center on helping corporations learn better avoidance behavior—that is, on reducing the risk of being complicitous in rights abuses, environmental harm, or corruption. The third consists of public/private partnership projects aimed at tackling particular problems in developing countries, the most prominent to date being programs to enhance awareness and prevention of Human Immunodeficiency Virus/Acquired Immune Deficiency Syndrome (HIV/AIDS). It is this latter mechanism that is the most oriented to concrete action where rights and security are imperiled.

In the spectrum of CSR initiatives, the GC is best characterized as a promotional endeavor. It relies on voluntary compliance and self-policing on the part of its corporate participants, and does not entail any mechanisms of external monitoring, verification, or sanctioning to ensure that the latter are actually living up to their commitments and claims. The GC typifies the attempt to develop alternative mechanisms of corporate governance to fill the gap created by the rollback of state-centered forms of regulation in the face of neoliberal hegemony, the growth of corporate power, and the emergence of new issues and problems resulting from globalization (Paine 2000). The initiative is a largely top-down attempt to generate a hybrid, voluntary system of engaging TNCs in socially and environmentally responsible practices in what has been termed the "new global public domain" by John Gerard Ruggie (2004), an academic who is the recently appointed UN special representative on business and human rights and a former special advisor on the GC.

Since its inception, however, the GC has been subject to wide-ranging criticism. These criticisms fall into three related areas. The first is ideology. Many activists see the GC as another step in the direction of the UN becoming closer to the interests of TNCs, a process that began in earnest in the early 1990s with the closure of the UN's Center on Transnational Corporations. ACFUN and other activist organizations see the GC as compromising the political and ideological neutrality of the UN while providing an opportunity for participating TNCs to exploit the UN's prestige for symbolic capital and public relations gains. Drawing on the communicational repertoire of the environmental movement, ACFUN and other critics have charged TNCs affiliated with the GC with "blue-washing," wrapping themselves in the UN flag as a way to enhance their public image as ethically responsible (Transnational Resource and Action Center 2000; CorpWatch 2002). Rather than representing an unconditional capitulation to an untrammelled ideology of corporate neoliberalism, however, others see the GC as redolent of "third way" politics that have attempted to give neoliberalism a more socially democratic face (Hughes and Wilkinson 2001).

The second area of criticism concerns the institutional implications of the GC. Observers from different political perspectives acknowledge that globalization has been accompanied by the expansion of corporate rights and power by making nation-state boundaries more permeable to economic transactions of all kinds (see Hughes and Wilkinson 2001; Paine 2000). This process is best symbolized by the growing importance of the World Trade Organization (WTO) and its ability to impose legally enforceable constraints on national governments. There have, however, been no comparable institutional developments with respect to corporate obligations and responsibilities. As an attempt to address these obligations and responsibilities, the GC in no way matches the authority and capacity of the WTO. Equally important, the formation of the GC represents an institutional separation of rights and responsibilities on terms that are not only uneven but also free the WTO from the need to concern itself seriously with the social, environmental, and ethical side-effects of neoliberal economics. While this institutional separation may diminish to some extent the WTO's legitimacy, it nonetheless simplifies its remit in terms of business as usual. The GC becomes the premier global forum in which these issues are taken up, but chiefly in the form of communicative, rather than material, action.

The third area of criticism concerns the specifics of the GC's aims, structure, and procedures. The focus of criticism here has been largely on what is missing, what the GC does not and cannot do, but what should nonetheless be done. The core criticism here is that the GC is just another scheme that relies on voluntary participation and self-policing by TNCs. It lacks any legally binding, enforceable mechanisms to ensure that TNCs are accountable for their actions and inactions. From the criticism of voluntarism flows a host of other reservations—namely, that the GC lacks a system to monitor corporate behavior, to ensure that participating TNCs report on their conduct in an objectively measurable, transparent, and verifiable way, and to ensure that problems are rectified successfully (Martens 2004; Simons 2004). Putting the accent on promoting corporate responsibility through socialization and communicative action means that the GC fails to achieve corporate accountability in a legally effective way (Williams 2004). The ideological and institutional critiques of the GC converge with these organizational and procedural criticisms. The GC and CSR generally do not address the root problem of how the balance of cultural, political, and economic power has been shifting in a direction that undermines democratic governance, nor do they offer a feasible instrument to promote social and economic development that is not compromised by the imperatives of competitiveness and profitability (e.g., Blowfield 2005; Blowfield and Frynas 2005; Frynas 2005; Jenkins 2005; Newell 2005; Shamir 2004). These criticisms have come from a variety of sources, including academics and even observers within the UN system itself (Bendell 2004; Utting 2002). The most comprehensive and sustained criticism, however, has come from social activists who see voluntary CSR schemes as simply a means to reproduce and legitimate existing power relations rather than bring about social and economic development of a more equitable and sustainable kind. ACFUN was the most vocal critic in the GC in the early 2000s. It is a network led by the U.S.-based corporate watchdog CorpWatch, and it draws its affiliates from among NGOs and activist organizations from the North and South, including the Brazilian Institute for Social and Economic Analysis, the Corporate Europe Observatory, the Thailand-based Focus on the Global South, and the International NGO Committee on Human Rights in Trade and Investment, which is based in India. Concerns about effectiveness, however, have also been expressed from within the GC. After the 2004 Leaders Summit, for example, NGO members of the GC, such as Amnesty International, issued a public statement criticizing the initiative for falling "far short of expectations" and calling for stronger measures to ensure corporate accountability (Amnesty International 2004). It is striking that the criticisms and recommendations from NGOs within the GC do not differ markedly from those being made by outside groups such as ACFUN.

The relationship between the GC and its civil society critics reflects general changes in the forms of contention and repertoires of action that have characterized the development of the global social justice movement. This movement is something of a hybrid of "old" and "new" social movements. Like the former, particularly the labor movement, it is concerned with issues of material inequality, security, and social well-being; like "new" social movements, it is also oriented toward issues of identity, cultural rights, and autonomy. It has a reticular structure, comprising a fluid network, or network of networks, whose nodes are different groups, organizations, and associations that come together out of shared interest in particular issues in a contingent and often temporary way (della Porta, Anretta, and Reiter 2006). This network structure has been facilitated by the development of new digital technologies, notably the Internet. These allow for low-cost, instantaneous communication that enhances mobilization capabilities and offers greater flexibility and responsiveness in decision making and campaigning. As Bennett (2003) has argued, communication has become the organizational logic of networked forms of social activism.

The importance of communication also extends to movement strategy and tactics. Social movements have long had an interdependent, if somewhat tenuous, relationship with the mainstream media (Smith et al. 2001). To some extent, however, this relationship has changed as the spread of digital media has decentralized and pluralized opportunities for alternative forms of communication. The implications are twofold. On the one hand, movements such as the social justice movement tend to function in terms of a strategy of permanent campaigning (Bennett 2003). On the other hand, the targets of activism are varied and are constantly shifting in response to new information, developments, and events. As a result, the role of communication is accentuated as the logic that ties together different tactics at the same time that it expands the movement's tactical repertoire. An increasingly important dimension of activism, and one that is especially pronounced in the case of CSR initiatives like the GC, is the constant surveillance and monitoring of major institutions like corporations, governments, and other governance bodies, and the accumulation, analysis, and publication of information about their actions and inactions in the form of reports, newsletters, and other forms of public discourse (see, e.g., Amnesty International 2005). Social justice activism has taken on an investigative, almost forensic, quality. Contention between social movements and their institutional targets increasingly involves the presentation and rebuttal of evidence, and gatherings such as the counter-summit are a way in which activists not only parody the practices of their targets but also make evidence-based claims publicly available for deliberation and debate.

Contention and Power Relations

The enhanced role that communication plays in transnational social movements also speaks to shifting configurations of power relations. Social movement research has generally seen changes in the forms, frequency, and intensity of contention in terms of the distribution of power and how this in turn shapes the distribution of other resources, opportunities, threats, and grievances. While not discounting the importance of power inequalities, it is important to recognize that the forms, frequency, and intensity of contention are also shaped by different modes or techniques of power, and by different ways in which power can be exercised and resisted. The repertoire of activities that social movement networks undertake—from lobbying to protest to humanitarian assistance to surveillance, monitoring, and the dissemination of information—is implicated in the exercise of power and the circulation of power effects. As Foucault has argued, modern forms of power in particular consist of more than simply practices of constraint and deprivation.

Power is productive inasmuch as it brings about new forms of social interaction, relationship, knowledge, and capacity. But even as it reproduces the interests of dominant classes, institutional power generates new forms of interaction and knowledge that challenge the status quo.

Foucault's conceptualization of power is particularly germane to understanding the struggle over issues such as corporate responsibility and accountability, because it captures the dynamic, contentious, and agonistic nature of power relations. This fluidity distinguishes relations of power from relations of domination, which are solidified, immobile, and immune to resistance (Foucault 1988a). While relations of domination do not disappear in modern society, relations of power become increasingly prevalent, inasmuch as social and political forces and capacities are focused on enhancing, shaping, and directing life and the social conditions of life, rather than on limitation and deprivation. Both power relations and relations of domination entail subjugation, but the two vary considerably in the ways in which they function. Domination is unilateral, coercive, and total; it functions through imposition; and its logic is repressive. Power, on the other hand, is the product and medium of social contingency (and the expansion of contingency is a defining feature of modernization). Power functions only in situations where those on whom it is exercised have the possibility of reacting otherwise. Contingency presupposes the possibility of different courses of action and can therefore be directed only at those who exercise a measure of freedom over their own actions. Those who exercise power may seek to totalize its effects, but these effects are never exhaustive, as the contingency of power relations allows for resistance and even reversal. Power relations are multilateral and open-ended, inasmuch as contingency multiplies the techniques and instruments of power and changes its operational logic from imposition to intervention. Power functions primarily not through constraining and preventing, though it may result in these effects, but through producing new patterns of social practice, together with discourses of knowledge and truth that legitimate and objectify these practices in an effective way.

Unlike domination, which acts in ways that are specific to particular situations or events, power functions continuously, because the objective of producing and shaping conduct means that the exercise of power is more than a self-referential undertaking. The function of domination is to reproduce domination; the function of power is to produce something new, to induce, encourage, incite, and direct. Power is not a commodity that can be possessed and accumulated; it is a kind of energy that exists only in its exercise and ramifications (Foucault 1980b). The exercise of power, moreover, is targeted not at people, but at their actions or conduct. Foucault (1988a) defines power in terms of the reflexivity of action, as an action upon action, whether someone else's or one's own. This means that the exercise of power seeks to internalize its effects in the subjectivity of those to whom it is directed, and become self-activating. Power, for Foucault, is about how we are made subjects in the dual sense: on the one hand, actors capable of self-reflection and rational conduct, of knowing and being known; on the other hand, actors marked by subjugation, bound to themselves and to others in relations that are asymmetric or hierarchical (1980a).

There are three aspects of Foucault's analysis of the power/struggle nexus that are valuable for understanding contention around the GC and the struggle for corporate accountability. First, power relations are bound up with the process of social problematization (Foucault 2000). The exercise of power presupposes that some condition, event, or mode of action is problematic in some way, and that it is capable of resolution or improvement. It is through problematization that the exercise of power is tied to the mobilization of ethical values and the production and circulation of knowledge in which the problematic is framed and explained. Second, Foucault (2003) argues that power does not function without resistance, struggle, and confrontation. The exercise of power is always (potentially) contentious. Power is leaky; the problems it addresses and seeks to subsume can escape its embrace to some extent, not the least because the exercise of power itself can be reflexively and contingently problematized. Third, the organization and focus of resistance and struggle are determined by the particular ways in which power is exercised. Power does not have a single, unitary identity or modality. It is finely differentiated in terms of the techniques through which it is exercised, the problems it addresses, and the ways in which it can be resisted and attacked. Given the contingent nature of power, these techniques may complement one another, or they may clash. Resistance and struggle are possible inasmuch as any technique of power can be challenged by deploying the same or some other technique of power as the basis for counterclaims, counterdemands, and counteraction.

Problematizing the Global Compact

Contention and controversy over the GC and corporate accountability have varied focal points and entail an array of different actors and interests. The field of contention is based largely on the triangular relationship between TNCs, the UN, and NGOs and other social movement organizations mobilized around social justice and environmental sustainability. Each of these comprises a network of individual actors whose own interests and stakes may vary and even conflict. Some international NGOs, such as Oxfam and

Amnesty International, are participants in the GC, whereas others, such as Greenpeace, are not. The same is true for large TNCs and labor movement organizations. More TNCs have been joining the GC, but it still seems to be viewed skeptically by U.S.-based transnationals whose size and scope make them crucial to its long-term feasibility. Because of this triangularity, the lines of engagement are more complex than in bilateral forms of struggle. The GC is trying to influence and cajole TNCs into taking action to respect and support its ten principles, and to encourage NGOs to join and engage in partnerships with TNCs to facilitate "best practices" learning. At the same time, activists are trying to put pressure on both the GC and TNCs to strengthen implementation, enforcement, and accountability measures with respect to human rights and environmental protection. TNCs, on the other hand, are generally attempting to resist stronger measures that they see as a tool to curtail their field of autonomy and advantage, while in many cases recognizing the need to espouse the discourse of social responsibility.

For its advocates, CSR initiatives are a solution rather than a problem. The problem lies in the social and environmental side-effects of the expansion of market relations that threaten the latter's long-term viability. Neoliberalism enhances the autonomy of the market, but the obverse is the increasingly transparent indifference, if not hostility, of the market to societal and environmental issues and values that cannot be calculated in terms of short-term cost and benefit. The property rights on which markets are based are exclusionary and resistant to democratic values that are not mediated through monetary exchange, and they have given TNCs too narrow a view of their own identity and potential. From the viewpoint of CSR advocates, then, the fundamental problem is one of lack: corporations lack sufficient awareness of the problems that market globalization fosters, as well as sufficient understanding of the role that they can and should play as "citizens" in circumstances where governments do not have the will and/or the capacity to act effectively to meet social and environmental needs. By casting this role in the language of responsibility rather than of obligation, CSR advocates soften both the attribution of causal blame for social and environmental problems and the strength of any normative requirement on TNCs to assume the costs and risks of remedial action.

There is nothing especially new in this discourse of the beneficent, ethically rational capitalist apart from a heightening of the stakes, particularly with respect to the environment. The theory of social economy arose in the early nineteenth century in response to the social problems resulting from the rapid growth of capitalism in Western Europe. What was deemed problematic was not the effect of market relations on the unequal distribution of wealth and power, but the impact of these inequalities on social relations and personal conduct. The problem was not poverty, which was seen as an incentive to industriousness and diligence, but pauperism, the tendency for many of the poor to be undisciplined, licentious, dissolute, unreliable, prone to criminality, and so on (Procacci 1991). The remedy lay in persuading capitalists to recognize their longer term, "enlightened" self-interest in addressing these social problems through educational intervention to ensure that paupers became the respectable poor. Philanthropy, as opposed to charity, entailed initiatives to reform the conduct of those who lost out in the competition for market success; it was not a case of simply providing supplementary compensation.

The morally self-righteous language has since largely disappeared, but the essential narrative remains untouched: like philanthropy before it, CSR is a supplement and complement to market relations. What has changed, however, is the scale of the problems. Globalization has closed off the opportunity for the problematic side-effects of market relations to be externalized; there are no more empty spaces in which to relocate the system's unwanted by-products, be they surplus populations or toxic emissions (Beck 1992). Appeal to the enlightened self-interest of global capital can no longer be confined to the local level. The globalization of problematic side-effects has given rise to a new discourse oriented around sustainability, or rather the unsustainabilty of business-as-usual practices concerned only with the maximization of short-term profit and shareholder value. Sustainability has obvious environmental connotations, and it signifies the way that the rhetoric of environmental responsibility has become a common aspect of the legitimation and reputation strategies of TNCs. Sustainability is also broad enough to subsume social as well as environmental problems, but without the need to radically reform the imperatives, objectives, or structures of the market system. Sustainability means simply finding less problematic ways to ensure system continuity and stability under conditions where externalizing social and environmental costs is less of an option. This turns CSR into a kind of prospective and preemptive form of crisis management.

In the case of the GC, the problem is framed primarily in terms of rights and the responsibility of TNCs to respect and support those rights. The assumption behind the GC is that respecting and supporting human, labor, and environmental rights will help ensure long-term viability of the global market system, enhance corporate legitimacy, and enable TNCs to see the rational benefits of ethical practices. The GC rightly assumes that human, environmental, and labor rights are constantly under threat of violation and abuse. The notion of respecting and supporting rights, however, frames the relationship between TNCs and rights abuses in an indirect way, as complicity or ignorance rather than as intent or indifference. In practice, therefore, respecting and supporting rights translate chiefly into better avoidance behavior: avoiding situations in which one might benefit from abuses carried out by others (e.g., host governments). Even in the case of labor rights, where TNCs are most likely to be in a position to commit violations, the problem is still defined in terms of avoidance: avoiding the use of forced labor, interference in workers' attempts to unionize, and discrimination in hiring and firing. To respect, even to support workers' right to freedom of association does not per se mean taking active steps to ensure that employees are unionized. Rights are notional. They entail the freedom to make claims or demands without fear of harm or disadvantage, but the realization of these demands is not necessarily guaranteed simply by the act of claims making.

For critics of CSR and the GC, the problem is a mixture of excess and lack: excessive power and autonomy on the part of TNCs and lack of a framework to ensure and enforce TNC accountability on the part of the GC. Criticism of the GC is part of a larger opposition on the part of the global social justice movement to neoliberalism and the growing autonomy of the market sphere at the expense of mechanisms of *social* control and democratic accountability. While social movement activists also tend to frame the problem through the lens of rights, their argument is that voluntary, self-policing systems of CSR, like the GC, are seriously inadequate, as they amount simply to a public relations exercise by TNCs whose public image is a primary ingredient of their marketing and consumer-relations strategies. CSR simply continues earlier practices of corporate philanthropy by softening symbolically the hard edges of market-generated inequalities and inequities, and generating additional forms of social dependency on the interests of organized capital. For activists, then, the problem with CSR is threefold: it is far too weak a mechanism for controlling corporate power and conduct; it reinforces relations of social dependence that are not subject to democratic decision making; and it functions as a way to enhance the commercialization and corporate control of the public sphere, where debate over social issues is distorted by the power of public relations.

Struggle and Strategy

Foucault insisted that wherever power relations function so too do relations of resistance, and it is resistance that gives power relations their contingent character. Foucault (1983) identifies three different types of resistance or struggle: against domination, exploitation, and subjection or "subjectivization." Struggles against domination are directed at loosening the grip of sovereign or state control, and are usually organized in terms of the extension and "reflexivization" of legal rights (the right to rights). Struggles against exploitation are characteristic of the working-class movement directed against economic power that separates people from the produce of their labor. Struggles against subjection are aimed at the exercise of power that ascribes differential social identities and ties people to these identities in individualizing ways. Although Foucault recognizes that any struggle can involve dimensions of all three types, he argues that one type of struggle tends to be predominant in any concrete situation. These struggles form a broad historical sequence, beginning in early modernity with struggles against domination (against the absolutist state), followed by struggles against exploitation during the period of industrialization, and culminating in "struggles against subjection, against forms of subjectivity and submission" in late modernity (Foucault 1983, 212).

Foucault's claim that struggles against subjection/subjectivization are becoming more important in late modernity echoes the argument that the focus of political contention is now concerned increasingly with "postmaterialist" values and the politics of identity or recognition that characterize the "new" social movements (Bennett 1998). For Foucault, these struggles against subjectivization are "transversal" (occurring across societies), aimed at immediate power effects rather than at underlying institutional structures, and concerned with both the status of the individual and the exercise of power based on "the privileges of knowledge" rather than on other resources such as wealth or coercion (1983, 211–12). While this characterization fits many of the struggles associated with identity or recognition politics in late modern societies, it does not fully represent a hybrid movement such as the global social justice movement. Activist challenges to the GC and CSR also resemble struggles against domination, inasmuch as they support the extension and substantiation of rights in the face of repressive or undemocratic governments, and against exploitation to the extent that they seek to strengthen the power of workers via freedom of association and to eliminate forced and child labor.

Where the movement challenging the GC and CSR does resemble struggles against subjection is in the areas of strategy and modes of activism. To the extent that struggles against subjection problematize identity and identity relations, they have a strong ethical and cultural component. Identity is first and foremost about the meaning and evaluation of the self (individual and collective), which lends itself to strategies of contention and repertoires of tactics that have a strong communicational orientation. In his analysis of power and strategy, Foucault (1983) argues that the exercise of power forms part of systemic "blocks" that also include relations of communication, as well as relations of material resources and capacities. These sets of relations, while analytically discrete, are empirically superimposed and interactive; each is implicated in the realization of the others—using "each other mutually as means to an end"—but in an uneven, contingent way (Foucault 1983, 218). In the case of struggles against subjectivization, whose initial objective is to change understandings, the exercise of power accentuates relations of communication and the use of communicative action.

While the movement challenging the GC and CSR has objectives that entail much more than changing understandings, this remains the initial—and recurrent—problem that mobilization must address. This problem is shared by all universalistic or altruistic movements to the extent that their main constituents are not the primary intended beneficiaries of activism (Gamson 1975; Melucci 1996). The problem is intensified, however, by the transnational nature of the central issues being addressed—namely, how to make TNCs more accountable for their human, labor, and environmental impact, particularly in the global South, and how to induce the GC to accept that stronger measures than a voluntary system of good intentions and self-reporting are needed. The movement is often dealing with problems that do not have an immediate, direct, or concrete impact in the global North. Threats to, or the actual abuse of, rights do not usually manifest themselves in the form of events that can be easily understood in terms of risk, crisis, or some other form of grievance conducive to large-scale mobilization. Framing, in other words, is problematic, and this accentuates the communicational stakes in the development and deployment of movement strategy.

The transnational, network form of movement organization also enhances the communicational dimension of activism. The movement for social justice has to mobilize and coalesce a disparate and dispersed constituency of members and supporters whose activism is itself often primarily communicational—petitions, letters, placards, leaflets, posters, public protests, symbolic culture jamming. The challenges of constituency mobilization and coordination are compounded by the need to establish lines of interaction with intended beneficiaries whose own social and cultural life contexts, experiences, and opportunities often differ significantly. Communication becomes critical as a means to manage these relationships, but also as a potential point of friction and additional problems whose solution lies partly in better communication. Communication becomes an integral and reflexive aspect of movement strategy that is key to ensuring the capacity to respond in a timely, flexible, and effective way to the actions of those who are better equipped with material and technical resources.

Because social movements typically lack access to significant material resources and capacities, communication-centered strategies are often directed at the exposure and ethical denunciation of both the actions and credibility of institutional opponents. Activism depends for its own credibility on opening up the breach between what institutions say—their claims to ethical responsibility and responsiveness—and how they actually behave. Activists attempt to use CSR as leverage to demonstrate how actions fall short of, if not contradict, claims. In any field of contention, strategy comprises not only objectives and the means to achieve these, but also the process of attempting to deprive opponents of opportunities, meanings, and other resources—their "means of combat"—to gain advantage (Foucault 1983, 225). By demonstrating not only how powerful institutions act in ways that are potentially harmful, especially to the socially vulnerable, but also how they are hypocritical and untrustworthy in failing to practice what they preach, social justice activists are able to mobilize additional normative resources that help to offset the disadvantages they face. By revealing the hypocrisy of their opponents, activists seek to deprive them of legitimacy by undermining trust, instilling doubt, and introducing risk into institutional environments.

The centrality of claims and counterclaims making to communicational politics carries with it the "postmodern" dilemma: how does the public decide the validity and merit of different, contesting views? Activists have been able to exploit this dilemma by exposing not only the breach between the words and actions of their opponents, but also the contradictions within their opponents' claims and practices. Critics of the GC, for example, have been able to use the UN against itself. In its criticisms of the GC, ACFUN has used the existence of a stronger model for securing corporate accountability that has been developed elsewhere in the UN system—namely, the UN Norms on the Responsibilities of Transnational Corporations and Other Business Enterprises with Regard to Human Rights, also known as the UN Norms for Business (UN Commission on Human Rights 2003). The Norms call for more stringent control over and accountability by TNCs than the GC's code of principles. Using an opponent's own norms and institutional processes as a basis for challenge helps to undermine credibility, reliability, and trust, and there are signs that this tactic has had some effect. While the GC still lacks any effective monitoring or binding decision-making capacity over its corporate affiliates, it has moved to strengthen what it calls "integrity measures" by introducing a third-party complaint mechanism and, in 2006, suspending the membership of 335 companies. What is striking, however, is that these companies were "delisted" not for failing to make progress in implementing the GC's principles, but for failing to *communicate* what progress, if any, they had made (Ethical Corporation 2007).

Power and Counterpower

Foucault argued that power is a force or energy that can be identified only in the manner of its exercise. Foucault's analyses of power were always concerned with the *how* of power rather than the *why*, and were focussed on the diverse techniques for exercising power (Foucault 1988b). Foucault identified four different "technologies" or modes of power—sovereignty, disciplinary power, regulation or "biopower," and pastoral power (e.g., Foucault 1977, 1983, 1988c, 2003). He saw each mode developing in something of a historical progression that begins with sovereignty in the premodern period, and extends into the modern period with the expansion of legal rights (the "democratization" of sovereignty), discipline, regulation, and secular forms of pastoral power closely tied to the growth and centralization of the state and its administrative apparatus. Each technology of power develops as social and demographic changes generate new problems that escape the purview of existing forms of power. For Foucault, the historical development of these different forms of power is cumulative, as each new mode problematizes and sharpens the functioning of existing modes rather than supplanting them. These different technologies of power become superimposed on one another and form a matrix of interacting techniques.

Each mode consists of particular techniques through which power is enacted, and operates at a particular level. Sovereignty functions largely through legal rights and the requirement that those subject to sovereign power respect and obey the law. Sovereignty is a totalizing mode of power, inasmuch as legality, right, and obligation apply to social aggregates such as populations. Discipline functions through techniques such as regimented drilling, training, surveillance, and testing aimed at making bodies more productive, efficient, and pliable or docile at the level of local institutions such as workplaces and schools. Discipline operates on an individualizing level. It is aimed at social normalization by making individual actions visible and legible to authority, and by encouraging self-discipline through the internalization of self-monitoring. Regulatory power also has normalizing or regularizing functions, but these are oriented to the promotion of security and the management of threats or risks to life at the level of populations. Regulation is realized through the application of science to measure, forecast, and generate knowledge about threats, and through the implementation of standards and practices to ensure the conditions that sustain life in areas such as health, hygiene, and public safety. Pastoral techniques, which are religious in origin and are revived and secularized in the modern period, consist in the exercise of power through caregiving oriented to individual welfare, self-knowledge, responsibility, and solidarity at the level of local communities.

Sovereignty (legal rights), discipline, regulation, and pastoral techniques extend and intensify the effects of power throughout all levels of social and personal life, and establish different rationalities for the exercise of power (order and justice, security and risk management, well-being and solidarity). Power relations infuse the "capillary" level of social life as the exercise and effects of power spread everywhere in the form of legal rights, socialization, regulation, normative and technical standards, surveillance, risk management practices, measurement procedures, testing, caregiving, confessional practices, and so on. The obverse of this growth in the differentiation and reach of power effects is a gradual narrowing and reduction in the capacity of the social system to externalize problems as a way of resolving them. The growth and differentiation of power techniques is a response to this narrowing, but also a factor that contributes to it by investing social spaces and processes with the rationalities of power. In this way, the permeation of power simultaneously intensifies the problematization of life as the exercise of power rebounds back on itself as an additional source of contentiousness: rights can conflict with rights, discipline can alienate, regulation can become rigid, and pastoral techniques can create dependency. As Foucault insisted, all forms of power are "dangerous" (2005, 266).

Power not only invests social relations with legal, disciplinary, regulatory, and pastoral force, but it also makes these relations contestable as points of challenge where the exercise of power is resisted, evaded, and even reversed. What this speaks to, however, is not a dichotomy of power and resistance, but to resistance as the exercise of counterpower. As Foucault (1980b) noted, the exercise of power by one means is resisted by the deployment of power by other means. Resistance does not function outside the logic of power; it is a reaction to an action upon actions. We invoke rights to limit the effect of discipline or regulation; we call for regulation and caregiving to offset the realization of rights for some at the expense of others; and those who challenge the exercise of power often succeed best when they impose some measure of discipline on themselves. Resistance compounds the logic of power while nullifying or qualifying its effects with the countereffects of other kinds of power.

The historical evolution of these different modes of power means that their relationship to one another is uneven. Contention over the GC and CSR demonstrates how legal right remains the primary point of reference for the exercise of power in ways that are not only legitimately binding but also accountable. Legal rights dovetail with regulatory modes of power, inasmuch as both are totalizing in scope and therefore lend themselves to the exercise of, and challenge to, power at the aggregate level of social relations. The struggle over the GC is in this sense straightforward in its objectives—namely, to replace a voluntary system of self-monitoring, self-reporting, and self-correction with a more binding, enforceable system of sanctionable regulation and accountability. The problem is that this goal cannot be implemented from within civil society alone, without governmental power. This problem is compounded by globalization, inasmuch as TNCs are often most likely to be complicitous in rights abuses or environmental harm in developing countries where governments lack the will and/or capacity to implement and enforce protection of rights. Moreover, enormous disparities in material resources, as well as the neoliberal privileging of property rights and market discipline over social welfare, have meant that TNCs enjoy far greater access to governments than do civil society groups.

Although civil society lacks the legally binding capacity to sanction corporate and governmental actors, it can nevertheless use the public sphere to pressure and influence these actors. Invoking and promoting the UN Norms for Business is not only a tactical device to gain leverage by using the UN against itself, it is also a more effective strategic tool with which to regulate corporate conduct and to ensure compliance with, and support and promotion of, human and environmental rights. The UN Norms for Business constitute a more stringent regulatory code that could eventually impose definite obligations and responsibilities on corporations in a way that identifies the boundaries between property rights and human rights. Unlike the GC's ten principles, which are defined in very general terms, the UN Norms for Business spell out in some detail the measures that TNCs should take to respect and implement labor rights (including the protection of children from economic exploitation), human rights, national sovereignty, consumer protection, and environmental protection.

The most significant difference between the UN Norms for Business and the GC is the fact that the Norms emerged from the UN Commission on Human Rights, while the GC represents a wholly new institutional creation. Because of their institutional location as part of the existing international human rights machinery, the UN Norms for Business will require greater scrutiny of TNC activity as it relates to human rights. The discussions around the Norms have noted that the discrepancies of power between states and corporate actors require efforts to hold nonstate actors accountable to international human rights laws, even though governments are technically the responsible parties to international treaties. The creation of a new institutional arrangement through the GC should then be seen as a conscious attempt to skirt established UN practices for human rights monitoring and reporting.

In 2005, the UN Commission on Human Rights authorized the creation of the office of special representative on the issue of human rights and transnational corporations and other business enterprises. Its mandate includes the development of standards of corporate accountability and methodologies for assessing the impact of business activities on human rights. Amnesty International, a major NGO participant in the GC, has actively worked to promote the Norms in the UN Commission on Human Rights and to educate the public and human rights practitioners about them. Amnesty International's website devotes hardly any attention at all to the GC, while providing extensive background on the history and current status of the Norms. These two competing schemes for global CSR offer substantially different possibilities for regulating the practices of TNCs. Because the Norms threaten to bring new scrutiny to corporate practices regarding human rights, they have faced strong resistance from TNCs, and one might also argue that they encourage more businesses to participate in the GC as way of heading off any effective international monitoring and sanctioning of corporate actions.

The elaboration of rights and the implementation of regulatory codes are necessary, but not sufficient, conditions to achieve corporate—and governmental—responsibility and accountability. Rights and regulation presuppose universality (rights) and standardization (regulation), which gives them breadth of coverage and enables them to be exercised at a distance through the institutional mediation of criminal, civil, and administrative law. But as modes of power, they are also leaky, and would remain so even if global institutional complexity did not expand the possibilities for evading legal and regulatory norms, and governments were committed to enforcing these norms. When legal requirements or regulatory standards are seen as restrictive, meeting them becomes a matter of the minimal level of performance necessary to avoid violation or noncompliance. Norms and standards easily become formalized, and this encourages a literalist interpretation that circumvents and threatens to undermine the concrete benefits that they are intended to achieve. This is particularly so under competitive conditions in which national government capacity and desire to implement transnational legal and regulatory structures have been weakened by neoliberal hegemony. One way to offset the restrictive implications of legal and regulatory structures may be to tie them to incentive structures. For example, the U.S.-Cambodia textile agreement offers a model for incorporating the effective regulation of labor standards into international trade agreements between developing and developed countries (Wells 2006). The agreement illustrates the feasibility of expanding regulatory oversight of human, consumer, and environmental and labor rights in developing countries via trade and development arrangements that secure market access and other forms of advantageous treatment in return for compliance with rights and standards.

One of the principal insights of Foucault's conceptualization of power is that different techniques of power work on different social levels and are organized in terms of different rationalities of value. Because modes of power are not only leaky but also dangerous, different techniques of power have to be used not only to complement but also to offset one another. Any attempt to make TNCs, governments, and other central institutions more responsible and accountable by submitting them to effective democratic governance has to deploy techniques of power on both the macro and micro levels: rights and regulation have to be supplemented by disciplinary and pastoral techniques, such as surveillance, monitoring, instruction, and provision of the means of material, social, intellectual, and emotional well-being at the local level. What facilitates this is the way that modes of power at the macro and micro levels are complementary in terms of their value rationalities. Though they function on different levels, discipline and regulation are oriented to order, security, and efficiency, while rights and pastoral techniques pertain principally to welfare, equity, and social cohesion. For each couplet, the mode of power at the local level is the means of substantiation of the mode of power at the macro level.

At the micro level, power functions through proximity rather than at a distance, and this reduces the possibility of mediating the ways in which power is exercised. For civil society actors such as NGOs, proximity is risky, not least because it carries the possibility of compromise or dependency. It is precisely this kind of risk that the GC itself poses inasmuch as it may function as a forum to regulate and discipline its civil society participants by incorporating them within an institutional framework of standardized procedures and practices. When power is exercised through proximity, autonomy is at stake. To preserve and enhance autonomy, activists and other civil society actors that lack material resources and are faced with restricted opportunity structures have to reduce risk by means of risk: they have to replace distance with uncertainty. Civil society actors have to deploy communication in ways that use the public sphere as an instrument of risk inducement in corporate and governmental environments. It is by making these environments uncertain and unpredictable that civil society actors can enhance their own autonomy and exert more effective pressure on institutional power centers in the direction of democratic responsibility and accountability. To accomplish this means engaging with corporations and governments on terms that are contingent and conditional rather than institutionally standardized.

Conclusion

Our analysis has sought to apply Foucault's conceptualization of power to the efforts by the international community to respond to corporate violations of human rights and other global norms. While this problem is defined in terms of rights and the balance of rights, it is also an issue of the different ways in which power is exercised on both the macro and micro levels of social organization. In addition, the GC demonstrates how different rationalities of value are privileged or disadvantaged through the exercise of power. We have shown how the attempts to expand global CSR regimes through the UN Global Compact and the UN Norms for Business have been limited in their ability to impact actual practices, and this is largely due to the fact that these arrangements fail to address fundamental imbalances of autonomy as well as imbalances in disciplinary and regulatory powers between TNCs and states. Moreover, neoliberalism has undermined the pastoral or caregiving capacities of states, further eroding their ability to respond to the challenges of economic globalization. Attempts to promote CSR as a remedy for corporate violations of social norms are problematic in that they have only minimal effects on autonomy as well as on disciplinary and regulatory power. What becomes clear is that any attempt to effectively curb socially harmful corporate practices will require efforts to fundamentally restructure power relations between states, international institutions, and TNCs. Instead of serving as partners in global CSR schemes, civil society actors would be more effective if they worked to reclaim the state—by which we mean reasserting its autonomy from markets, as well as its disciplinary, regulatory, and provisionary power over them.

Bibliography

Amnesty International. 2005. "Contracting Out Human Rights: The Chad-Cameroon Pipeline Project. http://web.amnesty.org/library/pdf/POL340122005ENGLISH/$File/POL34012o5.pdf.
———. 2004. "Global Compact Leaders Summit: NGO Participants Raise Concerns." http://web.amnesty.org/web/web.nsf/print/ec-letter-240604-eng.
Beck, Ulrich. 1992. *The Risk Society: Towards a New Modernity*. Trans. Mark Ritter. London: Sage.
Bendell, Jem. 2004. "Flags of Inconvenience? The Global Compact and the Future of the United Nations." ICCSR Research Paper Series No. 22-2004, Nottingham University, ISSN 1479-5124. http://www.globalpolicy.org/reform/business/2004/flags.pdf.
Bennett, W. Lance. 2003. "Communicating Global Activism: Strengths and Vulnerabilities of Networked Politics." *Information, Communication and Society* 6, no. 2: 143–68.

————. 1998. "The Uncivic Culture: Communication, Identity, and the Rise of Lifestyle Politics." *PS: Political Science and Politics* 31, no. 4: 41–61.

Blowfield, Michael. 2005. "Corporate Social Responsibility: Reinventing the Meaning of Development?" *International Affairs* 81, no. 3: 515–24.

Blowfield, Michael, and Jedrzej George Frynas. 2005. "Setting New Agendas: Critical Perspectives on Corporate Social Responsibility in the Developing World." *International Affairs* 81, no. 3: 499–513.

CorpWatch. 2002. "Greenwash + 10: The U.N.'s Global Compact, Corporate Accountability and the Johannesburg Earth Summit." http://www.corwatch.org/downloads/gw10.pdf.

della Porta, Donatella, Massimiliano Anretta, and Herbert Reiter. 2006. *Globalization from Below: Transnational Activists and Protest Networks*. Minneapolis and London: University of Minnesota Press.

Ethical Corporation. 2007. "The UN Global Compact—Surviving Without Annan." http://www.ethicalcorp.com/content.asp?ContentID=4928.

Foucault, Michel. 2005. "Is It Useless to Revolt?" In *Foucault and the Iranian Revolution: Gender and the Seductions of Islam*, ed. Janet Afaray and Kevin B. Anderson, 263–67. Chicago and London: University of Chicago Press. Originally published in *Le Monde*, May 11–12, 1979, 1.

————. 2003. *"Society Must Be Defended": Lectures at the Collège de France 1975–1976*. Trans. David Macey. New York: Picador.

————. 2000. "Governmentality." In *Power: Vol. 3 of the Essential Works of Foucault 1954–1984*, ed. James Faubion, trans. Robert Hurley and others, 201–22. New York: New Press.

————. 1988a. "The Ethic of Care for the Self as a Practice of Freedom: An Interview." In *The Final Foucault*, ed. James Bernauer and David Rasmussen, trans. J. D. Gauthier, 1–20. London and Cambridge, MA: MIT Press.

————. 1988b. "On Power." In *Michel Foucault. Politics, Philosophy, Culture: Interviews and Other Writings 1977–1984*, ed. Lawrence Kritzman, trans. Alan Sheridan, 96–109. New York and London: Routledge.

————. 1988c. "Politics and Reason." In *Michel Foucault. Politics, Philosophy, Culture: Interviews and Other Writings 1977–1984*, ed. Lawrence Kritzman, trans. Alan Sheridan, 57–85. New York and London: Routledge.

————. 1983. "The Subject and Power." In *Michel Foucault: Beyond Structuralism and Hermeneutics*, ed. Herbert Dreyfus and Paul Rabinow, 208–26. 2nd ed. Chicago: University of Chicago Press.

————. 1980a. "Truth and Power." In *Power/Knowledge: Selected Interviews and Other Writings 1972–1977*, ed. Colin Gordon, trans. Colin Gordon, Leo Marshall, John Mepham, and Kate Soper, 109–33. New York: Pantheon Books.

————. 1980b. "Two Lectures." In *Power/Knowledge: Selected Interviews and Other Writings 1972–1977*, ed. Colin Gordon, trans. Colin Gordon, Leo Marshall, John Mepham, and Kate Soper, 109–33. New York: Pantheon Books.

————. 1977. *Discipline and Punish: The Birth of the Prison*. Trans. A. Sheridan. New York: Pantheon Books.

Frynas, Jedrzej George. 2005. "The False Developmental Promise of Corporate Social Responsibility: Evidence from Multinational Companies." *International Affairs* 81, no. 3: 581–98.

Gamson, William. 1975. *The Strategy of Social Protest*. Homewood, IL: Dorsey.

Greenleaf Publishing. 2004. "The U.N. Global Compact: A Primer on the Principles." http://www.greenleaf-publishing.com/pdfs/rtbprime.pdf.

Hughes, Steve, and Rorden Wilkinson. 2001. "The Global Compact: Promoting Corporate Responsibility?" *Environmental Politics* 10, no. 1: 155–59.

Jenkins, Rhys. 2005. "Globalization, Corporate Responsibility and Poverty." *International Affairs* 81, no. 3: 525–40.

Joint Civil Society Statement on the Global Compact and Corporate Accountability. 2004. http://www.globalpolicy.org/reform/business/2004/07gcstatement.pdf.

Martens, Jens. 2004. "Precarious 'Partnerships': Six Problems of the Global Compact between Business and the U.N." New York: Global Policy Forum. http://www.globalpolicy.org/reform/business/2004/0623partnerships.htm.

Melucci, Alberto. 1996. *Challenging Codes: Collective Action in the Information Age*. Cambridge: Cambridge University Press.

Newell, Peter. 2005. "Citizenship, Accountability and Community: The Limits of the CSR Agenda." *International Affairs* 81, no. 3: 541–57.

Paine, Ellen. 2000. "The Road to the Global Compact: Corporate Power and the Battle over Global Public Policy at the United Nations." New York: Global Policy Forum. http://www.globalpolicy.org/reform/papers/2000/road.htm.

Procacci, Giovanna. 1991. "Social Economy and the Government of Poverty." In *The Foucault Effect: Studies in Governmentality*, ed. Graham Burchell, Colin Gordon, and Peter Miller, 151–66. Chicago: University of Chicago Press.

Ruggie, John Gerard. 2004. "Reconstituting the Global Public Domain—Issues, Actors, and Practices." *European Journal of International Relations* 10, no. 4: 499–531.

Shamir, Ronen. 2004. "The De-Radicalization of Corporate Social Responsibility." *Critical Sociology* 30, no. 3: 669–89.

Simons, Penelope. 2004. "Corporate Voluntarism and Human Rights: The Adequacy and Effectiveness of Voluntary Self-Regulation Regimes." *Relations industrielles/ Industrial Relations* 59, no. 1: 101–42.

Smith, Jackie, John McCarthy, Clark McPhail, and Boguslaw Augustyn. 2001. "From Protest to Agenda Building: Description Bias in Media Coverage of Protest Events in Washington." *Social Forces* 79, no. 4: 1397–1423.

Transnational Resource and Action Center. 2000. "Tangled Up in Blue: Corporate Partnerships at the United Nations." http://www.corpwatch.org/downloads/ tangled.pdf.

United Nations Commission on Human Rights. 2003. "Economic, Social, and Cultural Rights: Norms on the Responsibilities of Transnational Corporations and Other Business Enterprises with Regard to Human Rights." http://www.unhcr.ch/huridoca.nsf/(Symbol)/E.CN.4.Sub.2.2003.12.Rev.2.En?Opendocument.

United Nations Environmental Programme. 2002. *Guide to the Global Compact: A Practical Understanding of the Vision and Nine Principles.* http://uneptie.org/ outreach/compact/docs/gcguide.pdf.

United Nations Global Compact. 2006. "The Ten Principles." http://www. unglobalcompact.org/AboutTheGC/TheTenPrinciples/index.html.

Utting, Peter. 2002. "The Global Compact and Civil Society: Averting a Collision Course." *Development in Practice* 12, no. 5: 644–47.

Wells, Donald. 2006. "'Best Practice' in the Regulation of International Labor Standards: Lessons of the U.S.-Cambodia Textile Agreement." *Comparative Labor Law and Policy Journal* 27, no. 3: 357–76.

Williams, Oliver. 2004. "The U.N. Global Compact: The Challenge and the Promise." *Business Ethics Quarterly* 14, no. 4: 755–74.

CHAPTER 10

Illusions of Control

Janie Leatherman

The exercise of power in global politics—through technologies, institutions, and discourse—has become more complex and more fluid as globalization has increased the connections and struggles among states, international organizations, transnational corporations (TNCs), and nongovernmental organizations (NGOs), as well as among individuals and illicit actors. Following Foucault, this volume has explored how different techniques of power have evolved—techniques ranging from sovereign and disciplinary power to regulation or biopower and pastoral power—and what their productive effects have been in terms of global politics today. As the state has expanded its bureaucratic structures and functions, it has been closely associated with these types of power, from premodern forms of sovereign power to modern techniques of discipline, regulation, and pastoral power. More recently, scholars have debated whether or not the state can survive the pressures imposed by globalization and competition from other—sometimes more powerful—actors such as TNCs.

This volume has examined how the state has adapted by using its power to colonize global regimes of surveillance, supervision, and regulation, extending its bureaucratic reach and discursive terrain. The state has been challenged by other actors, such as the global media, the United Nations (UN), and TNCs, but it has also been able to harness them to its own purposes, extending its gaze and erasing the significance of national boundaries, differences among identities, and alternative sources of authority in global politics. The U.S.-led "war on terror" is a prime example of these dynamics.

There are new, and often troubling, questions about the ways in which these economies of power have led to self-policing and the policing of the "other." As Foucault writes, we have become the objects of our own subjugation.

This has led to acquiescence and docility—even in the face of sweeping and bald lies told by public authorities—as well as to intolerance of difference. There is a longing, especially in the West and in the United States post–September 11, for imperial control: an end to disorder.

Thus, the war on terror occupies a central point of reference for many of the chapters in this volume, although the aim is to unsettle its predominance, its ubiquitousness, especially its "normalness." In the United States, the war on terror is *the* discursive vehicle for defending freedom. It provides the template to justify disastrous U.S. imperialist adventures and the disciplining of populations, both domestic and foreign, to its imperial prerogatives, and it legitimates the high cost incurred in terms of lives, torture, and treasure. Disciplinary regimes in global politics and on the domestic front in the United States and other countries are pervasive. Though rooted in nostalgia for the past, they are decidedly postmodern, and also "leaky." As Knight and Smith argue in chapter 9, "the exercise of power is always (potentially) contentious," and it is leaky because "the problems it addresses and seeks to subsume can escape its embrace to some extent." That leakiness highlights the limitations of imperial control through force and coercive means, and it also points to the opportunities to counter it through alternative discourses and technologies of power.

What challenges stand in the way of producing alternatives? This concluding chapter takes up these questions, *first* by problematizing global regimes of supervision and surveillance. It looks at how the productive effects of these regimes operate in terms of their economies of power, discourses, undermining of democratic accountability, and disciplining of identities. The *second* part of the chapter takes up the problems and possibilities of resisting. It draws from Foucault and focuses especially on the capillary power of global Panopticons—and their leakiness.

Global Regimes of Surveillance and Supervision

Globalization has presented a crucial dilemma in the configuration of power and authority in the late twentieth and early twenty-first centuries. The key problem is the disjuncture between the territorial boundedness of the state and pressures to secure the state by closing off access to it by external enemies and would-be (unwanted) immigrants. In contrast, the deterritorialized global capitalist system demands open borders and free movement of goods and peoples. In chapter 5, Kim Rygiel refers to this as an "economic/security paradox."

This paradox is at the root of the longing for a simpler past, and it is manifested in the primacy of the hegemonic masculinity that has shaped

U.S. foreign policy, especially since the attacks of September 11. While much of the policymaking that has emerged post–September 11 was already under development during the previous decade (e.g., confronting disorder and chaos in the third world after the collapse of Communism—see George H. W. Bush 1990), the attacks on the World Trade Center, the Pentagon, and U.S. airlines on September 11 stunned Americans and opened new political space for the (largely) preconceived assertion of a much more aggressive and punitive foreign policy. The exercise of such arrogance by the United States—with the goal of imposing its own will on the international community, while denying the UN and other authorities any role or legitimacy—is a clear display of hegemonic masculinity.

Hegemonic masculinity is a socially constructed role that leads to an aggressive, nationalist orientation. It places self-interest and self-aggrandizement over and above the global public good, and feminizes other states and actors that use *either* consensus building or terrorist strategies. Hegemonic masculinity is one type of masculinism (Hooper 2001; Connell 1995). What is crucial in understanding hegemonic masculinity is how it functions at the level of the whole society to underwrite male advantage and power and subordinate other masculinities (nonwhite, racialized Others, class differentiated, or gay men), as well as women (Leatherman 2005).

The end of the Cold War might have opened up space for alternatives to a punitive U.S. regime of global supervision. That possibility was encapsulated in an event on another September 11—precisely eleven years to the day before the September 11, 2001, terrorist attacks on the United States. President George H. W. Bush gave a speech to a joint session of Congress on September 11, 1990, to galvanize support for the (first) war against Iraq. As Achcar (2002, 2) writes, "President Bush understood immediately the great benefit he could reap from a military action that was so legitimate in terms of international law: the first military action in the history of the [UN] to receive active or passive approval from all five permanent members of the Security Council and the great majority of the General Assembly." More important, however, was the chance to overcome the Vietnam syndrome, which Ronald Reagan, his predecessor, had failed to achieve. (Instead, Reagan was heir to the "emasculation" of U.S. force in Beirut—the 1983 attacks on the U.S. Embassy, which left 63 dead; followed by suicide attacks on marines serving in a multinational force, leaving 242 U.S. marines dead—and author of the invasion of the small Caribbean island of Grenada, code named "Operation Urgent Fury").

George H. W. Bush's speech to Congress in 1990 contained both idealist and realist arguments to map out his vision of a "new world order."

However, the idealist arguments were more lip service than commitments. Thus, he

> limited himself to describing what was possible in 1990—but only *possible*—without promising to make it happen. The world was in fact "at a unique and extraordinary moment" then, with "a rare opportunity to move toward a historic period of cooperation." A "new world order" could have been the outcome of the end of the Cold War: "a new era—freer from the threat of terror, stronger in the pursuit of justice, and more secure in the quest for peace." It could have been an era in which "the nations of the world, East and West, North and South, can prosper and live in harmony," while "the rule of law supplants the rule of the jungle" and the strong respect the rights of the weak.
>
> (Achcar 2002, 4, emphasis in original)

In contrast, the part of the speech that did focus on commitments emphasized the vital economic interests at stake—the danger of Iraq controlling 20 percent of global oil reserves and threatening its neighbors, which control the "lion's share of the world's remaining reserves." There was "no substitute for U.S. leadership" in the face of such tyranny. "The world is still dangerous, and surely that is now clear. Stability is not secure. American interests are far-reaching. Interdependence has increased. The consequences of regional instability can be global. This is no time to risk America's capacity to protect her vital interests" (George H. W. Bush 1990).

George H. W. Bush's doctrine for a new world order laid the foundations of a global regime of supervision that emerged unchallenged post–9/11. The first Gulf War in 1991 was a prelude to his son's—George W. Bush's—September 2002 National Security Strategy (NSS). This was the first comprehensive rationale for pursuing an aggressive and preemptive national security strategy against a hostile threat, especially from rogue states and terrorists (i.e., the global South). Its origins, which can be traced back to a 1992 Defense Planning Guidance draft report by Paul Wolfowitz, laid out the Bush administration's approach to foreign policy for dealing with terrorists, regional conflicts, economic growth, development assistance, and promotion of democracy. It is triumphalist in tone, emphasizing the "victory of the forces of freedom" over Communist enemies in the Cold War, and it warns of new threats on the horizon from terrorists and rogue states—that is, "enemies of civilization"—a refrain that echoes his father's rhetoric. Most significantly, the NSS 2002 is premised on a doctrine of ensuring the perpetuity of U.S. power and enforcing it through unilateral and proactive means, including anticipatory self-defense. Gone is the façade of commitments to peace and prosperity between the global North and South. As Achcar (2002, 4) notes:

> Considered from this point of view, the events of September 11, 2001, can be legitimately interpreted by contrast as the deepest point so far in a descent into terrorism that is the corollary of the widening gap, in the course of the eleven intervening years, between reality and the conditions for global peace and justice described in Bush's speech of September 11, 1990. In a world in which inequality is increasing inexorably, inside each society as well as among nations, in which the law of the jungle and the principle of "might makes right" reign supreme, the barbarism on one side inevitably engenders the barbarism on the other. "The threat of terror" in all its diverse forms, ends up weighing heavily on everyone.

Economies of Power

The U.S. global regime of supervision laid out in the NSS 2002 now colonizes many institutions and discourses with multiple and reinforcing economies of power. It relies fundamentally on war. As Nowacki and Gutterman argue in chapter 4, "People seek discipline because they cannot stand disorder, and in wartime they cannot stand weakness and submission to an 'enemy.'" The tentacles of the war on terror reach out globally through many states and international bodies (such as TNCs, NGOs, and international organizations), as well as downwards to the level of the individual in society. The many dimensions of these overlapping regimes of surveillance and supervision have been sketched in this volume in chapter 2 by Mertus and Rawls, who describe the U.S. regime on torture; in chapter 3 by Krista Hunt, who explores its hegemonic, patriarchal manifestations in the George W. Bush administration's war on terror and co-optation of women's rights through its efforts to expand the global capitalist system deep into the global South through the cheap labor of women; in chapter 4 by Nowacki and Gutterman, who illustrate its workings through the magical vehicle of the missile defense shield and the protection of the "normative family"; in chapter 5 by Kim Rygiel, who reviews the new developments in the governmentality of citizenship as a global regime to control the movement of people and carry out surveillance on enemies; by Riaz and DiMaggio and Michael Dartnell in chapters 6 and 7, respectively, who explore the regime of supervision in the context of the media or "global presence," and its relationship to the discourse and the war on terror. For his part, Dartnell concludes that "Television images from the Iraq conflict ... reconfigure the Iraq conflict into something that is happening to a collective Euro-Americaland ("us") rather than as a catastrophe for the Iraqis." It is a narrative that reproduces the great "civilizing mission" and all that the first world represents.

In chapter 8, Evelyn Bush's discussion of discipline and resistance in diplomacy in the context of the UN Declaration on HIV/AIDS also, in many ways, shows how the global regimes of supervision—rooted in hegemonic masculinity and based in the West on the close relationship between conservative Christians and the Bush administration—have formed alliances with other conservative religious forces and states (e.g., the Vatican, the Organization of the Islamic Conference [OIC], and Islamic states) to subordinate other masculinities and sexualities and to discipline women's reproductive rights (see also Buss and Herman 2003).

The global regimes of supervision that have emerged after the end of the Cold War and that have gained great currency under George W. Bush, in particular, enjoy expansive economies of scale. This is part of the reason that they are insidious and difficult to resist or subvert through alternatives. For example, the operation of the regime of torture set up by the Bush administration counts among its tools the Panopticon of the Patriot Act and its surveillance capabilities (including unconstitutional provisions), the abuses of Guantanamo, Abu Ghraib, and the many other unnamed prisons in Iraq, and the CIA gulag of secret prisons throughout Europe and elsewhere in the world, including Afghanistan. As Mertus and Rawls argue in chapter 2, it is this large economy of power that makes it "more difficult ... to limit the degree of pain inflicted upon the criminal." The images of torture have been widely disseminated from Abu Ghraib—and thus turned into public displays. They reinscribe the sovereign power of the United States on bodies of the "Other" and underscore the powerlessness of these subjects. It is a form of public branding. Another insidious aspect of this economy of power is the great dissymmetry it displays between the "all powerful sovereign" and the powerless subject. Prisoners abused at Abu Ghraib, Guantanamo, and elsewhere have their personal humiliation etched on the global public consciousness (see also Puar 2005; Puar and Rai 2002). Their humiliation by staged homosexual acts and other abuses avenges the victims of September 11, but it also demonstrates that resisting American power is dangerous. The worst possible form of discipline can be enacted on those who resist, on anyone. This is because, as Foucault argues, "punishment must be spectacular so as to frighten the others." It is the "virtue of example" (1980, 155).

Border controls also play into the global regime on terror, and target not only would-be terrorists, but anyone who attempts to resist the regime. In October 2007, two American pacifists were refused entry to Canada because their names were on a Federal Bureau of Investigation (FBI) watch list that is primarily devoted to criminals and individuals suspected of terrorism. One of the pacifists, Medea Benjamin, was the founder of an NGO in San Francisco and the organizer of sociocultural trips to poor countries. She subsequently joined Code Pink—a pacifist women's organization that demonstrates in front of the White House (which is forbidden) and also attends Congressional hearings, where they interrupt officials reporting on the war, calling on them to "Tell the Truth." So, these pacifist women, who are "guilty of the crimes of interrupting lying speeches," are among those tracked because of the danger they represent even to Canada (which welcomed conscientious objectors in opposition to the Vietnam War). As Courtemanches (2007, 1) writes, "As for Mrs. Benjamin, if she wants to return to Canada, she will have to pay $200 for a three-day permit and submit herself to a 'rehabilitation process' that includes a long interrogation on her 'criminal' past and fingerprinting. In short, in this ever-more American country [Canada], protest and pacifism have become crimes that interdict entry to the territory."

Loss of Democratic Accountability

The new global regimes of surveillance and supervision under the war on terror are also menacing because of the ways in which they shut down or elide democratic accountability. The Patriot Act is an important example. As noted in a *New York Times* Op Ed piece entitled, "Spies, Lies and FISA" (2007),

> After 9/11, the Patriot Act made it even easier to conduct surveillance, especially in hot pursuit of terrorists. But that was not good enough for the Bush team, which was determined to use the nation's tragedy to grab ever more power for its vision of an imperial presidency. Mr. Bush ignored the FISA law [the 1978 Foreign Intelligence Surveillance Act, or FISA that requires a warrant to intercept international communications involving anyone in the United States] and ordered the National Security Agency to intercept phone calls and e-mail between people abroad and people in the United States without a warrant, as long as the "target" was not in this country.

Another such sleight of hand occurred in 2007, when the Bush administration rushed through Congress a bill to authorize eavesdropping on communications between foreigners who pass through U.S. computers. In that legislation, Congress fixed this loophole, but then also authorized spying without the approval of the Foreign Intelligence Surveillance Court (FISC) ("Spies, Lies and FISA 2007). These strategies turn on its head the traditional formula of transparency in democracies. As Nowacki and Gutterman point out in chapter 4, the actions of government are now opaque and the lives of its citizens are in the light.

Similar maneuvers to elide democratic accountability are found in the Bush Administration's policy on torture. The scope of the administration's deceit on torture policy became clearer in October 2007 at "the disclosure of secret Justice Department legal opinions permitting the harsh interrogation of terrorism suspects." The documents, first reported by the *New York Times* on October 6, consisted of two separate 2005 legal opinions from the Justice Department, which "authorized the CIA to barrage terror suspects with a combination of painful physical and psychological tactics, including head-slapping, simulated drowning and frigid temperatures." These memoranda were written shortly after the Justice Department had declared in December 2004 that torture was "abhorrent" (Stolberg 2007; Johnston and Shane 2007). Frank Rich reports that these "'enhanced interrogation techniques' have a grotesque provenance. 'Verschärfte Vernehmung,' enhanced or intensified interrogation, was the exact term innovated by the Gestapo to describe what became known as the 'third degree.' It left no marks. It included hypothermia, stress positions and long-time sleep deprivation" (Rich 2007).

Many of the chapters in this volume also document the loss of democratic accountability under the gaze of the new global Panopticon. Rygiel (chapter 5) cites this with the displacement of control of citizenship to other states and nonstate governing authorities—including private companies. This involves both power from top-down and capillary power—so the global regime of citizenship functions parallel to, and in conjunction with, other economies of power designed to ensure discipline through self-governing, self-policing, and individuals policing others (as Rygiel reports on a Fedex employee program, and Time Warner's American Online, Western Union, and Wal-Mart). The combination of new technologies, new discourses, and new regimes of surveillance and supervision have the effect of normalizing such conduct. It becomes insidious also in part because it is now mundane. Repeatedly every day, CNN encourages its viewers to be its eyes, ears, and reporters—to log on to its website and upload images from their cell phones, digital cameras, and video recorders. Elsewhere, individual citizens monitor politicians on the campaign trail; and Jimmy Justice turns the tables and monitors the traffic police (Celizic 2007).

Disciplining Identities

Global regimes of supervision and surveillance are also dangerous because of the economy of power for disciplining of identities. In chapter 3, Krista Hunt illustrates how liberation for women in Muslim countries is subject to their own nation's liberation of the market place. The identity they are assigned is as cheap labor, but not at the expense of being good wives and consumers. Setting Western fashion as the benchmark (apparel, makeup, design) is another way to encode their participation as docile, faithful wives in the larger global marketplace.

The missile defense shield, one of the tools of the war on terror, serves similar purposes in terms of policing women's identity and role in society. As Nowacki and Gutterman show in chapter 4, "in the rhetorical war to define and defend the "homeland," the missile defense shield serves as a magical vehicle that does not simply promise future safety, but reifies the mythical past and a projected future of gender stability and domestic order." Missile defense rhetoric puts the family at the center of what must be protected, using patriarchal norms and identities of the family, and playing on (especially women's) nostalgic desires for security and safety. As Nowacki and Gutterman argue, the political economy of this discourse depends partly on its manipulation of threat, from both external and internal forces, and the way these are collapsed (see also Baker 2006). So, the shield ensures the sanctity of the traditional family (nuclear, conservative, white, Christian) not only from "terrorists" abroad, but also from the "enemy within," who struggles for abortion and reproductive rights, gay marriage, and so forth.

Women who carry out roles outside of this normative frame are also disciplined, as the example of Pfc. Lynndie England illustrates. Michael Dartnell reports in chapter 7 on photographs of her posing with nude inmates in sexually humiliating positions, showing how the military tolerated gender, racial, and sexuality hierarchies among U.S. military personnel. England's dominance "illustrates the danger of masculinizing women in warfare and the need to punish those who do not submit. The message is that gender equality and women's sexual empowerment unleash female masculinity and aggressive predatory behavior." The celebration of the normative good women is also racialized. Shoshana Johnson, an African American female soldier captured in Iraq, is framed not as innocent like the white, blonde Jessica Lynch, but as victim, and she is marginalized and relegated to the background. Lynch is instead a celebrity, sexually innocent, racially pure, a symbol of the power and reach of the U.S. military, as Dartnell argues.

Making Space for Resistance

What kinds of spaces can be opened up to contest the abuses of power that emerge from these disciplinary maneuvers? What kinds of power can activists deploy to counter state and corporate power and reinvigorate the state as an instrument for social responsibility? Knight and Smith's chapter (9), though sobering in its assessment of the UN's capacity to limit corporate power through the technology of the Global Compact (GC), nonetheless offers some answers to these questions by drawing from Foucault's conceptualizations of power. Their argument highlights his urging that because different technologies of power are dangerous, they need to be used not only to complement but also to offset one another.

Foucault himself was often questioned about where he stood as an intellectual—the contribution he sought to make with his work. He expressed many times the sentiment that he was widely misunderstood, though this did not concern him especially.[1] However, he emphasized that the questions

> I am trying to ask are not determined by a preestablished political outlook and do not tend toward the realization of some definite political project ... I am attempting ... to open *up* problems that are as *concrete* and *general* as possible, problems that approach politics from behind and cut across societies on the diagonal, problems that are at once constituents of our history and constituted by that history ... And it has been necessary to try to raise them both as present-day questions and as historical ones, as moral, epistemological, and political problems.
>
> (1984b, 376, emphasis in original; see also Foucault 1984a, 384)

While Foucault resisted identifying himself as being situated at some particular location on a political "chessboard," he nonetheless did see his role, as an interviewer put it to him, "as linking an analysis with a type of action that is not ideological in itself, and thus which is harder to name ... You help other people get their own struggles going in specific areas; but that is certainly an ethics, if I may say so, of the interaction between theory and practice; it consists in linking the two. Thinking and acting are connected in an ethical sense, but one which has results that have to be called political" (1984b, 376–77). Largely agreeing with this characterization, Foucault responded with the example of Poland (where he had lived for a year earlier in his life), which at the time of the interview was under martial law. While recognizing that "we can't dispatch a team of paratroopers, and we can't send armored cars to liberate Warsaw," he argued that we still "have to raise the problem of Poland in the form of a nonacceptance of what is happening there, and a nonacceptance of the passivity of our own governments. I think this attitude is an ethical one, but it is also political; it does not consist in saying merely, 'I protest,' but in making of that attitude a political phenomenon that is as substantial as possible, and one which those who govern, here or there, will sooner or later be obliged to take into account" (ibid.). While recognizing the imperative as well as the dangers of revolutions[2] (e.g., the Iranian revolution about which he also wrote), Foucault cautions, "One does not dictate to those who risk their lives facing a power. Is one right to revolt, or not? Let us leave the question open" (1994d, 452).

Ultimately, Foucault's commitment was to "look closely, a bit beneath history, at what cleaves it and stirs it, and keep watch, a bit behind politics, over what must unconditionally limit it. After all, that is my work" (1994d, 453).

To this end, he was also ethically committed to understanding how people can "unblock" their history and "engage in inventing a future for themselves," as he saw the Poles struggle to do in October 1982. He describes the Solidarity movement as having accomplished a certain number of things that could not be "quashed," an experience that can no longer be "obliterated." He is referring to "the consciousness they had of all being together." He continues:

> That is paramount. Thirty-five years of the previous regime had convinced them, finally, that the invention of new social relations was impossible. In a state like that one, each individual can be consumed by the difficulties of his own existence. One is in every sense of the word, "occupied." This "occupation" is also the solitude, the dislocation of society ... but now [what surfaced from their shared hatred of the regime] was clearly formulated in words, discourses, and texts, and it was converted into the creation of something new and shared in common.
>
> (1994b, 467–68)

Foucault thus saw the possibility of transformation of society (see for example, 1994e). His role was to raise questions about this in a way that would not lead to solutions springing from the head of "some reformist intellectual;" rather, it would come from years and decades of the hard work of people at the grassroots level—those directly affected. His aim was not to "dictate how things should be," but instead to "pose problems, to make them active, to display them in such a complexity that they can silence the prophets and lawgivers, all those who speak for others or to others" (1994a, 288). He saw political changes as follows:

> In this way, it will be possible for the complexity of the problem to appear in its connection with people's lives; and consequently, through concrete questions, difficult cases, movements of rebellion, reflections, and testimonies, the legitimacy of a common creative action can also appear. It's a matter of working through things little by little, of introducing modifications that are able if not to find solutions, at least to change the given terms of the problem.
>
> (1994a, 288)

The conclusions of this study nevertheless pose troubling questions about the possibilities of creating new spaces, of "unblocking" our history, and of escaping our own "occupation." Efforts to establish alternative discourses and power relations have to work through or overcome several developments. First, the close relationship between states and private corporations under the global regimes of surveillance and supervision reviewed in this volume raise the specter not only of the state colonizing other institutions, but also of the eventual hollowing out of the state. As many of the functions of the state are downsized (in the global South, it has been structural adjustment), outsourced, and privatized, the public sphere itself—where debate, dialogue, and contestation should take place under conditions of transparency and accountability in a democracy—is vanishing.

Naomi Klein (2007) has referred to this development as "disaster capitalism: the new economy of catastrophe" (48). Shock and awe is not only about military operations but also about profit making, the division of the world into red and green zones—the superwealthy, and the desperately poor. As Klein explains it,

> Like most people, I saw the divide between Baghdad's Green and Red Zones as a simple by-product of the war: this is what happens when the richest country in the world sets up camp in one of the poorest. But now, after years spent visiting other disaster zones, from post-tsunami Sri Lanka to post-Katrina New Orleans, I've come to think of these Green Zone/Red Zone worlds as something else: fast-forward versions of what "free-market" forces are doing to our societies even in the absence of war.
>
> (2007, 48)

The devastating impact of disaster capitalism is more evident in poor countries than it is in wealthy ones. A natural disaster like a tsunami can bring the poor countries to their knees; in the West the infrastructure has a more robust history. But the signs of its erosion and the implications are already present. After the collapse of a major highway bridge in Minneapolis, Minnesota, in the summer of 2007, the *Wall Street Journal* called for privatizing bridges as a solution in dealing with America's crumbling infrastructure. The speed with which this solution was broached should not be surprising. Klein notes that think tanks in Washington have already been on a hostile

> campaign to privatize the essential functions of the state. As a May 2007 cover story in Business Week explained, "In the past year, banks and private investment firms have fallen in love with public infrastructure. They're smitten by the rich cash flows that roads, bridges, airports, parking garages and shipping ports generate—and the monopolistic advantages that keep those cash flows as steady as a beating heart ... Investors can't get in fast enough."
>
> (Klein 2007, 49)

Klein further documents how "the military industrial complex that Dwight D. Eisenhower warned against in 1961 has expanded and morphed into what

is best understood as a disaster–capitalism complex, in which all conflict-
and disaster-related functions (such as waging war, securing borders, spying
on citizens, rebuilding cities, treating traumatized soldiers) can be performed
by corporations at a profit" (2007a, 50). Even academics are drawn into
profit making in war. For example, the Pentagon has hired anthropologists
to accompany 26 American combat brigades in Iraq and Afghanistan (Rohde
2007). Many of the same companies at work in Iraq (e.g., Halliburton's
former subsidiary Kellogg, Root and Brown; Blackwater; Parsons) snatched
up extremely lucrative contracts in New Orleans. Klein (2007, 51) argues
that this privatization is so pervasive in Washington that it has led to the
creation of a "fully articulated state-within-a-state that is as muscular and
capable as the actual state is frail and feeble." This is evident partly by the
lack of state control over the outsourced functions. For example, the U.S.
State Department, following a shooting spree by Blackwater security guards
in Iraq (leading to the deaths of 17 Iraqis on September 17, 2007), was
forced to deploy dozens of its own diplomatic security service agents to Iraq
in an attempt to monitor Blackwater convoys that were in Iraq under a
multiyear $1.2 billion contract with the department to provide it with
security (Broder 2007)!

The corporate shadow state thus operates in the global North much like
shadow economies operate in the global South. They both rely on the state,
and enrich themselves through close ties to its political elite (clientalism) for
access to revenues, contracts, and concessions. From this perspective, global
warming looms lucrative. This is a parallel system over which citizens have
no claims, no control. Fraud and corruption are rampant (Klein 2007, 51;
Nordstrom 2004; Rose 2007; and on how this happens in West Africa, see
Ghazvinian 2007).

Meanwhile, studies show that the gap between the rich and the poor grows
wider, even in the heart of Panopticon. In the United States, the widening
of the income gap has been dramatic since 2000—in fact, the richest
Americans' share of the national income has hit a postwar record, exceeding
the highs of the 1990s: the wealthiest 1 percent earned 21.2 percent of all
income in 2005, while the poorest 50 percent earned just 12.8 percent
(Ip 2007; see also Baker 2007, 38, on the impact of such a wealth–poverty
divide in Manhattan).

Second, along with the vanishing state and the privatization of the public
sphere and the duties of government, there is a public perception of a drift
toward postideological politics. Baker (2007, 39), for example, argues that

as repugnant as George W. Bush's brand of social conservatism has been, it
is not ideology that is at the heart of his administration's failure but his

personality, for in the post-ideological world the politics of personality are all
that remains. The worst excesses of the Bush regime have stemmed directly
from its leader's character—that is, its rampant cronyism, its arrogance and
egotism; its peremptory, bullying tone and methods; its refusal to brook
criticism from within or without; its frighteningly authoritarian impulses; its
need to create enemies as a means of governing; its impulsiveness and naïveté;
its outright contempt for the law; and its truly staggering ability to substitute
its own versions of what it wishes the world to be for any recognition of
objective reality.

I contend, nevertheless, that this notion of politics being emptied of ideology is merely a sign of the extent to which market globalization and institutions backing its expansion—like the war on terror—have become ubiquitous.
The public's senses are deadened to violence, suffering, poverty, and politics.
Despite pervasive lies and repeated failures of magical devices like the missile
defense shield, the public has not protested—not much. John Cory writes,

> Modern America now spies on its citizens, conducts warrantless wiretaps,
> suspends habeas corpus, creates "free speech zones" to corral protestors out
> of sight of sensitive royal eyes, and politicizes the very justice system meant to
> protect people's rights by turning it into a fraternity of God-fearing Republican
> conservatism. Neocon America rewards hate speech with celebrity, reviles the
> very immigration that built this country, and sells out to the highest lobbyist
> while poisoning its people. Preemptive war trumps truth, and death is glorified
> by those who never have to sacrifice an ounce of flesh. America has become
> the personal ATM machine of Bush and the GOP while their corporate
> cronies line their pockets with the lives of our loved ones.
>
> (2007, 1)

Citing Dr. Martin Luther King Jr.'s admonition that "'Our lives begin to end
the day we become silent about things that matter,'" Cory concludes that
"Americans have become orphans of the great silence" (ibid.).

Resistance depends partly on knowing that the state has set a line to be
toed, and on being able to find that line and know where and how to begin
to push it back—as a human rights activist who fled Egypt explained to me
a couple years ago. Americans, she contended, don't even know there is a
line to look for. Thus, resistance lies in coming out of the comfort zone of
docility (for some, "safety"; for others, resignation or acquiescence). Indeed,
as the chapters in this volume have shown, the global regimes of discipline
and punishment cannot operate only from the top down. The Panopticon
depends also on self-subjugation. This partly requires docility, but it also
requires a predisposition on the part of individuals in society to police one

another. At this level, the Panopticon works on capillary power. This is where it achieves its greatest economy of power. *But* this is where the power of the Panopticon is also potentially the leakiest. Where the Panopticon is leakiest is also where the greatest opportunities for resistance and employing alternative modes of power—like pastoral power—open up.

Foucault sees pastoral power as having several key components in a secular context, drawing from its origins in Christian institutions. These include a power that is prepared to sacrifice itself for the life and well-being of its community—as distinct from royal power, which demands a sacrifice of its subject for the throne; a power that looks not only after the whole community, but also after each individual through that person's life; and a power that is exercised in the context of people's conscience and with an ability to direct it. Thus, pastoral power is both "coextensive and continuous with life" and is "linked with the production of truth—the truth of the individual himself." In practical political and institutional terms, this means caring for people's health, well-being (i.e., adequate wealth or standard of living, a living wage), security, and protection (Foucault 1994c, 333). For a world that lives with extremes of wealth and poverty, it also means a global new deal—that should also include the environment (Felice 2003; Singer 2004).

The challenge of the twenty-first century is to find the political technologies with which to bring a new pastoral power not only within states, but also into global discourses, institutions, and practices. In this volume, we have at least mapped out the barriers to this endeavor, the problems that exist with the current technologies of power, and their weaknesses—the illusions of control. The first steps in creating alternative spaces has to come from each of us individually, and then as individuals collectively working to bring pastoral power to bear on the production of truth, by being true to ourselves. As Solzhenitsyn puts it, "Live not by Lies" (1974). This is in everyone's hands to do. Collectively, it will start to change the world.

Notes

1. For example, he said, "here have been Marxists who said I was a danger to Western democracy—that has been written; there was a socialist who wrote that the thinker who resembled me most closely was Adolf Hitler in *Mein Kampf*. I have been considered by liberals as a technocrat, an agent of the Gaullist government; I have been considered by people on the right, Gaullists or otherwise, as a dangerous left-wing anarchist ... and so on. Fine, none of this matters ..." (1984b, 376).

2. For example, in his essay "Useless to Revolt," Foucault also cautioned "the power that one man exerts over another is always perilous. I am not saying that power, by nature is evil; I am saying that power, with its mechanisms, is infinite

(which does not mean that it is omnipotent, quite the contrary). The rules that exist to limit it can never be stringent enough; the universal principles for dispossessing it of all the occasions it seizes are never sufficiently rigorous. Against power one must always set inviolable laws and unrestricted rights" (1994d, 453; see also Jabri 2007).

Bibliography

Achcar, Gilbert. 2002. "Introduction: From One September 11th to Another." In the *Clash of Barbarism: September 11 and the Making of the New World Disorder*. Monthly Review Press, 1–4. http:/www.monthlyreview.org/cobxcerpt.htm.

Baker, Kevin. 2007. "A Fate Worse than Bush: Rudolph Giuliani and the Politics of Personality." *Harper's Magazine*, August, 31–39.

———. 2006. "Stabbed in the Back! The Past and Future of a Right-Wing Myth." *Harper's Magazine*, June, 31–42.

Broder, John M. 2007. "State Department Plans Tighter Control of Security Firm." *New York Times,* October 6, 1–2. http://www.nytimes.com/ref/membercenter/nytarchive.html.

Bush, George Herbert Walker. 1990. "Toward a New World Order." A speech by George H. W. Bush, Joint Session of the United States Congress, Washington, D.C., September 11. http://en.wikisource.org/wiki/Toward_a_New_World_Order (accessed October 14).

Buss, Doris, and Didi Herman. 2003. *Globalizing Family Values: The Christian Right in International Politics*. Minneapolis: Minnesota University Press.

Celizic, Mike. 2007. "Video Vigilante Turns Tables on Traffic Enforcers." www.msnbc.msn.com, August 17. http://www.msnbc.msn.com/id/20311210/ (accessed October 14).

Connell, R. W. 1995. *Masculinities*. Berkeley: University of California Press.

Cory, John. 2007. "Once upon America." *Truthout*, July 4, 1–2. http://truthout.org (accessed July 5).

Courtemanche, Gil. 2007. "Stephen Harper's Smoking Trails." *Le Devoir*, Saturday and Sunday,October 7–8, 1–2. Trans. Leslie Thatcher. http://www.truthout.org/docs_2006/100807G.shtml (accessed October 8).

Felice, William F. 2003. *The Global New Deal: Economic and Social Human Rights in World Politics*. New York: Rowman and Littlefield.

Foucault, Michel. 1994a. "Interview with Michel Foucault." In *Michel Foucault: Power*, ed. James D. Faubion, 237–97. Essential Works of Foucault 1954–1984, ed. Paul Rabinow, vol. 3, trans. Robert Hurley et al. New York: New Press.

———. 1994b. "The Moral and Social Experience of the Poles Can No Longer Be Obliterated." In *Michel Foucault: Power*, ed. James D. Faubion, 465–75. Essential Works of Foucault 1954–1984, ed. Paul Rabinow, vol. 3, trans. Robert Hurley et al. New York: New Press.

———. 1994c. "The Subject and Power." In *Michel Foucault: Power*, ed. James D. Faubion, 327–48. Essential Works of Foucault 1954–1984, ed. Paul Rabinow, vol. 3, trans. Robert Hurley et al. New York: New Press.

―――. 1994d. "Useless to Revolt?" In *Michel Foucault: Power*, ed. James D. Faubion, 449–53. Essential Works of Foucault 1954–1984, ed. Paul Rabinow, vol. 3, trans. Robert Hurley et al. New York: New Press.

―――. 1994e. "What is Called 'Punishing'?" In *Michel Foucault: Power*, ed. James D. Faubion, 383–93. Essential Works of Foucault 1954–1984, ed. Paul Rabinow, vol. 3, trans. Robert Hurley et al. New York: New Press.

―――. 1984a. "Polemics, Politics, and Problemizations." In *The Foucault Reader*, ed. Paul Rabinow, 381–90. New York: Pantheon Books.

―――. 1984b. "Politics and Ethics: An Interview." In *The Foucault Reader*, ed. Paul Rabinow, 373–80. New York: Pantheon Books.

―――. 1980. "The Eye of Power: A Conversation with Jean-Pierre Barou and Michelle Perrot." In *Power/Knowledge. Selected interviews and Other Writings 1972–1977*, ed. Colin Gordon, trans. Colin Gordon, Leo Marshall, John Mepham, and Kate Soper, 146–65. New York: Pantheon Books.

Ghazvinian, John. 2007. *Untapped: The Scramble for Africa's Oil*. New York: Harcourt.

Hooper, Charlotte. 2001. *Manly States*. New York: Columbia University Press.

Ip, Greg. 2007. "Income-Inequality Gap Widens." *Wall Street Journal*, October 12. http://www.truthout.org/ (accessed October 15).

Jabri, Vivienne. 2007. "Michel Foucault's Analytics of War: The Social, the International, and the Racial." *International Political Sociology* 1, no. 1 (March): 67–82.

Johnston, David, and Scott Shane. 2007. "Debate Erupts on Techniques Used by C.I.A." *New York Times*, October 5, 1–2. http://www.nytimes.com/ref/membercenter/nytarchive.html.

Klein, Naomi. 2007. "Disaster Capitalism: The New Economy of Catastrophe." *Harper's Magazine*, October, 47–58.

Leatherman, Janie. 2005. "Gender and U.S. Foreign Policy: Hegemonic Masculinity, the War in Iraq, and the UN-doing of World Order." In *Gender and American Politics: Women, Men, and the Political Process*, ed. Sue Tolleson-Rinehart and Jyl J. Josephson, 103–26. 2nd ed. New York: M.E. Sharpe.

National Security Strategy of the United States of America (NSS). 2002. The White House. September 17. http://www.whitehouse.gov/nsc/nssall.html.

Nordstrom, Carolyn. 2004. *Shadows of War: Violence, Power, and International Profiteering in the Twenty-First Century*. Berkeley and Los Angeles: University of California Press.

Puar, Jasbir. 2005. "On Torture: Abu Ghraib." *Radical History Review* 93, no. 1 (Fall: 13–38.

Puar, Jasbir, and Amit Rai. 2002. "Monster, Terrorist, Fag: The War on Terrorism and the Production of Docile Patriots." *Social Text* 20, no. 3 (Fall): 117–28.

Rich, Frank. 2007. "The 'Good' Germans among Us." *New York Times*, October 14. http://truthout.org.

Rohde, David. 2007. "Army Enlists Anthropology in War Zones." *New York Times*, October 5. http://query.nytimes.com/gst/fullpage.html?res=9403E1D8143BF93 3A25753C1A9619C8B63 (accessed October 16).

Rose, David. 2007. "The People vs. the Profiteers." *Vanity Fair*, November, 1–10. http://truthout.org/docs_2006/printer_1000807a.shtml.

Singer, Peter. 2004. *One World (Terry Lecture Series): The Ethics of Globalization*. Yale University Press.

Solzhenitsyn, Alexander. 1974. "Live Not By Lies." http://www.columbia.edu/cu/augustine/arch/solzhenitsyn/livenotbylies.html (accessed October 15).

"Spies, Lies and FISA." 2007. Editorial. *New York Times*, October 14. http://www.nytimes.com/ref/membercenter/nytarchive.html.

Stolberg, Sheryl Gay. 2007. "Bush Says Interrogation Methods Aren't Torture." *New York Times,* October 6. http://www.nytimes.com/ref/membercenter/nytarchive.html.

Index